American Unexceptionalism

THE NEW AMERICAN CANON

The Iowa Series in Contemporary Literature and Culture

Samuel Cohen, series editor

American Unexceptionalism

The Everyman and the Suburban Novel after 9/11

Kathy Knapp

UNIVERSITY OF IOWA PRESS, IOWA CITY

University of Iowa Press, Iowa City 52242

www.uiowapress.org
Printed in the United States of America

Design by Omega Clay

The University of Iowa Press is a member of Green Press Initiative and is committed to preserving natural resources.

Printed on acid-free paper

Library of Congress Cataloging-in-Publication Data
Knapp, Kathy, 1960–
American unexceptionalism: the everyman and the suburban novel after 9/11 / Kathy Knapp.
pages cm. — (The New American Canon: the Iowa series in contemporary literature and culture)
Includes bibliographical references and index.
ISBN: 978-1-60938-228-5, 1-60938-228-5 (pbk)
ISBN: 978-1-60938-251-3, 1-60938-251-x (ebk)
1. American fiction—21st century—History and criticism.
2. Suburban life in literature. 3. September 11 Terrorist Attacks, 2001—Influence. 4. Authors, American—21st century—Political and social views. I. Title.
PS374.S82K63 2014
813'.609—dc23 2013043057

For Bob and Phyll

Contents

Acknowledgments

Writing can feel like a lonely endeavor, but in truth every sentence in this book has benefited from the fine insights, suggestions, and support of a multitude of friends, colleagues, and family members.

My thanks must begin with Lenny Cassuto, the Grand Poobah of advisers and a fantastic friend. He read and reread the following pages countless times, each time with exhaustive comments and fresh enthusiasm. He cheered me on and propped me up when things got really tough. And along the way he reminded me to take a walk, grab a meal, watch some *Wire*, and keep things in perspective.

Anna Mae Duane, friend, colleague, and mentor extraordinaire, has likewise read these pages over and over and has been a bottomless source of wisdom, advice, support, encouragement, and good cheer.

I am blessed with many terrific colleagues at UConn. Clare Eby has been an incredibly generous reader, advocate, and friend. Cathy Schlund-Vials offered feedback early on that set my project in motion. The members of my American Studies writing group—Anna Mae, Martha Cutter, Shawn Salvant, Mike Gill, and Alexis Boylan—provided comments late in the game that led to important fine-tuning. Bob Tilton and Margaret Breen have been sounding boards and supporters. Pam Bedore, Ellen Carillo, and Serkan Gorkemli are my comrades-in-arms. Fiona DeMerrell and Judy DiLaurenzio have covered for me and kept me laughing.

In addition, I am deeply indebted to several top-notch scholars in the field for their invaluable help at various stages. Cathy Jurca provided pages of thoughtful comments at the dissertation stage that gently guided me to challenge my assumptions. Gordon Hutner offered suggestions and support early on that launched this project. Andy Hoberek, Min Hyoung Song, Aaron DeRosa, and Lee Zimmerman gave me feedback that stretched my thinking and took my work in new directions. Sam Cohen has been a great editor and a good guy every step of the way.

Thanks go also to Elisabeth Chretien at University of Iowa Press, who has been helpful and accommodating in ushering this book into print, and to Charlotte Wright, this book's managing editor, and Margery Tippie, its copy editor, who have handled it with great care and attention to detail. Early versions of Chapters 1 and 2 were originally published in *American Literary History* and *Twentieth-Century Literature*. Thanks to those journals for permission to include that material here.

Finally, I owe everything to my home team: they have read and revised, compiled and formatted, cooked and cleaned, and kept the fires burning throughout this long, arduous process. Christopher, Michael, and Peter Knapp confound my thesis by being truly exceptional young men. I am also hugely appreciative of their extraordinary mates—Lola Diane, Genevieve Parshalle, and Jacob Graham, respectively—who make us all happier for being part of the brood. Emma Knapp has grown up with this book, and her laughter and wine deliveries have kept me buoyed throughout. And then there is Steve, where it all starts and ends. We clamb this hill thegither, love.

Introduction

The Suburb and the Everyman in Transition

When Matthew Weiner, the creator of the hit television series *Mad Men*, announced in 2011 that the show would stop production after its seventh season, fans immediately began to wonder how the story of Don Draper, its iconic white upper-middle-class 1960s advertising executive, would conclude. Among the many speculations that circulated, several astute observers suggested that the answer lay in the series' opening titles. In what is clearly meant to evoke Richard Drew's haunting photograph of September 11, 2001, the animated sequence features the silhouette of a man in suit and tie toppling in slow motion from the window of a skyscraper. Noting the likeness, Tom Junod observes that "for all its American-Century trappings," *Mad Men* is "set squarely in the age of American decline."[1] But as the show's critical and popular success paradoxically also implies, narratives centering on white middle- and upper-middle-class male experience are themselves on the rise in the post-9/11 era.

New York Times critic Charles McGrath made a similar observation in a 2004 article entitled "Heading Home to Adultery and Angst," which celebrates the arrival of writers such as Tom Perrotta and Chang-rae Lee and their return to the well-trod suburban terrain of "Updike and the ghost of Cheever" (E1). Though McGrath credits these new writers with conferring fresh hipness on a literary tradition largely abandoned as "too old, too square, too white and middle class" (E1), the novels that draw his attention—Lee's *Aloft* and Perrotta's *Little Children* as well as subsequent acclaimed suburban novels like Richard Ford's *Lay of the Land* (2006), Philip Roth's *Everyman* (2006), Eric Puchner's *Model Home* (2010), Joshua Ferris's *The Unnamed* (2010), and Jonathan Franzen's *Freedom* (2010)—all center on such old, square, white middle-class male protagonists. Why this apparently retrograde return? More immigrants and people in poverty now live in the suburbs than in urban areas,[2] so these narratives of middle-class, middle-aged white male angst seem oddly out of step, especially in the context of the traumatic events of 9/11 and a tense, ongoing aftermath that by 2004 had left the populace not only shaken but fearful, angry, and bitterly polarized.[3]

These novels demand to be read in precisely that context of recent events. Such a claim may seem counterintuitive. In his book *After the Fall: American Literature Since 9/11* (2011), Richard Gray charges that, by and large, post-9/11 American novels merely "assimilate the unfamiliar into familiar structures. The crisis is, in every sense of the word, domesticated" (30). Elizabeth Anker offers a politicized version of Gray's critique in her argument that the post-9/11 novel revolves around the "metaphor of male mid-life crisis" born of "a longing to return to a bygone era of American omnipotence wherein white, heteronormative, patrician masculinity was still sacrosanct" (468). The post-9/11 novels that Anker and Gray examine, in other words, may register catastrophe and chaos, but they do so in order to give voice to the nostalgic impulse for order and male authority.

The path of writers once again "heading home" to suburbia in order to focus on the typical existential woes of the beleaguered white male would appear to confirm these scholars' charge that the events of 9/11 and their aftermath have resulted in an insular and reactionary body of fiction. It is my contention, however, that the male-authored suburban novel's very insistence upon the quotidian and the domestic provides the basis for its unique contribution to the growing corpus of post-9/11 literature. The novels I examine in the following chapters for the most part assiduously avoid engaging the event itself and the divisive politics that came after 9/11 so as not to devolve into the same "us versus them" thinking that these works collectively work to counteract. Instead, they circle it—and in the process define it anew.

The novels that concern Gray and Anker—among them Jonathan Safran Foer's *Extremely Loud and Incredibly Close* (2006) and Don DeLillo's *Falling Man* (2007)—vividly return readers to the day's devastation with characters whose lives are destroyed when the Twin Towers, the nation's most potent icon of economic might, come crashing down. But these cataclysmic novels are not the only ones to address 9/11. The post-9/11 male-authored novels that I engage take place in the sprawling terrain that stretches out beyond the Twin Towers—the postwar suburbs that since the end of World War II have likewise served as a powerful advertisement of US dominance to people around the globe by projecting "a standard of living commensurate with the nation's status as the leader of the 'free world,'" as Robert Beauregard puts it (6). This fiction, however indirectly, grapples with the implications of the apparent decline of the United States' economic, geopolitical, and moral authority both before and after 9/11. These novels concern themselves not with the conditions of large-scale catastrophe but instead with those of an anxious everyday that is often as banal as it is nerve-wracking. The protagonist of Tom Perrotta's *Little Children* contends with the exigencies of child care and the looming threat of a sexual predator at the same time. In Franzen's *Freedom*, highway congestion and suburban sprawl compete with mountaintop removal and the war in Iraq in raising its protagonist's blood pressure. Far from devolving into the trivial, in these novels the main character's concerns are ultimately subsumed by events that render his environment uncertain and impermanent, so that his personal troubles are finally exposed for what they are: the inconsequential luxuries of a dated past. These novels all corroborate the assessment of Ford's protagonist in *The Lay of the Land*, that "*before* is everlastingly gone. There is only everlastingly *after*" (458). The "familiar structures" that have long supported the suburban novel—stasis, angst, alienation—are rendered irrelevant if not unfamiliar. Further, these novels resist the "desire for closure" that Samuel Cohen identifies in some post-9/11 traumatic narratives, which may be "too quick to heal the wounds" they uncover in their desire to reaffirm readers' wishful belief "that everything turns out all right for America in the end" (161).

The suburban novels I examine share a narrative vision that turns upon a fulcrum of determined open-endedness that operates like the insidious color-coded threats that nibble at the edges of post-9/11 consciousness. Ford's *The Lay of the Land*, which I discuss in the first chapter, ends with its protagonist quite literally in midair—he is on a plane, headed for the Mayo Clinic, the prognosis for his prostate cancer unclear. The protagonist of Lee's *Aloft*, the focus of my second chapter, is last seen standing in a hole in his own backyard that just as easily represents either a fresh start or a fresh grave. These novels advance an aesthetic of contingency that provides the basis for a new suburban literary tradition. The pervasive sense of uncertainty that hovers over *The Lay of the Land* and *Aloft* becomes almost unbearable in Franzen's *Freedom*, which I examine in Chapter Three. The news of the day—9/11, but more particularly the war in Iraq, an economy running amok, and an environment on the brink of collapse—fuels its protagonist Walter Berglund's unbridled rage. In contrast to the noise that characterizes *Freedom*, Philip Roth's diminutive *Everyman* is certainly a much quieter novel but no less unnerving, as I'll demonstrate in my fourth chapter. Here, the novel's white middle-class protagonist is a frail senior citizen who relocates to a retirement community in New Jersey to ease his anxiety after the Twin Towers attacks. The novel may seem paltry when compared to Roth's grandly ambitious American Trilogy, *American Pastoral* (1997), *The Human Stain* (1998), and the post-9/11 alternate-historical novel, *The Plot Against America* (2004). But while those sweeping works look back to consider the nation's fraught history, *Everyman* centers on a character doing his best to contend with a distraught everyday while also coming to terms with the mistakes of his past—a reckoning that is all the more poignant since the novel begins at its protagonist's graveside.

Ford, Lee, Franzen, and Roth are not the new writers that McGrath champions but are well-established authors. However, as my first four chapters illustrate, in terms of setting, mood, and especially characterization, the post-9/11 suburban novels of these writers feel fundamentally different from earlier works in which they cover the same approximate turf. Amid the real and metaphorical rubble of 9/11, these authors concern themselves not so much with crisis, but with what comes after in order to "engage productively with an otherwise scary and unmanageable world," as Franzen himself put it in an interview after *Freedom*'s publication (Grossman 48). Ford, Lee, Franzen, and Roth seize the post-9/11 moment to hold their white middle-class male protagonists accountable for both their actions and their inaction. In the wake of devastating loss, *Freedom*'s Walter Berglund, for instance, finally directs his rage inward in order to confront the hard truth of his own prideful intractability—a process that not only subdues but softens him so that he becomes more compassionate and forgiving. Significantly, female novelists who take the suburb as their setting similarly evince a spirit of forgiveness in their depictions of white middle-class men whose bearings are unsettled by their experiences. In my final chapter, I consider suburban novels by established female authors, such as Anne Tyler's *Digging to America* (2006), Gish Jen's *World and Town* (2010), and A. M. Homes's *May We Be Forgiven* (2012), all of which feature flawed male characters who ultimately learn to take a measure of responsibility for themselves and others.

In her examination of twentieth-century suburban novels such as Sinclair Lewis's *Babbitt*, Sloan Wilson's *The Man in the Gray Flannel Suit*, and John Updike's *Rabbit* tetralogy, among others, Catherine Jurca has criticized what she identifies as the "empowering rhetorics of victimization" by which the white male suburban protagonist deflects blame for the privilege he enjoys (19). Jurca asserts that "nothing comes more naturally" to these affluent everymen "than feeling bad—maltreated, rather than angry or guilty—about being the white middle class" (19). The main character of Eric Puchner's post-9/11 suburban novel *Model Home*, on the other hand, may have plenty to feel bad about—he has lost his home, his family, and his livelihood thanks to a real estate deal gone sour—but the novel makes clear that the devastation that befalls not only him but his entire family results directly from his own greed and dishonesty. As Puchner's novel illustrates, the new suburban novel takes its white male protagonist to task for upholding the neoliberal values of individualism, private property ownership, and upward mobility that, as we shall see, have both supported and masked white male privilege. At the very least, these novelists have caught up with critics who have dismissed this fiction for overstating and universalizing middle-class woes, weaving, as Andrew Hoberek notes, "narratives of individual dispossession that enforce [the middle class's] cultural dominance rather than seeking a potentially more useful affiliation with those . . . outside the magic circle of capital" (32). The calamities that punctuate these suburban novels suggest that this charmed sphere is a delusion.[4]

There are, in fact, plenty of concrete reasons why the suburban setting is crucial to an aesthetic of contingency, not least of which being that, of the 2,800 people killed in the Twin Towers, almost 1,400 were from the suburbs of New York, New Jersey, and Connecticut.[5] Any remaining illusion of security and certainty was shattered that day as suburbia was cast, at least for the moment, into the realm of uncertainty and catastrophe. The suburban setting also best answers Gray's call for a new novelistic form to match the new realities reshaping the United States. He cites several statistics that indicate immigrants, especially those from outside of Europe, are radically transforming the nation (22–23), but what he does not mention is that the majority of these immigrants now live in the suburbs, alongside an increasingly poor and steadily graying population.[6] Put simply, the entrenched image of suburbia as an exclusive haven of white privilege no longer pertains.[7] Further, these communities now contend with congestion, crumbling infrastructure, insufficient affordable housing and health care, schools ill-equipped to deal with the needs of a diverse student body, and increased crime, all while their tax bases are shrinking.[8] If the postwar suburbs have historically provided a suitable stage for a glittering master narrative of American prosperity built around the care, feeding, and sheltering of the fetishized nuclear family, these same suburbs now tell a story of American decline. Thus, the cohort of writers who have returned to this beat do not offer the postwar suburb as a retreat from the larger world but suggest instead that the world has come to the suburbs.[9]

The question persists: if the suburbs themselves are no longer defined by a sense of stability and ease nor by blinding whiteness, what can we glean from post-9/11 suburban novels that center on the experience of the kind of materially comfortable middle-class, middle-aged white everyman who has been a staple feature of suburban fiction since its inception? In the first place, it does not detract from the range of victims killed on 9/11 to note that three quarters of them were, in fact, white middle-class males.[10] Who better to speak to and for a nation that must suddenly contend with the "endemic uncertainty" that now characterizes a "world risk society" than the arguably complacent white, middle-class everyman (Beck 12)?

Unquestionably, these novels register the wide-ranging distress of the historical present through the all-too-familiar "insecurities of white, upper-middle-class manhood" (Anker 6). Yet by no means do these novels reinscribe white male privilege, either by valorizing their protagonists or by suggesting that they are victims. As Kaja Silverman has claimed, historical trauma —whether a war, an earthquake, or a large-scale terrorist attack—has the capacity to "interrupt or even deconstitute what society assumes to be its master narrative" (55). Certainly the events of September 11 profoundly unsettled a nation that had been lulled by the longest economic boom in its history. But the speed with which the government and the media sought to return the nation to a pre-9/11 status quo was likewise staggering. In the days following the crisis, politicians and pundits moved quickly to transform overwhelming trauma into resounding victory: victims became heroes, and the events of that day yet another demonstration of our indomitable national character.[11]

American Unexceptionalism, on the other hand, argues that through their depictions of unremarkable everymen who are neither victims nor heroes, male-authored post-9/11 suburban novels counteract the narrative of American innocence and resolve swiftly marketed by the mass media and the Bush administration. In her psychoanalytic examination of several films in the immediate post-World War II era, Silverman hopefully proffers the idea that "the typical male subject, like his female counterpart, might learn to live with lack" (65). Gordon Hutner notes that in the immediate postwar era that lack was quickly filled by narratives that told the story of our preternatural national resilience. The audience for these stories were Americans desperate to have their cherished myths restored (243). Similarly, in his discussion of several twenty-first-century popular culture texts, Hamilton Carroll asserts that the events of 9/11 and their aftermath have accelerated rather than derailed efforts to recuperate white male privilege. He cites the "everyday hero" who emerged immediately after September 11 in the figure of the firefighter as well as the extraordinary public servant Jack Bauer, the counterterrorist agent and retrograde hero of Fox TV's wildly successful drama *24*. Both Bauer and the firefighter are advanced as patriots who bespeak a reinvigorated and particularly aggressive form of American exceptionalism (19–20).[12]

Clearly, the feeble, elderly, and anonymous everyman at the center of Roth's *Everyman* cannot compete with these robust and "exemplary citizens" who rise to extraordinary circumstances in order to serve the common good and keep the world safe for democracy. Indeed, it is my central argument that the post-9/11 suburban everyman demonstrates how to live with lack by being so obviously lacking, and effectively counters the narrative of American exceptionalism by being so emphatically unexceptional. *American Unexceptionalism* follows the rise, decline, and reconstitution of the suburban literary tradition from its postwar roots to the harrowing present, but not to argue that its newest iteration reasserts the centrality of the white middle-class male perspective. Instead, these books reorient that perspective. The post-9/11 suburban novels I examine all feature protagonists past their prime whose trajectories defy the logic of upward mobility to trace alternate routes down and out. These everymen are brought low by sickness, financial ruin, and devastating loss. Their stories possess a new set of conventions, and they teach a different set of lessons to a humbled middle-class readership.

Contested Masculinity and the Pre-9/11 Suburban Novel

The unexceptional everyman certainly is not new to suburban literature. Earlier iterations of the species were imagined as misunderstood victims who have always been "plagued," McGrath asserts, "by spiritual emptiness and a sense of collective purposelessness" (E1). As I will elaborate in the following chapter, whatever we may make of them today, iconic postwar everymen such as Cheever's Neddy Merrill (from "The Swimmer"), Updike's Rabbit, and Richard Yates's Frank Wheeler were cast as "frustrated poets of a sort" who possess "almost visionary clarity and sensitivity" (McGrath). By the 1990s, however, in what amounts to a dystopian orgy of mass destruction, those writers who deigned to use the suburbs as their setting took it upon themselves to violently punish their alienated protagonists, whom they now characterized as plagued by self-pity, solipsism, deviancy, avarice, and cowardice. These stories send their entire worlds up in flames real and metaphorical.[13] Novels such as David Gates's *Jernigan* (1992) and *Preston Falls* (1998), Jeffrey Eugenides's *The Virgin Suicides* (1993), Rick Moody's *The Ice Storm* (1994), T. C. Boyle's *The Tortilla Curtain* (1995), A. M. Homes's *Music for Torching* (2000), and Jonathan Franzen's *The Corrections* (2001) depict the white middle-class everyman's limited agency and resigned disengagement as pathetic smokescreens meant to hide in plain sight his single-minded, childish self-interest and refusal to take responsibility for himself, his family, or the larger world. In *Music for Torching*, Paul Weiss assuages his boredom by smoking crack, wearing his wife's nightgowns, having his genitals tattooed, and indulging in not one but multiple simultaneous extramarital affairs that require a standing reservation at the local motel. After he attempts to burn his house down, he sighs, "You can't control everything" (41). What he really means, of course, is that he has no desire to take responsibility for his own actions. Thus, he is positively triumphant when the insurance adjuster agrees to cover the damages under what he terms "the stupidity clause" (137).

These novels, written on the eve of 9/11, feature suicide, horrific accidents, environmental disaster, school shootings, incest, and economic meltdown, perhaps to indicate that the familiar structures of suburbia—home, family, community—are irrevocably broken. Many of these novels —*Music for Torching, The Ice Storm, The Tortilla Curtain*—punctuate this point in their depictions of the violent deaths of children. Not one but all five of the daughters of Mr. Lisbon, the spineless, effeminate father *in The Virgin Suicides,* kill themselves. In *The Corrections,* Franzen suggests simply that all of the children have fled the crumbling suburbs, leaving the decrepit and demented paterfamilias, Alfred Lambert, to mind the fort until he or the fort falls down.

It would appear that these novels are collectively determined to destroy once and for all a suburban literary franchise built on the premise of the white middle-class male-as-victim. Especially when read in the context of these novels' particular historical moment—against the backdrop of an identity politics in full flower—these 1990s suburban novels that depict detestable everymen getting their just deserts seem to contribute to the radical effort to dismantle the "hegemony of whiteness and maleness" that Kathleen Fitzpatrick argues has been "long served by the structures of traditional humanism" that she deems "an influence that has for centuries supported . . . the putatively universal ideals that function to reinforce the hierarchies of racism, sexism, heteronormativity, ethnocentricity, nationalism, and individualism" (202). Fitzpatrick follows scholars such as Donna Haraway, Ruth Frankenberg, Toni Morrison, George Lipsitz, and David Roediger who have called attention to the power and privilege that inhere in an abstract individualism that renders the white male subject invisible—as the very term "everyman" implies. As I will elaborate in my chapter concerning Philip Roth's novel *Everyman,* the white male represents the standard against which difference is measured.[14]

To be sure, the everyman's unspoken claim to the normative informs earlier versions of the male midlife crisis novel in which the "fantasy of victimization" is conceived of as a universal existential dilemma (Jurca 9). By the 1990s, however, white middle-class male despair had become a culturally specific tale of woe: masculinity was now portrayed as being crushed by "the twin pressures of domestic multiculturalism and identity politics on the one hand, and the globalization of labor and economics, on the other" (Carroll 3). Fitzpatrick analyzes this cultural shift in her discussion of a cadre of white male writers, including Franzen, DeLillo, Thomas Pynchon, and David Foster Wallace. She says that these novelists embrace their supposed marginalization in order to reserve for themselves the claim to high literary art. Carroll looks to pop culture to show how white men in general "manage the stakes of their own failure" (4). He argues that they "participate in the broader and more pernicious culture of white male injury or victimhood" that blames women and people of color for getting all of society's benefits (9, 4). The broadly held sense of crisis among white middle-class men during the 1990s is evident in the success of novels such as Chuck Palahniuk's *Fight Club* (1995), a novel about an emasculated man who goes to extremes to reclaim his manhood, and Robert Bly's self-help book, *Iron John: A Book About Men*, which spent sixty-two weeks on the *New York Times* bestseller list. These texts intervene in order to valorize and heal wounded white masculinity. In contrast, many 1990s suburban novels appear to work intently to discredit white male victimization.

Take, for example, the smug protagonist of Boyle's *The Tortilla Curtain*, Delaney Mossbacher, a self-proclaimed "liberal humanist" (3). A faithful husband, the primary caregiver for his stepson, and an ardent environmentalist, Delaney ostensibly represents the new, improved version of the white middle-class male—that 1990s phenomenon, the Sensitive New Age Guy. Yet the novel makes immediately evident the odious assumptions upon which the "structures of traditional humanism" and Delaney's unearned privilege have been built when he hits an undocumented immigrant with his car and brushes him off with a twenty-dollar bill, explaining away the inadequacy of the gesture by telling his wife, "I told you—he was *Mexican*" (15; emphasis original). Delaney leaves the man bleeding and injured, but the damage, he believes, is of no real consequence since the victim is already marked by racial, ethnic, and class difference. Indeed, Delaney subsequently imagines *himself* to be the victim, haunted as he is by the Mexican's spectral presence and convinced that the immigrant camping in "his" canyon is sullying it. After putting Delaney's childish self-absorption and sense of entitlement on full display, the author gleefully concocts both a fire and a flood that topples the liberal humanist Delaney and the structures that support him: he and his entire gated community, Arroyo Blanco (White Stream), are washed away in an angry, muddy torrent. *The Tortilla Curtain* is of a piece with the other pre-9/11 novels I've mentioned, which chastise their protagonists in similarly brutal fashion.

But as savagely as these novels may treat their odious, self-pitying white male characters, they work craftily to reinstate white male authority in general. Sally Robinson argues that white masculinity is not the victim of identity politics, after all, but instead plays strategically according to its rules in order to reclaim for itself the centrality it has always enjoyed. In her analysis of 1970s and 1980s middle-class male-authored fiction, Robinson takes note of the "wounded white men" who populate these works. These characters' "undeniable attraction to masochism" represents their efforts "to come to terms with the feminist critique of male power and privilege" (11). These "masochistic narratives," Robinson maintains, "defer closure and resolution" and depict white men who take pleasure in their own injury and disempowerment (11). In this way, Robinson argues, the novels she examines—among them Updike's *Rabbit Redux* (1970) and *Rabbit Is Rich* (1981) and Philip Roth's *My Life as a Man* (1974)—attempt to gather for their protagonists the sympathetic recognition that is the victim's due. By the 1990s, however, novelists writing in this tradition proffer protagonists who may feel they are victimized, but who are themselves responsible for inflicting wounds on themselves and others, primarily because they are so reprehensibly irresponsible. Far from being open-ended, these stories bring devastating closure to the narrative of white male self-pity. With the harrowing conclusion to *Music for Torching*, for instance, Homes effectively argues that the "fantasy of victimization" is not simply delusional but dangerously immoral. Paul, the novel's feckless protagonist, fits Robinson's masochistic model: he has had his genitals tattooed at the behest of a dominatrix lover, and they get dreadfully infected. But any humor the reader might derive from Paul's willful disempowerment is wiped out by the novel's searing conclusion. Paul's youngest son, Sammy, is taken hostage and shot by a classmate who is the son of one of Paul's many lovers. The danger signs were there all along—Paul knew that the boy's father spent his weekends playing war games and that he kept firearms in his house; he knew that the boy had bullied his son in the past; and he saw the abject terror in his son's eyes when he picked him up from a sleepover at the boy's house. But Paul chose to ignore the evidence because it might interrupt his own pursuit of pleasure. Throughout the novel Paul feigns powerlessness, but in the novel's final scene he truly is powerless. The story's damning final words, "It's over," definitively mark an end to a genre that has passed its expiration date.

Critics have excoriated Homes for the "arbitrarily violent" ending to *Music for Torching* (Clover), but the novel's conclusion is all the more disturbing for its prescience: the Columbine school shootings took place shortly after its release. *Music for Torching* is singular among the novels I've listed because it was written by a woman, but it functions in the same way that the male-authored novels do in the way that it implicitly but emphatically seeks to recover white male authority. If, as Carroll suggests, "white masculinity has learned to manage the stakes of its own failure," pre-9/11 suburban novels manage those stakes first of all by raising them to terrifying heights. These novels blame their deeply flawed everymen for the problems they depict—the demise of the family, imperiled youth, ecological ruin, world financial meltdown—to demonstrate in no uncertain terms the devastating consequences of failed patriarchy. The trope of the endangered child is frequently employed to play on readers' sympathies, and to make an urgent case for the necessity of a strong parent who will restore order to the family and protect its weakest members.

To be sure, pre-9/11 novels may dispense with a particularly degenerative strain of white masculinity, but they also capitalize on the reader's inclination to sympathize with the weak and the needy by offering in its stead a vulnerable but fundamentally decent version of the white middle-class male who deserves to be nurtured: the young son who is prematurely called to duty when his errant father abdicates all responsibility. This scenario marks the conclusion of David Gates's *Jernigan*, in which the eponymous everyman, an unemployed, unrepentant drunk, abandons not only his damaged girlfriend and her sexually abused daughter but also his own sixteen-year old son. Teetering and brandishing a gun as he makes his grand exit, he slurs, "You're the man of the family now" (231). In *The Virgin Suicides*, a motley crew of neighborhood boys valiantly attempts to rescue the Lisbon girls—after their hapless father fails—from their controlling mother and a home that has become literally noxious. Mere children themselves at the time of the girls' suicides, the would-be rescuers are helpless to change anything and can impose order only long after the fact with a collective narrative that does not solve the mystery of the girls' misery. All the story does is attest to the boys' own good intentions. In the novel's final paragraph, they conclude that "it didn't matter in the end how old they had been or that they were girls, but only that we had loved them, and that they hadn't heard us calling, still do not hear us, up here in the tree house" (248). All but eliding the fact that these lovesick boys are now middle-aged men with "thinning hair and soft bellies," and in what amounts to a bait-and-switch maneuver, the novel's collective narrator re-presents white middle-class manhood so that it is not only absolved of the sins of its fathers but is reimagined as the injured party (248). In the final analysis, the story is not about the Lisbon sisters, after all, but about the collective narrator, who as "custodians of the girls' lives," retain the power to author the story and determine its meaning (224).

The Virgin Suicides and all the other novels I've discussed in this section variously undermine the figure of the white middle-class male-male-as-victim, but they resurrect this very same figure by way of an inchoate version of him that deserves the reader's sympathy. Rick Moody's *The Ice Storm*, for instance, works in a similar fashion to *The Virgin Suicides*. Though the novel chronicles the terrible fallout from the misbehavior of selfish, swinging upper-middle-class suburbanites in the 1970s, the narrative ultimately belongs to these characters' sensitive son, Paul Hood, who is left to sort out the pieces. As with Eugenides's novel, the conclusion only fleetingly reminds readers that twenty years have passed since the events described, so that the young narrator is himself a middle-aged white male. More disturbingly, in the final scene of *Music for Torching*, it is Paul Weiss's older son, Danny, who at age twelve takes action while his father stands paralyzed, charging the building and scooping up his younger brother after he has been shot. The description of the adolescent boy with his younger brother in his arms, his shirt covered in blood, elicits the reader's deep sympathy: "Help me," he pleads (353). Danny is thus both victim and hero who, if properly cared for, could grow into the father figure that the narrative desperately calls for.

The Corrections, published immediately before 9/11, alters the shape of this outline only slightly. In this case, the shamelessly devious and irresponsible white middle-class male and his kind, innocent son are conflated in the character of Chip Lambert. Wantonly self-absorbed throughout the novel, in the final pages, Chip is mystically transformed by the demise of his authoritarian father into a dutiful son, and the only one his dying, demented father trusts, since "you looked at Chipper and you knew he'd never lie to you. There was a sweetness to Chipper that nobody else could counterfeit" (555). Throughout the novel, Chip has been anything but sweet or honest. Yet in the final pages the description turns miraculously apt: forgiven of the financial debt he owes his sister if only he will assume responsibility for the father she herself cannot handle, a new version of Chip develops—a son who wipes his father's chin and who in short order falls in love, becomes a father himself, marries, and takes a full-time teaching job. Rendered blameless by his sister, it is he who emerges as the novel's hero by reestablishing order and reaffirming forsaken family values. In her review dated September 4, 2001, Michiko Kakutani lauded the novel for painting a "harrowing portrait of America in the late 1990's—an America deep in the grip of that decade's money madness and sick with envy, resentment, greed, acquisitiveness, and self-delusion" (Kakutani). Kakutani is just one of the critics who credited *The Corrections* with diagnosing a nation in dire need of correction. What the novel also offers, though, in the form of its duly chastened and fully corrected white male protagonist, is a prescription that will make it well: a fully refurbished patriarchal order.

It should come as no surprise that immediately after 9/11, it is precisely a strong patriarchal figure that cultural critic Frank Rich, in an op-ed in the *New York Times*, summons to the scene:

> On a day when countless children in America lost their fathers, the rest of us started searching for a father, too. When a nation is under siege, it wants someone to tell us what to do, to protect us from bullies, to tell us that everything's O.K. and that it's safe to go home now. It's an impulse, perhaps, that we never outgrow. (n.p.)

Rich is just one among many of the putatively liberal cultural intelligentsia who in the aftermath of 9/11 not only predicted but earnestly yearned for a return to so-called family values and a strong patriarchal order. One week after *Vanity Fair* editor Graydon Carter made his now infamous proclamation that the age of irony had come to an end and just two weeks after the Twin Tower attacks, Roger Rosenblatt, in a *Time* magazine essay, concurred that "people may at last be ready to say what they wholeheartedly believe. The kindness of people toward others in distress is real. . . . And the preciousness of ordinary living is real as well—all to be taken seriously, perhaps, in a new and chastened time. The greatness of the country: real. The anger: real. The pain: too real" (n.p).[15] Given that these pronouncements were made just days after 9/11, the sense of injury and the hunger for security they express is understandable. There is no question that the events of that day were horrifying. But these commentators also articulate a "them vs. us" mentality that is troubling. Consider, for instance, Rosenblatt's call to " the good folks in charge of America's intellectual life" to embrace a new sense of "seriousness":

> Are you looking for something to take seriously? Begin with evil. The fact before our eyes is that a group of savage zealots took the sweet and various lives of those ordinarily traveling from place to place, ordinarily starting a day of work, or—extraordinarily—coming to help and rescue others. Freedom? That real enough for you? Everything we cling to in our free and sauntering country was imperiled by the terrorists. (n.p.)

Rosenblatt's insistence on our national innocence in contrast to the "savage" "evil" that detests our freedom immerses itself in the rhetorics of American exceptionalism in general and what Svetlana Boym identifies as restorative nostalgia in particular. As I will discuss more fully in the first chapter in my analysis of Richard Ford's Frank Bascombe trilogy, Boym notes that restorative nostalgia places the emphasis on *nostos*, which means "return home," with home being conceived not as a "duration but a perfect snapshot," rather than on *algia*, which means "loss" (41). Those who enlist this sort of nostalgia, Boym asserts, are engaged in a rebuilding project that figures the idealized home as under attack. The project of restorative nostalgia is thus particularly suited to nationalist aims, since it works to foment a desire to return to the established order. We can surely see the degree to which the Bush administration rushed to craft just such a recuperative narrative. In his address to the Joint Session of Congress on September 20, 2001, President Bush championed our exceptional national unity and strength, celebrating "the decency of a loving and giving people who have made the grief of strangers their own. My fellow citizens, for the last nine days, the entire world has seen for itself the state of our Union—and it is strong" (Bush, Joint Session). But the President quickly segued from this healing narrative to a revenge plot that figures our nation as an idyllic home that must be defended against a vicious enemy: "Tonight we are a country awakened to danger and called to defend freedom. Our grief has turned to anger, and anger to resolution. Whether we bring our enemies to justice, or bring justice to our enemies, justice will be done" (Bush, Joint Session). The Bush administration would stick to this script in its efforts to justify two wars, the violation of the Geneva Convention, extraordinary renditions, torture, racial profiling, and the abuse of civil liberties under the so-called Patriot Act, all in the name of the putative freedom that accounts for our amorphous enemies' wrath.

More insidiously but arguably just as troubling, those who create and comment on culture proved equally eager to contribute to this reassuring narrative. This is precisely the project that Anker and Carroll claim drives the post-9/11 texts they analyze. Anker examines literary fiction and Carroll concentrates on pop-cultural artifacts, but they both conclude that all of these works purposefully "evince deep nostalgia for an earlier epoch of American greatness " (Anker 468). The return home to suburbia that McGrath heralds might likewise speak to the universal desire for the sense of security and the desire to go home that Rich describes. Without question, the moment offers novelists the opportunity to revisit and further empower the nascent white male father figure augured by the pre-9/11 suburban novel.

Curiously, however, these male-authored post-9/11 suburban novels do not work to reestablish stability, nor do they offer the white middle-class male as a father figure with the ability to protect those under his care from harm. In *Aloft*, when his daughter goes into premature labor while aboard his single-engine plane, Jerry Battle does his best but is unsuccessful in bringing her to safety. In *The Lay of the Land*, Frank Bascombe intervenes when heavily armed thieves invade his neighbors' home, but they are killed anyway. Unlike the white "everyday heroes" that Carroll examines, such as the Marvel Comics firemen or, more particularly, the middle-class everyman character Clint Eastwood plays in the 2008 film, *Gran Torino*, who lays down his own life for the sake of his ethnically shifting community, the protagonists that I examine do not suffer from white knight syndrome. Or if they do, circumstances cure them of the illusion that they possess any special power to control or mitigate outcomes.[16]

Post-9/11 novels pointedly do *not* seize an occasion when white middle-class men did happen to comprise the majority of the day's victims to revive the all-too-familiar figure of the besieged everyman. Instead, these novels introduce a new specimen altogether: a middle-class, middle-aged white male who holds himself accountable both for his failures and his failure to act. *Aloft*'s protagonist, Jerry Battle, has made a business of burying shame and paving over painful memories. But after his daughter confronts him with the damage he has done to her and her brother by preventing them from coming to terms with their mother's death, Jerry must ruefully conclude that had he not insulated himself so well, "no doubt things could have been different between us, much different" (315). These protagonists' soul-searching are not hollow acts of contrition meant to absolve them of past mistakes but are considered, fraught reevaluations of the assumptions that have supported their privilege and shaped their self-pitying narratives: the "structures of traditional liberal humanism" that have imagined the everyman as a heroic antihero pitted against a hostile society (Fitzpatrick 202). The Twin Towers themselves can be read as the concretization of that double-edged narrative. Their architecture once both secured and obscured the white middle-class male's privilege. His position as a worker bee in the world's tallest hive bolstered his claim to victimization at the hands of an all-consuming, dehumanizing corporate culture, but the salary he took showed how he benefited at the same time. In the aftermath of 9/11, with those structures reduced to rubble, the novelists I examine in *American Unexceptionalism* expose the hypocrisy of this Janus-faced narrative by taking a clear-eyed look backward at the postwar suburban aesthetic to implicate the white middle-class everyman at its center.

These novels engage the very rubrics of the established male midlife crisis narrative in order to reassess and rewrite it. Richard Ohmann offers a particularly useful outline of this tradition in his analysis of the "structure of feeling" that underwrites what he identifies as "pre-canonical" texts written between 1960 and 1975—among them, the first two installments of Updike's *Rabbit* tetralogy and Roth's *Portnoy's Complaint* (1969). These are midlife crisis novels, he asserts, that imagine their white middle-class male protagonists as alienated by the rampant consumerism, numbing working conditions, and fierce competition that characterize what is variously labeled a "sick society," "the establishment," and "the system" (210). These "personal illness stories," as Ohmann calls them, "transform deep social contradictions into a dynamic of personal crisis, a sense of there being no comfortable place in the world for the private self" (217). As I discuss in the first chapter, this man-against-society formula may have arguably served a purpose in the novels written within Ohmann's time frame. But by the early 1980s, and after Margaret Thatcher's infamous declaration that society has ceased to exist, this battle had been rendered meaningless (Thatcher n.p.). The isolated suburbanites who roam listlessly in male midlife crisis novels from this point on merely affirm the prerogatives of a loosely organized neoliberal society that celebrates self-actualization over the common good.

It is exactly this equation that authors such as Ford, Lee, Franzen, and Roth seek to rewrite in their post-9/11 suburban novels. Further, these established writers return to the suburban setting to take stock of their role in contributing to this flawed narrative. As per Rosenblatt's directive, and as opposed to their pre-9/11 counterparts, these post-9/11 texts are not ironic but deeply felt. But far from reiterating a dangerous "us versus them" mode of inquiry, the novels in question offer white middle-class everymen who conduct self-inventories and find themselves seriously lacking. Ford's Frank Bascombe, a real estate broker, comes to terms with his own role in nurturing a suburban ethos of personal property ownership that has been especially profitable for him. He could be speaking for the novelist himself when he avers, "In other words, I'm implicated" (47). To be sure, these post-9/11 midlife crisis narratives offer new iterations of the "illness story" to provocatively suggest that the fictional white middle-class everyman and the society he opposes share the same affliction: a predilection for valorizing individual desire, the sole purpose of which is to keep in motion the wheels of production and reproduction upon which our market-driven liberal democracy turns.

Before turning to these established authors' treatment of the male midlife crisis narrative, however, let me pause to consider relative newcomer Joshua Ferris's novel *The Unnamed* (2010), which vividly illustrates the reformulation of the personal illness story. The white middle-class male protagonist, Tim Farnsworth, does not suffer the usual malaise or sense of alienation we have come to expect. A senior partner at a white-shoe law firm, he loves his work, his wife, his daughter, and the material fruits of his success. However, he contends with a strange and debilitating medical condition for which there is no precedent, diagnosis, or treatment: a random compulsion to walk aimlessly to the point of exhaustion.

In setting and theme, the novel evokes Cormac McCarthy's 2006 post-apocalyptic novel, *The Road*. In counterpoint to the purposeful journey that McCarthy's unnamed protagonist undertakes with his son to the coast, Farnsworth embarks on circular and pointless odysseys across a treacherous landscape of suburban sprawl, littered Walmart parking lots, and vast expanses of industrial wastelands that breed predatory crime. With the exception of the nuclear unit of wife and daughter and colleagues who are only concerned with billable hours, *The Unnamed* is devoid of extended family members, prying neighbors, or any sort of community whatsoever, thus perversely confirming that Thatcher's vision has come true: society has ceased to exist. Vaguely futuristic in feeling and stripped bare of any historical referents that would locate it in time, the novel takes place in a no man's land sometime after what Francis Fukuyama has notoriously identified as "the end of History," signaled by the triumph of the liberal democratic state and technologically driven capitalism. In contrast to Fukuyama's assertion that the major alternatives to liberal democracy have reached the point of "total exhaustion" (Fukuyama 1989, 3), Ferris's novel suggests that it is liberal democracy itself that is exhausted, as evidenced not only by the depleted landscape but also by Farnsworth's deterioration: both body and soul grow increasingly wretched before giving out entirely in the novel's foregone conclusion. Farnsworth's "disease," ceaseless, compulsive motion for its own sake, parodies the ethos of upward mobility, which the story implies has likewise accomplished nothing other than exhausting limited resources. Indeed, Farnsworth's aimless treks, which take him across the country and back again, render him a perverse embodiment of rugged individualism: he dies demented and alone, his sole reward being that "he never [has] to rise again" (310).

Whereas *The Unnamed* clearly diagnoses the illness that afflicts individual and society alike in a fully evolved neoliberal democracy, the novels I concentrate on in the following chapters—Ford's *The Lay of the Land*, Chang-rae Lee's *Aloft*, Jonathan Franzen's *Freedom*, and Philip Roth's *Everyman*—move beyond critique to make a modest but bold adjustment by conceiving of their white middle-class everymen no longer in opposition to society but in relation to it. Consider, for instance, the difference between Richard Yates's much-praised 1960 novel, *Revolutionary Road*, and Lee's novel, *Aloft*. Yates's prototypical suburban novel concludes with an image of a middle-class, middle-aged white male willfully sealing himself off from the world's unpleasantness by turning off his hearing aid. The novel thus participates in the genre's entrenched habit of schooling its readers in the rules of disengagement. In striking contrast, Lee's novel features a detached protagonist, Jerry Battle, who is chided by his daughter into being "more wise and generous and self-sacrificing" than he has been over the past sixty years (316). Jerry duly takes this advice to heart when he expands his home to provide housing for his noisy, messy, extended family, itself a microcosm for the suburbs' sprawling, diverse, and ill-housed population. Lest Jerry's gesture be mistaken for the beneficence of the suspect figure of the white knight, however, the household follows a new set of rules that require everyone to contribute according to his or her abilities, thereby stressing interdependence over independence and advancing a new model for middle-class being and belonging.

These are by no means utopian novels, however. As I've noted, these works are insistently open-ended and even downright bleak, nostalgic only in their emphasis on *algia*, or loss. But in their depictions of crisis and, more importantly, its anxious, ongoing aftermath, they advance an aesthetic of contingency that inaugurates a new suburban literary tradition, the basis of which is connectedness rather than alienation. If the pre-9/11 male-authored suburban novel offers the figure of the son who might carry the torch in order to preserve white male privilege, these post-9/11 novels give the last word to their female characters, who locate in suffering and despair the common grounds for empathy and an ethos that favors social justice over individual desire. In Roth's *Everyman*, it is not the unnamed protagonist's bitter, estranged sons but his beloved daughter, "besmirched only by her unstinting generosity," who arranges his funeral and speaks on his behalf (105). All of these male-authored suburban novels nod toward the warming influence of their main characters' daughters, sisters, wives, and girlfriends in order to overturn male-gendered neoliberal values of individualism, privacy, and competition that originally provided their foundation. Correspondingly, the novels I examine in my final chapter, suburban novels written by women after 9/11, hold their white middle-class male characters accountable and displace them from their traditional seat at the head of the table, but they also offer them a provisional spot at a new table whose shape is still being determined.

While these male- and female-authored novels may not be overtly political, they do work to reshape their readers' political consciousness and perhaps even facilitate change by encouraging middle-class readers to "learn to live with lack," as Silverman puts it (65). These novels' commitment to that objective is especially fitting when considered in the context of the 2008 economic meltdown. In the 2010 film *The Company Men*, a middle-class, middle-aged white everyman who has recently lost his job in the corporate downsizing that followed the Great Recession of 2008 implicitly compares his situation to that of the victims of 9/11: "The world didn't stop. The newspapers still came in the morning. . . . My life ended, and nobody noticed." This character sees the two events in opposition to each other, but as his comparison makes clear, they are entwined in the middle-class imagination. As the passage quoted above also suggests, this character and the other recently unemployed "company men" the film depicts—all white upper-middle-class males—are inclined toward self-pity and a determination to get their former lives and occupations back rather than toward soul-searching and a willingness to imagine a new reality.

Recent suburban literature, however, has likewise conjoined these events in order to foster something akin to what Christopher Hayes calls in *Twilight of the Elites* (2012) a "radicalized upper middle class": those who have been spurred by the events surrounding 9/11 and the financial meltdown to recognize that they have more in common with the working class and poor than with the wealthy few above them (230). In Eric Puchner's novel *Model Home* (2010), for instance, the protagonist's (self-inflicted) financial woes are temporarily overshadowed by a devastating explosion in the middle of the novel that leaves his son permanently disfigured by third-degree burns; the two crises turn out to be inextricably bound up with one another, and together they offer a scathing critique of the false premise of upward mobility. The tenets of capitalism have not only failed to sustain these characters but have leveled them. Unlike *The Company Men*, the novel eschews self-pity and extends beyond critique to suggest new alliances and new modes of being that might overturn this dehumanizing ethos. Like its pre-9/11 counterparts, Puchner's novel features a son who must answer for the sins of his father. But unlike those earlier novels, which offer up a fully ameliorated filial substitute for the failed patriarchy, in *Model Home* the son has been damaged beyond recognition and repair. He thus learns that there are "two planets, the one where unburned people lived, filled with music and light and strolls on the beach, and the other one," populated, for instance, by an Afghani girl whose melted face has been horrifyingly captured in a photograph that hangs in the L.A. burn unit where he has been treated (344). Acknowledging that he will never return to the former planet, he assumes his position in the latter world, where he gives and receives comfort and care among his fellow burn victims.

If this body of literature has historically been faulted for its limited vision, it has now gained a depth of field that self-consciously folds the personal into the political and considers the have-nots along with the haves in order to forge a community of readers who are now accountable to the larger world. *American Unexceptionalism* reads the post-9/11 suburban male midlife crisis novel not only against the backdrop of its particularly vexed cultural moment, but also in the context of earlier iterations to chart the various registers with which this genre has deigned to speak to, for, and about its middle-class readers since its inception in the postwar era. If the genre once sought to shape and instruct a rising middle class, it now addresses a middle class in decline.[17] Rearticulating middle-class experience in this manner is not without its problems, as Derek Nystrom has recently pointed out. In a discussion about *The Company Men*, he notes that such efforts at building solidarity among the classes "often obscure as much as they reveal about differently situated experiences of social vulnerability" (n.p.).[18] As I will discuss in the chapters ahead, however, in varying degrees the novels I engage, which all happen to feature recently unemployed or underemployed upper-middle-class men, call attention to the range of suffering and disenfranchisement felt by different socioeconomic groups in order to redraw the suburban community and the white male's place within that community.

■ ■ ■

In the first chapter, "The Canonical Everyman: Richard Ford's Frank Bascombe Novels and the Challenge to Neoliberal Suburbia," I trace the postwar suburban novel from its literary roots to its latest incarnation, centering on Ford's trilogy, *The Sportswriter* (1986), *Independence Day* (1995), and most recently *The Lay of the Land* (2006). Taken together, these novels chart the shifting cultural, political, and economic landscape that has shaped the concerns of the suburban literary tradition and accounted for its rise, decline, and reconstitution. I therefore begin with a discussion of Ford's first two Bascombe novels in order to mark the radical shift in tone and theme that arrives in the final post-9/11 installment. In *The Sportswriter* Ford consciously dons the mantle of his literary predecessors by introducing an everyman who invokes (as Frank Bascombe's name suggests) Yates's Frank Wheeler, as well as Sinclair Lewis's George F. Babbitt and Updike's Harry "Rabbit" Angstrom. Like his predecessors, Bascombe is a heroic antihero alienated by the deadening environment of his suburb. But unlike any of these forebears, the Bascombe we encounter in *The Sportswriter* during the era of Reagan and Thatcher does not contend with a community that demands from him conformity and boosterism. Instead, his suburb, the fictional Haddam, New Jersey, fetishizes property and privacy. Thus, while Ford's novel may operate squarely within the established postwar suburban literary tradition, and may similarly purport to diagnose a sick society, it conveys another meaning entirely in its validation of the individual who pursues his own aims. When Bascombe returns to Haddam in the second installment of the trilogy, *Independence Day*, he once again traces the trajectory of his literary progenitors, who, like Cheever's suburban everymen, are not "eagles," but "canaries soon caged," as Irving Howe bitterly notes ("Realities" 131). *Independence Day*, like *The Sportswriter*, therefore reconfirms the established order by fully recommitting its protagonist to his patriarchal role. Indeed, in the novel's conclusion, which features a Fourth of July parade that Bascombe has helped to underwrite, he is figured as a beneficent town father.

This exordium prepares for my analysis of Ford's latest installment, *The Lay of the Land*, in which Ford advances an aesthetic of contingency that challenges the story of upward mobility that has been written into the suburban ethos. The novel is rife with the sense of anxiety and vulnerability that characterized the New Jersey suburbs in the aftermath of 9/11: within the first several pages, a senseless murder and a terrorist attack at the local hospital bespeak the sense of danger that has come to characterize this formerly ostensibly secure terrain. Strategically, however, the novel takes place over the Thanksgiving weekend of 2000, when the presidential election between Bush and Gore was as yet undecided. This pre-9/11 vantage point allows Ford to implicitly examine the conditions that precipitated that day's horrific events without devolving into the sort of finger pointing that would result in a counterproductive "them vs. us" ethos. To be sure, Ford also takes the occasion to reassess the individualistic assumptions that provided the foundation for his previous two novels and consider how these premises might likewise have played a role in fomenting the conditions that have led us to the edge of disaster. In this manner, Ford tills the ground for a new aesthetic to take root, one that no longer trains its eye on individual experience but instead posits a world where interconnection is not only possible but necessary.

Frank Bascombe represents one kind of everyman—that is, one who has inherited the tradition as if by birthright. In my second chapter, "The Assimilated Everyman and the Business of Forgetting: Postwar Living Memorials and the Posttraumatic Suburb in Chang-rae Lee's *Aloft*," I examine a different strain of the genus: the assimilated everyman, whose residence in the suburbs is owing to the massive changes ushered in by the postwar era—not only suburbanization but the comprehensive, unprecedented benefits of the GI Bill, which transformed an ethnic working class into middle-class homeowners. Lee's novel merits close attention because it directly questions the universal claims that the very term "everyman" implies. In Lee's formulation, the suburban everyman is a cultural construction built immediately after World War II to peddle a new social order predicated upon the "good life" of consumption and upward mobility. To be sure, the returning (white) vet was the putative raison d'être for the free-market initiatives articulated by the massive development of single-family suburban homes. Lee offers not one but three generations of suburban everymen, all with personal fortunes bound up with this triumphalist narrative: Jerry, born in 1945, shares a birthday with the postwar moment; his father Hank (The Tank), who changed the family name from Battaglia to Battle and moved the family landscaping business to the new suburbs because they were a "veritable goldmine" (290); and Jerry's son, Jack, who is currently running that landscaping business into the ground. All three men demonstrate skill at denial of their shared history of loss and shame.

I present a historical account of the postwar move toward "living memorials"—the playgrounds, ball parks, and swimming pools that represent the foundation of the Battle family landscaping business—to argue that the impulse to deny a traumatic past is essential to a national narrative that has historically depended upon quick burial of a vexing past of poverty, genocide, and nuclear death in order to smooth the ground for a future of leisure, ease, and prosperity. Lee's "Battle" men are as detached as their suburban literary precursors, but, in a shift, the novelist now holds these assimilated everymen accountable as accessories after the fact for their role in plowing under and paving over this history. But the lucrative business of forgetting, Lee suggests, has lost its currency in the wake of 9/11. The final scene of the novel finds Jerry in a hole in his own backyard, sifting through the "archeological fragments" of lost toys, shoes, and broken pottery that represent the sum of his life. These shards are reminiscent of the jetsam that littered lower Manhattan in the days after September 11. Lee's post-9/11 novel may feature a protagonist left standing in the rubble of his former existence, but the razed earth uncovers an alternative history that breaks free of binary conceptions of exclusion versus inclusion, both of which have supported a master narrative built upon the tenets of private property ownership, individual enterprise, comfort, and stability. Instead, it imagines a hodgepodge household that levels these core values in order to prepare the ground for a radically different structure altogether.

In the first two chapters I argue that in the wake of 9/11 Ford and Lee have reimagined the white middle-class everyman as a figure whose awakened moral consciousness ultimately spurs him to become socially relevant in a world characterized by contingency and calamity. In contrast, in the third chapter, "'How to Live?': The Case for Failure in Jonathan Franzen's *Freedom*," I show how Franzen's latest novel, *Freedom*, reengages the suburban midlife crisis genre in order to argue for the relevance of irrelevance. Franzen's fiction has always dramatized the marginalized role of the white, straight, middle-class liberal male, and *Freedom*'s everyman, Walter Berglund, is no different: he concedes that he has been "left behind with the dead and dying and forgotten" (480). In an earlier context, we might read the novel's unrelenting negativity as the means by which its disillusioned protagonist justifies inaction—a move that has the added benefit of once again casting the straight white male as society's latest victim. I trace Walter's development over the course of the novel from a prototypical 1990s Sensitive New Age Guy to his latest incarnation, the Angry White Man, to argue that in *Freedom*, in contrast, it is ultimately Walter's willingness to embrace his own obsolescence that provides the foundation for the novel's ability to be "socially useful" in an environment marred not only by the terrorist attacks of 9/11 but by two seemingly endless wars waged to feed an insatiable market (Grossman 48).

I implicate the novel with Lee Edelman's and Judith Halberstam's queer antisocial aesthetic, articulated in their polemics, *No Future: Queer Theory and the Death Drive* (2005) and *The Queer Art of Failure* (2011) respectively, in order to argue that *Freedom* similarly rejects what they read as a triumphal futurist agenda that guarantees the perpetuation of the existing social order from one generation to the next with its sunny promise that tomorrow will be better than today. In *Freedom*, Franzen offers humiliation, failure, and loss as an antidote to the narrative of upward mobility. In this case, failure and loss no longer provide an excuse for resigning oneself to the status quo, as they arguably have in Franzen's earlier fiction. Instead, despondency forms the basis for an aesthetic that works purposefully to reject the existing social order and resist the tyranny of the future. Walter's commitment to stem population growth might be read as a literal attempt to reverse the imperatives of reproductive futurism, but his desire to effect lasting change is based on his eventual embrace of his own mortality. Earlier in the novel, in a moment of dismay over his lack of control in a world run amok, Walter wonders plaintively, "How to live?" He ultimately finds his answer by staring into the void of his own obsolescence. The novel does not point its readers toward a brighter future but compels us instead to confront what Martin Luther King called the "fierce urgency of now." Yet for all of the novel's stridency, it ends on a note of forgiveness and compassion, as Walter sees in his estranged wife's eyes the lack that defines them both, and us all. Not simply coming to terms with but embracing an aesthetic of failure and impermanence, the novel imagines new alliances and new avenues that the middle-class reader might explore.

Chapter Four, "Dead Man Walking: Philip Roth's Engagement with the Everyman Tradition and the Reimagination of Middle-Class Identity," considers Roth's aptly titled *Everyman*, which takes to its logical conclusion the aesthetic of failure advanced by Franzen through its depiction of an anonymous white suburban middle-class everyman who is dead before the novel even starts. In a further illustration of the failure to progress, the novel ends just as it begins, with the unremarkably dead body of its aged and anonymous everyman on the operating table. Like Roth, I bring my own discussion full circle in order to fully consider the implications of the corpse that frames *Everyman*. I begin with a look back at a novel Roth wrote almost a decade before, *American Pastoral* (1997), in order to examine the impossibly youthful everyman at its center, Seymour (the Swede) Levov. Taken together, the robust Seymour and the depleted everyman narrate a history not only of the life and death of the male body but of the mythos of American exceptionalism and national resilience that that body has served and protected. I examine these novels in the context of Rosemarie Garland-Thomson's seminal study, *Extraordinary Bodies: Figuring Disability in American Culture and Literature* (1997), to underscore her observation that, at best, we are all only "temporarily able-bodied" (14). In *American Pastoral* Roth engages the suburban everyman tradition in order to call attention to the stakes involved in its depiction of a preternaturally resilient figure with the uncanny ability to rise from the ashes of his experience (such as Updike's Rabbit, for instance, who at the end of *Rabbit Redux* [1971] escapes his burning house and finds his way back to his estranged wife's bed). A variation of the "everyday hero" that Carroll explores, the eternally fit white American everyman is possessive individualism's beloved mascot: he is patriotic not so much because he can defend his country but, more importantly, because he requires nothing from it.

In contrast, the ashes-to-ashes trajectory that Roth's post-9/11 *Everyman* traces brings to a self-conscious end the tradition of the everyman who stands in heroic opposition to society in a manner that only strengthens it by contributing to the mythos of the rugged individual. In his stead, Roth offers an everyman whose frailness and preordained death advance a poetics of prostration that not only admits but affirms what the protagonist of *American Pastoral* could not: "the assailability, the frailty, the enfeeblement of supposedly robust things" in a move that radically reimagines a suburban middle-class male identity that has hitherto been predicated upon security and upward mobility (*American Pastoral* 426).

My final chapter, "That's What She Said: The Everyman in Recent Suburban Fiction by Anne Tyler, Gish Jen, and A. M. Homes," considers the depiction of white males in post-9/11 suburban novels written by established female authors, such as Anne Tyler's *Digging to America* (2006), Gish Jen's *World and Town* (2010), and A. M. Homes's *May We Be Forgiven* (2012). I invoke these novels to ask two questions: first, what role do they assign the figure of the white male everyman, given that by the year 2050 whites will be the minority and males a minority within that minority in the United States? Second, I've argued that suburban novelists make a unique contribution to the emerging post-9/11 perspective by training their focus on the everyday and the domestic in order to craft a moral framework for middle-class experience in a world characterized by uncertainty and impermanence. To what extent does this new aesthetic demand that we reconsider female-authored novels that have been marginalized for their supposedly limited "domestic" perspective?

This chapter builds on the discussion launched by Elaine Showalter in her essay "The Female Frontier." Showalter observes that in the wake of John Updike's death in 2009, (male) members of the literati wondered who remained to "fly the flag for the great American novel." The candidates these writers and critics advanced, unsurprisingly, were almost all male. This omission is reflected in the contretemps that erupted after the publication of Franzen's *Freedom*, in which several female authors expressed their anger over the privileging of male-authored over female-authored fiction. Clearly, female authors continue to struggle for recognition in an arena in which (white) male authors and critics set the standards. The novels I examine in this chapter, like their male-authored counterparts, may focus on quotidian circumstances, but they share an expansive vision that explores the fraught relationship between the personal and the political.

Significantly, these novels do not marginalize white masculinity (which would participate in the tradition of the white male as victim), but instead ultimately offer him a part, albeit a decentered and as yet-to-be-written one, in the nation's next chapter. As it happens, all three of these female-authored novels feature white male protagonists who are recently unemployed educators. And similar to the male-authored novels I examine, the white male characters in these works are past their prime: they contend with chronic, debilitating conditions such as heart trouble, a history of strokes, and cancer. But the female-authored novels in question by no means seek to reinstate their male protagonists to their former positions at the head of the class, nor do they work to garner sympathy for them. Instead they advance characters whose experiences with joblessness and illness drive them to chart a new course of action and to understand themselves as just one part of a shifting community of similarly fragile human beings. Jen's *World and Town*, for instance, depicts sixty-eight-year old widow Hattie Kong and her complicated relationships with a newly arrived family of Cambodian refugees as well as the middle-aged WASP Carter Hatch, a former lover, colleague, and adversary. As Hattie and Carter become reacquainted, she forces him to answer for his past mistakes. But she also serves as a bridge between him and her Cambodian neighbors. In its depiction of a complex web of affiliations that is often contentious but ultimately fruitful, the novel is indeed sensitive to the various ways that race, class, age, gender, geography, and history affect where one falls on the spectrum of misery and vulnerability.

The male-authored post-9/11 suburban novels I've examined are noteworthy for their portrayals of female characters who instruct their male counterparts on "how to live with lack," a move that radically alters their aesthetic, which now privileges interconnection and the common good over individual experience. Similarly, the novels I engage in this chapter are more interested in the long, ongoing aftermath of catastrophe than they are in crisis itself. Homes's *May We Be Forgiven* dispenses with the brutal act that implicates its white male protagonist in the first 40 pages of a 481-page novel. The novel instead devotes itself to a suburban everyman who must reckon with his role in destroying one family in order to assume a place in a new, radically altered version. These novels take a long view in order to reorient middle-class consciousness and, not incidentally, challenge entrenched assumptions concerning the role of the domestic and the feminine in the evolving literary canon.

▪ ▪ ▪

Michael Rothberg has justly argued that although American novelists immediately added their voices to those of pundits claiming that the 9/11 attacks gave rise to a new era, "the *form* of their works does not bear witness to fundamental change" ("Failure" 152). Franzen rebuts Rothberg when he asserts that "to do something new is not to develop a form for the novel that has never been seen on earth before. It means to try to come to terms as a person and a citizen with what's happening in the world now and to do it in some comprehensible, coherent way" (48). The suburban subgenre continues to be a novel of manners, meant to represent and instruct its middle-class readers in appropriate modes of behavior. But these novels reconceive middle-class experience by imagining it in the context of a world no longer represented as stagnant and stultifying but, instead, as unstable and frightening. All of these post-9/11 suburban novels, whether written by men or women, depict unexceptional, imperfect middle-aged white everymen who contend with loss, failure, illness, and mortality to counteract a triumphalist narrative of American exceptionalism that is itself past its prime. These open-ended stories thus map out new territory that is as vast and rich as it is complex and uncertain. The twenty-first-century suburban novel offers readers new and flexible ways to imagine identity, belonging, and accountability in a demanding age.

American Unexceptionalism

1

The Canonical Everyman

Richard Ford's Frank Bascombe Trilogy and the Challenge to Neoliberal Suburbia

The Sportswriter, *Independence Day*, and the Neoliberal Suburb

In what would launch one of the more fabled literary feuds of recent history, Colson Whitehead issued a scathing review of Richard Ford's short story collection, *A Multitude of Sins* (2002), in which he asserts, "The characters are nearly indistinguishable. If I were an epidemiologist, I'd say that some sort of spiritual epidemic had overtaken a segment of our nation's white middle-class professionals" ("The End of the Affair" n.p.). Unquestionably, the assorted characters of these stories should be recognizable to anyone even remotely familiar with the established male-authored suburban literary tradition. Almost all, Whitehead notes, are in one stage or another of an adulterous affair; they are suitably isolated, with neither friends nor acquaintances; if they have children, they are somewhere offstage; and they all suffer from "self-absorption, vague yearnings and a nagging sense of incompleteness." These are protagonists, in other words, who remind Whitehead of Ford's most famous disaffected white-middle-class professional, Frank Bascombe of *The Sportswriter* (1986) and *Independence Day* (1995). But if that protagonist, given the space of (at the time) two capacious novels, eventually earns our "good will, and a great deal more," the characters who populate the stories in *A Multitude of Sins* are odious whiners whose "Awkward Pang[s] of Simmering Dissatisfaction" and "Awkward Pang[s] of Muted Epiphany" amount to nothing, as far as Whitehead is concerned ("The End of the Affair" n.p).

Ford did not take this review well at all. As the story goes, it became a source of simmering dissatisfaction for the author himself, who years afterwards approached Whitehead at a cocktail party and spat on him.[1] But it would also appear he took this criticism to heart, since the Frank Bascombe we encounter in his third novel of the trilogy, *The Lay of the Land* (2006), bears scant resemblance to the interchangeable sniveling and solipsistic middle-class white protagonists that Whitehead describes, or even to the aimless, alienated character we have come to know in the first two Bascombe novels. Once characterized as "dreamy" and drifting, this Frank has remarried and is deeply committed to his wife; he has forged a close, satisfying relationship with his daughter; he abounds with both friends and acquaintances; and it is not vague malaise that he suffers but an uncertain prognosis for his prostate cancer and an even more tenuous future vis-à-vis a world no longer defined by stasis and stagnation but by instability and danger.

As I outline in my introduction, the events of 9/11 and their fraught, ongoing aftermath have impelled writers who use the suburbs as their terrain to reimagine white middle-class experience and draft a new blueprint for the suburban literary tradition. Perhaps the reconstitution of the suburban novel and the white everyman at its center is most vividly illustrated not by one of the younger writers newly taking up these concerns, but by a (relatively) older one who has been the keeper of this tradition for the past twenty-five years. Ford's Bascombe trilogy charts the meandering course of its middle-class white male protagonist, ultimately taking him, in the last installment, a full 180 degrees, from known territory where he is master of a dull destiny to unmapped terrain ruled by chance. In this fraught, frightening environment, the personal problems that plagued the "indistinguishable" white male suburbanites that Whitehead derides are exposed for what they are: the inconsequential luxuries of a past that has suddenly become dated. Indeed, I would contend that though Ford participates fully in the established suburban literary tradition in his first two Bascombe novels, with *The Lay of the Land* (2006) he poses a serious challenge to the assumptions that have provided the foundation for its ethos and he tills the ground for a new aesthetic to take root.

Before turning to *The Lay of the Land*, and in order to appreciate the radical shift in perspective it represents, it is necessary to examine Ford's earlier engagement with the suburban genre and, most especially, to take note of the cultural transformations the first two novels register and negotiate. Though Whitehead has duly observed the demographics that demarcate Bascombe and his ilk, most scholars remark upon his status as a white upper-middle-class suburbanite incidentally rather than recognizing it as constitutive of his character.[2] Catherine Jurca is the exception: based on *The Sportswriter* and *Independence Day*, she anticipates Whitehead's critique, declaring Bascombe to be one more in a line of purportedly amiable but displaced suburbanites, wallowing in disingenuous self-pity as a means of justifying his self-centered, irrelevant existence. Whitehead and Jurca call attention to what mainstream critics take for granted: the characteristics that earn Frank the label of "everyman." I will explore more thoroughly the stakes involved in this figure's bodily construction in my fourth chapter in relation to Philip Roth's aptly named *Everyman* (published the same year as *The Lay of the Land*, in 2006). As far as the critics are concerned, however, it goes without saying that he is white and middle to upper middle class. As Whitehead indicates, the universalized everyman is also afflicted by "Awkward Pang[s] of Simmering Dissatisfaction" and has a tendency to wax philosophical on "life, death, and the meaning of it all" (Sawyers).[3]

There is no question that Frank Bascombe begins as a card-carrying member of a group of seminal fictional suburbanites that includes Sinclair Lewis's Babbitt and John Updike's Harry "Rabbit" Angstrom. Jurca might well be describing Bascombe in her summation of Rabbit's trajectory over the course of his tetralogy when she notes that he "runs. He returns. . . . he runs again. . . . He returns again, and some thirteen hundred additional pages record his enduring fantasies of flight" (162). In the first two installments, Bascombe likewise tries to escape the ills of his station—marital trouble, alienation from his children, career dissatisfaction—by heading to Florida before returning to the fictional suburb of Haddam as a real estate broker (like Babbitt) in order to endure afresh variations of the same miseries. Perhaps just as suggestive, however, is the name Ford originally intended for his everyman: Slocum, after Joshua Slocum, the mariner who circumnavigated the globe single-handedly, since, as Ford explains, that is a "subtextual conceit" of the first novel: "sailing alone" (D. Lee n.p.). Similar to Neddy Merrill, who in Cheever's iconic story "The Swimmer" (1964) charts a course across suburbia by swimming from one backyard swimming pool to another until he ends up semi-naked, alone, and locked outside of his own home, the Frank Bascombe we encounter in *The Sportswriter* is likewise isolated and adrift in a hostile environment.

This iteration of the alienated everyman is so familiar that it is easy to miss the dramatic reformulation of the logic that undergirds it. Lizabeth Cohen notes that the original proponents of postwar suburbanization championed an idealistic vision of shared abundance as "buyers from all walks of life," whether "engineer or factory worker, teacher or state trooper," lined up to purchase homes side by side (200). But if promoters celebrated the suburbs' putative egalitarianism, social critics and fiction writers disparaged the rigid social codes and bland conformity that these instant communities engendered, issues that no longer apply in recent fiction, since the suburbs have come to be characterized by the fetishization of private property. In the postwar era, William Whyte, Herbert Gans, and David Riesman among others made careers out of observing the customs of new suburbanites, whom they condescendingly found to be extremely eager to blend with one another and participate in a vast array of formal and informal group activities, facilitated by a process Whyte called "leveling," which enabled residents of mixed social classes to see eye to eye as long as the more educated were willing to disguise their "advantages," since tolerance among residents almost always went "downward," not upward (39).[4]

The alienated suburbanites who populate the high-minded if middlebrow fiction of Cheever, Yates, and Sloan Wilson, for instance, all seek to distance themselves from their socially energetic, eagerly conforming neighbors, sharing Cheever character Charlie Flint's plaintive cry to preserve him from "dinner parties . . . and madrigal singers, political discussion groups, recorder groups, dancing schools, confirmation classes, committee meetings, and lectures on literature, philosophy, city planning and pest control" (Cheever 290). These characters struggle to find privacy in communities where the never-ending whirl of coffee klatches, block parties, and PTA meetings are de rigueur.

As Andrew Hoberek explains, such narratives of "threatened individuality . . . simultaneously obscure and reveal concerns about downward class mobility" among a professional-managerial class who had come to feel that their collective and individual agency had been subsumed by the rise of the Organization and so came to distrust "organization as such" (8). Robert Beuka similarly calls attention to the "financial uncertainty" that unsettles many of Cheever's upper-middle-class suburbanites in order to claim that his fiction represents "a complex critique of postwar class consciousness" (69). I would argue instead that Cheever's stories are part of a body of postwar fiction that actually encouraged class consciousness among a readership of newly arrived low-and mid-level white-collar suburbanites whose aspirations and alliances were still up for grabs. Beuka astutely observes, for instance, that Cheever and his colleagues depict a postwar suburban landscape characterized by regimentation and surveillance that makes their protagonists pine for "lost natural landscapes" (90). Their longing for an idealized past, however, is part of a larger nostalgia for what Hoberek identifies as the "putative autonomy of the property-owning old middle class" who have been converted into a new middle class of white-collar corporate workers (8). As one of Cheever's narrators wistfully puts it, he and his brethren belong to "that enormous stratum of the middle class that is distinguished by its ability to recall better times" (Cheever 137). In their desire for space from their prying neighbors and their frequent reveries for the halcyon days of yore, the protagonists of Cheever's postwar middle-class fiction directed readers to disdain the new suburban experiment that promoted democratic notions of broadly shared interests, privileges, and responsibilities and identify instead with the values of individualism, privacy, and property ownership associated with the established upper middle classes.

By the time Ford entered the fray with the first Bascombe novel, *The Sportswriter* (1986), this transformation was complete. The suburbs had transmogrified from "instant communities" populated by what Gans calls "hyperactive joiners" (Putnam 209) to spaces that value privacy above all else, causing Ford's protagonist to opine that he moved to the suburbs in the first place because he wanted to live where he "knew no one and no one knew me" (*Sportswriter* [hereafter *SW*] 39). Bascombe's desire for anonymity registers a profound shift in the suburban ethos that can be explained at least in part by the suburbs' evolving demographics. As I discuss in my introduction, these sprawling suburbs have undergone profound changes. The suburbs are now home to the majority of the nation's immigrants and people living in poverty.[5]

These dramatically different demographics render all the more glaring the fact that Haddam, New Jersey, the fictional suburb that Frank Bascombe inhabits in *The Sportswriter* and *Independence Day*, is, in fact, an exclusive bastion of white upper-middle-class privilege. Robert Putnam notes that as the suburbs exploded, and in panicked response to their increasing ethnic, racial, and economic diversity, they fragmented into "a sociological mosaic—collectively heterogeneous but individually homogenous, as people . . . sorted themselves into more and more finely distinguished 'lifestyle enclaves,' segregated by race, class, education, life stage, and so on" (209). This homogeneity has had the strange effect of decreasing rather than increasing civic engagement: where Gans found a community of eager beavers, ethnographer M. P. Baumgartner, who sojourned in the suburbs in the 1980s, found a culture of isolation and what she calls "moral minimalism" (13), with residents seeking privacy from, rather than connectedness with, their neighbors. Baumgartner notes that in contrast to the early postwar suburbs, "it is not uncommon for people to know few of their fellow residents" (11).

In truth, however, the transition from a group-based ethos to one best summed up by the phrase "mind your own business" has been oddly seamless, perhaps because the shift is more natural than it first appears. As Lizabeth Cohen indicates in her own account of the suburbs' increasing class segmentation, the bond between suburbanization and mass consumerism—initially the basis of "egalitarian hopes" that wealth could be widely and evenly shared—rendered "market concerns paramount in decisions about how and where one lived" (202). Home pricing, loan practices, and zoning ordinances further redefined for new suburbanites the transformation of the home, once conceived of as "a longstanding emotional investment in a particular neighborhood, ethnic community, or church parish," into a commodity that determines both net worth and social status, with home buyers increasingly selecting "among homogenous suburbs occupying distinctive rungs in a clear status hierarchy of communities" (202).[6] Unsurprisingly, Ford's protagonist offers his stately Tudor house as evidence of his upper-middle-class credentials, assuring readers that with its "comfortable, overstuffed entities" and "faded orientals," it "represents other aims" than his nurse girlfriend's "little 1-BR condo" up the turnpike (*SW* 57). Suburbanization, Frank's careful distinction indicates, has not so much expanded but consolidated the realm of the established upper-middle and upper classes by advancing their central premise: the primacy of private property ownership.

Indeed, though postwar suburbanization appears to be the result of a final wave of New Deal initiatives, built into the very foundation of these houses are the neoliberal ideals that by the 1970s would be so pervasive as to be unassailable. The purchase of the hearts and minds of newly minted suburbanites represents just one strand of the vast range of political agendas, national interests, and global events that David Harvey traces in his book *A Brief History of Neoliberalism* (2005), in which he argues that neoliberal values have "become incorporated into the common-sense way many of us interpret, live in, and understand the world" (3).[7] Harvey points out that the founding fathers of neoliberal thought, supported by big business interests, cannily couched their agenda in the core values of human dignity and individual freedom, equally compelling to protesting students, disenfranchised minorities, and globally minded humanitarians. Neoliberal ideals were especially compelling to suburbanites, however, since the premium placed on private property literally located their personal worth and financial security in their own backyards.

In a 1985 article entitled "A Downpour of Literary Republicanism," Joe David Bellamy makes the case that neoliberal ideals had by then so thoroughly saturated the culture that they had infected literary output: the then *au courant* minimalist/realist trend embraced by writers such as Raymond Carver, Bret Easton Ellis, and Richard Ford acts as a "conservative response to inflation—underutilization of capacity, reduction of inventory, and verbal joblessness" (36). Bellamy emphasizes that these authors participate in an aesthetic that is not necessarily politically motivated—hence, writers as diverse as Bobby Ann Mason and Raymond Carver, whose work centers on rural and working-class characters, are stylistically linked with Ann Beattie and Jay McInerney, for instance, whose work chronicles the lives of privileged "yuppies." Nevertheless, these writers' spare style and their tendency to convey their narratives through a single perspective rather than the multiple perspectives employed by contemporaneous postmodern writers is wholly consonant with a national ethic that favors privacy and the rights of the individual over the community, an ethos that is especially at work in fiction concerned with the travails of self-absorbed suburbanites.[8]

If his earlier novels originally qualified him, with the publication of *The Sportswriter,* Ford secures his place on Bellamy's list of minimalist writers who corroborate Margaret Thatcher's now-infamous assertion that "there is no such thing [as society]! There are individual men and women and there are families" (n.p.). Unlike his literary progenitors, Bascombe is neither alienated nor stifled by society, since "society" has ceased to exist in his privileged corner of the world. Instead, "editors, publishers, Time and Newsweek writers, CIA agents, . . . business analysts, [and] the presidents of a number of large corporations that mold opinion" all occupy "big secluded houses" (*SW* 5). Social engagement has been reduced to occasional "chitter-chatter across the driveways and hedges," and while his predecessors craved privacy from their prying neighbors, Frank himself feels "as invisible as Claude Rains in the movie [*The Invisible Man*]" as he roams the "winding, bowery streets" after dark to peer in others' rooms, since it is "the only way neighbors here can be neighborly" (51, 339).

This shift in the suburban ethos reorganizes our understanding of Frank's disengaged stance as well as the role of the suburban everyman in general. Postwar suburban fiction has been roundly criticized for its stock characterization of the alienated white male at its center and its tendency to imagine his sense of dispossession in "abstractly individualized terms," as Hoberek puts it (8). But the suburban subgenre's value has arguably rested in its ability to find meaning in quotidian experience that is centered on the middle-class people who are both the subjects and the readers of these novels. Timothy Aubry, for instance, argues effectively that middlebrow novelists such as Cheever, Sloan Wilson, and Richard Yates, "like the New York Intellectuals who scorned them, were cultivating a particular attitude vis-à-vis mainstream American culture that would enable both assimilation and a capacity for critique" (*Reading as Therapy* 6). One might argue that Frank's progenitors, in their determination to distance themselves from their community, could be characterized as inner directed, to borrow David Riesman's term for the person who maintains "a delicate balance between . . . his goal in life and the buffetings of his external environment" (16). Especially in the era of McCarthyism, the suburban protagonist who seeks to distinguish himself from the crowd might have served as an example for his middle-class readers, even if his author was simultaneously maligned for selling his soul to the marketplace.[9]

By the 1960s and '70s, however, the middle-class fiction of Cheever, Updike, and others had settled comfortably into the literary establishment, which itself had made awkward peace with that same marketplace. Richard Ohmann describes a "common class" of "literary agents, editors, publicity people, reviewers, buyers of hardbound novels, taste-making intellectuals, critics, professors, most of the students who took literary courses, and in fact the writers of the novels themselves" who "emerged and grew up with monopoly capitalism" and who, more importantly, benefited by it (209). This "nearly-closed circle" of like-minded people, awkwardly caught between a ruling class whose institutions it managed and a working class it supervised, dealt with this social contradiction by eliding it. Ohmann argues that the middle-class protagonist's dispossession does not highlight or remediate society's ills but instead sidesteps them with stories of personal illness.

The Frank Bascombe we encounter in *The Sportswriter* clearly belongs to the "nearly closed circle" that Ohmann describes. Thanks to the money from selling the film rights to his short story collection, Frank has access to all of the bourgeois trappings of his neighbors, and he and his wife quickly establish themselves among the town's "writers and editors" with whom they enjoy "rounds of cocktail parties" (*SW* 40). He also clearly follows the trajectory laid out by Ohmann, which is to say he is an unhappy person who moves toward happiness, but his story reads very differently in the late suburban landscape of Haddam circa 1985. "Society" has indeed ceased to exist, at least in the carefully quilted suburb Frank depicts, so that his determination to live in a place that is "in most ways 'neutral'" renders Frank merely part of the "other-directed" herd who have likewise come to suburbia seeking its amenities and moral minimalism (*SW* 40).

If Ford's everyman is meant to instruct his readers, he teaches well Thatcher's message of "every man for himself." Per Ohmann's rubric, Frank's is indeed a story of personal illness: after the death of his oldest son, unwilling to confront his own grief or console his wife and remaining two children in theirs, he is lost in a solipsistic state he calls "dreaminess" but which might more aptly be called selfish indifference. It is certainly with selfish indifference that Frank treats Walter Luckett, an acquaintance who commits suicide after visiting Frank in search of counsel the night before. Frank offers Walter nothing beyond an obligatory drink because, he says, "It's too late in the night. I'm ready for bed" (181). One might assume that such dismissiveness would be a source of guilt for Frank in hindsight. Yet echoing Thatcher's assertion that "it is our duty to look after ourselves" (n.p.), Frank coldheartedly concludes that "what happened to Walter on this earth is Walter's own lookout" (*SW* 353). Walter's suicide nevertheless precipitates Frank's requisite existential crisis, leading him to decide that "it's high time for a new quick age to dawn" (352). He pulls up stakes and heads south, where he marvels at the feeling "of being released" (375). If we are meant to understand this as a victory, however, it is a hollow victory at best. Frank's is not an escape from a stultifying world that had threatened to engulf him but a mere departure from a loosely organized constellation of similarly indifferent individuals to whom he has given nothing and has received nothing in return. Ford's aim may be to undercut the shallow "life-forever lie of the suburbs" (319), but with the novel's conclusion, he fails outright, since Bascombe merely takes advantage of what Jurca asserts is the prerogative of the suburban homeowner by exercising his "freedom to live where and how one pleases" (7). Frank's revelatory flight from late suburban Haddam to a breezy beach in Florida thus merely reaffirms the neoliberal values it purports to challenge.

Frank's failure to be cured may explain why novelists working the suburban beat in the 1990s cast the formerly amiable if flawed everyman as loathsome and beyond redemption. As I discuss in my introduction, in these millennial novels the suburban protagonist's determined detachment is not the function of his desire for autonomy but the result of his stunted growth. Such is certainly the case with the woefully immature everyman of A. M. Homes's novel, *Music for Torching* (1999), pointedly situated in so-called Cheever country, the tony, established suburbs of Westchester County, New York. The protagonist's reprehensibly selfish behavior leads to the devastating disaster that concludes the novel. A. M. Homes has explained that the apocalyptic vision she shares with her contemporaries challenges the assumption that "you'd made it when you got to the suburbs. . . . The two-kids, two-cars myth has been exposed for what it is, and what we're hearing and seeing now is from the perspective of the first generation that grew up in the decline of that dream" ("Children of the Cul-de-sac," 83). She and her colleagues do not offer a counternarrative to what they perceive to be a deadening ethos. Instead, they merely pronounce the genre dead.

Scholar James Berger notes that apocalypse simplifies the world, putting "an end to ambiguity and doubt" (56); as Sam Cohen suggests, with the end of the Cold War American novels of the 1990s found "narrative closure difficult to resist" (161). Though hardly triumphalist, these apocalyptic endings certainly provide one kind of closure by petulantly sweeping the pieces off the board. But in ending the game without offering an alternative set of rules, they simply clear the slate for the status quo to reassert itself. Further, the odious everymen of these pre-9/11 suburban stories are so cartoonishly drawn that readers can't possibly identify with them (shudder that they might) and are invited instead to enjoy a sense of moral superiority.[10] If the suburban novel's chief function had originally been to represent and instruct its readership by way of protagonists who are "analogous to us" (Ohmann 213), these damning narratives offer nothing to a readership whose world has grown increasingly complicated.

On the one hand, Frank Bascombe's return to Haddam as a real estate broker in *Independence Day* (1995), peddling the "the silly fragrant dream" (*SW* 319) of the suburbs to "schmos" (*Independence Day* [hereafter *ID*] 58) seems to capitulate to the possessive individualism that has come to characterize the suburban ethos. On the other hand, Ford deserves credit for revisiting terrain his fellow writers have abandoned in order to constructively challenge, instruct, and direct his readers. Frank's return is after all motivated by born-again civic-mindedness: five years after leaving Haddam ostensibly for good, Frank experiences a "deep-beating urgency" that leads him back with a "new feeling of great purpose and a fury to suddenly do something serious for my own good and possibly even others', but also with the feeling of renewal . . . that immediately translated into a homey connectedness to Haddam itself" (93). Frank's newfound optimism and community spirit are a welcome change from the self-interest that usually dictates the everyman's choices, but Haddam itself hardly feels homey. Its property values have plummeted, fueling a collective "sense of a wild world being just beyond our perimeter, an untallied apprehension among our residents" (5). A fortress mentality has replaced the amiable disinterest of the "lifestyle enclave." Throughout the novel, therefore, Frank's behavior is prompted by an admirable but arguably misguided desire to restore small-town values to Haddam. In other words, Ford employs his everyman to temper the heartlessness of neoliberal ideology with his own wholesome brand of kumbaya capitalism.

Though Ford wrote *Independence Day* at the height of the Clinton administration, it takes place over Independence Day Weekend of 1988, as campaigning between the senior George Bush and Michael Dukakis is heating up and the economy is languishing after the market correction of 1987. This backward glance notwithstanding, the novel is infused with the pragmatic and conciliatory spirit of Clinton's centrist brand of politics that seeks to humanize not only the suburbs but the nation, perhaps because the nation itself has become one big, dyspeptic suburb: *Independence Day* is ostensibly a "road" novel, yet Frank's journey, a father-son trip to

Cooperstown, does not offer the expected escape but instead a horrific, looping landscape marked by gun-toting security guards; toxic waste dumps masquerading as Dream Houses; rotating chains of Friendly's restaurants, strip malls, Comfort Inns, cineplexes; and, everywhere, traffic. Ruled by a logic of "endless capital accumulation and economic growth no matter what the social, ecological, or political consequences," late suburbanism has indeed given way to near-apocalypse (Harvey 181).

Ford himself asserted in an interview that he wanted the novel to reconsider the tendency to equate independence with individualism, noting that although "independence in the most conventional sense means . . . putting distance between yourself and other people," he wanted to explore "if independence could in fact mean a freedom to make contact with others" (Majeski n.p.). Accordingly, Ford revises the everyman as conceived by his literary forefathers, for whom "maturity is equated with independence" and an "invulnerability to society itself" (Ohmann 213). He appoints the clear-eyed Alexis de Tocqueville his novel's patron saint: the local boys' academy is named after him, and Frank keeps Tocqueville's *Democracy in America* on his bedside table. Frank's approach to his work as a "residential specialist" reflects the Tocquevillian description of "self interest rightly understood," so that citizens behave according to "an enlightened regard for themselves," which "constantly prompts them to assist one another and inclines them willingly to sacrifice a portion of their time and property to the welfare of the state" (Tocqueville 2:122).

The novel nostalgically advances a return to an older ideal in which the community serves as what Alan Wolfe calls a "Tocquevillian laboratory of democracy"—a refuge from the anonymity of mass society (182). Over the course of the novel, Frank undertakes a series of initiatives in order to create the conditions that would transform the cold, impersonal "lifestyle enclave" that Haddam has become into what Robert Bellah calls "a community of memory": a socially interdependent group "who participate together in discussion and decision making and who share certain practices" (333). Such a community is "defined in part by its past" and, more importantly, by "its memory of its past" (333). Of course, Frank's determination to bring old-fashioned community values to Haddam also invests him with the sense of power and control once ostensibly enjoyed by the small-property-owning, entrepreneurial old middle class that Hoberek identifies.

To that end, Frank makes several investments in his community to restore it and him to their imagined former glory. First he purchases two houses in the black section of town in order to provide "affordable housing options" while protecting his "financial backside and establishing a greater sense of connectedness" (*ID* 27). He also takes over writing his real estate firm's monthly "Buyer vs. Seller" guide, seeing an opportunity to convince his readers and fellow residents, "almost all Republicans" who "love Reagan like Catholics love the pope," that "Governor Dukakis has in mind more 'pure pocketbook issues' than most voters think" (6). Frank is an avowed Democrat, but as we later learn in *The Lay of the Land*, he is a Democrat who will embrace Clinton's centrist policies, convinced that the two parties can meet on financial ground where they can all agree.

Frank makes one more small investment that hearkens back to a bygone era of simpler times: a roadside drive-in restaurant—Bemish's Birch Beer Depot, the sort of place he remembers as " 'the real meeting place' for all the kids and the grown-ups too" (130). He spins this investment off into a portable hot dog stand, which he donates for use at the Independence Day parade in order to raise funds for the orphaned children of a murdered colleague. The final scene of the novel sentimentally places Frank on Constitution Street as the trumpets, cymbals, and drums celebrate our national history, making Frank's "heartbeat quicken" as he feels "the push, pull, weave and sway of others" (451). In contrast not only to the disastrous endings of the 1990s suburban novels I describe in the introduction, but to a similar scene in Updike's *Rabbit at Rest* (1991), in which the eponymous antihero lurches his way through a Fourth of July parade straining against an impending heart attack, *Independence Day* resoundingly concludes with Frank basking in good will as he assumes his place as Haddam's beneficent town father.

Ford's novel thus crafts a convincing case for a return to old-fashioned community by trumpeting the "Third Way" argument of the Clinton administration that profit and the common good do not have to be mutually exclusive. He also attempts to restore the suburban everyman to his familiar role as both representative of and an example for his suburban readers. Jurca has pointed out that the suburban novel "sympathetically treats affluent house owners" as the victims of "sentimental dispossession" (7). In *Independence Day* Ford uses the same tactics to imagine sentimental *re*possession: Frank makes the case for commitment to rather than disavowal of the suburbs, with himself in the center.

Yet in his sentimental portrait of a communal history meant to induce in readers a longing for an idealized past, Ford once again actually perpetuates the very agenda he had purportedly hoped to undercut. Svetlana Boym distinguishes between two types of nostalgia—restorative and reflective. Throughout *Independence Day*, but most especially in the final scene, Ford relies upon restorative nostalgia, which Boym asserts depends upon "invented traditions" to offer "a comforting collective script for individual longing" that allows for the "secular transformation of fatality into continuity, contingency into meaning" (42). As Frank finds himself awash in a sense of contented belonging at the Fourth of July parade, he participates in precisely the type of "recreated practice[ ] of national commemoration" that Boym suggests is "politically manipulated . . . with the aim of reestablishing social cohesion, a sense of security, and an obedient relationship to authority" (42). In *Independence Day* Ford succumbs to the national myth of exceptionalism that reinforces the rampant individualism the novel sought to challenge in the first place. Cohen notes that the end of the Cold War prompted a revival in triumphalist narratives that offer readers tidy, affirming endings (161)—and that is what Ford offers in *Independence Day*. It takes nothing less than the cataclysmic events of September 11 to destroy once and for all the structure of feeling that Ford has inhabited in the first two Bascombe novels.

The Lay of the Land and the Millennial Suburb

New York Times book reviewer (and novelist) Will Blythe questioned whether the male midlife crisis novel—born, he says, in the 1960s "when an increasing level of economic prosperity and a loosening level of morality freed men to stare rapturously at their navel"—has reached its own midlife crisis (13). Blythe credits Ford's Bascombe trilogy for keeping the genre afloat "by not having much of dramatic import happen," so that "everydayness . . . take[s] on the miraculous sheen of the seen-for-the-first-time" (13). One could counter that getting shot in the chest by an automatic weapon, as Frank Bascombe does in *The Lay of the Land*, qualifies as a dramatic event. Further, Ford's characterization of "everydayness" is hardly miraculous but is instead harrowing and uncertain. Bascombe himself, however, remains decidedly unmiraculous, so that he is indeed the right man for the moment.

As with *Independence Day*, Ford sets his novel in the recent past in order to assess the present moment. That present moment of 2006 was particularly fraught in the New Jersey suburbs after which Ford's fictional Haddam was modeled, since only New York City sustained more losses than New Jersey in the 9/11 attacks.[11] *The Lay of the Land* instead takes place over the Thanksgiving weekend of 2000, when the presidential election between Bush and Gore was as yet undecided, the Twin Towers had yet to crumble, and other matters of "dramatic import'—the wars in Afghanistan and Iraq, Hurricane Katrina—were still ahead, so that New Jersey suburbanites' sense of the "wild world . . . just beyond our perimeter" is still perceived as "an untallied apprehension among our residents" (*ID* 5). Nevertheless, the novel is rife with foreboding signs of the devastating events to come. The novel begins with news of a teacher in Texas who is the victim of a random shooting. Frank goes to have his usual lunch at Haddam's hospital and finds there has been a terrorist attack and the grounds are swarming with counterterrorist agents. Later he and his friend Wade Arcenault will take in the spectacle of watching a local landmark building come crashing to the ground. Near the end of the novel, a pair of heavily armed teenagers besiege Frank's neighbors' house. And in the novel's final image, Ford invokes and personalizes the events of September 11 by placing his everyman on a plane: "We are going down fast now. Our craft dips, shudders hard, and I feel myself afloat. . . . A bump, a roar, a heavy thrust forward" (*Lay of the Land* [hereafter *LOL*] 485). These premonitory moments admonish the reader that times have indeed changed, even in the supposedly changeless suburbs, and the stakes are much higher.

A pre-9/11 vantage point also enables Ford to implicitly examine the conditions that precipitated that day's horrific events. Without doubt, Ford's focus on the 2000 election and Bascombe's repeated reminders to readers that he voted for Gore are meant to presage that the Bush presidency will prove disastrous. Yet Ford also takes the occasion to unblinkingly reassess the assumptions that provided the foundation for the previous two novels and consider how these premises might have played a role in leading civilization-as-we-know-it to the brink of the unknown. If *Independence Day* concluded with Frank basking in the warmth of a sustaining community he helped build, in *The Lay of the Land*, he is doomed to find his way in a nightmarish landscape of his own making. As Frank wends in and around Haddam, the novel recalls the conceit of Frank Capra's postwar film, *It's a Wonderful Life*. In that film, the everyman George Bailey is made to see how his corner of the world might fare without him to protect it from the avaricious Mr. Potter. In Ford's formulation, Frank and his fellow Haddamites are all Potters, and he must reckon with the hellish world he has helped to create, a world resulting from an ethos that has reduced freedom to free enterprise and private property. As Harvey argues, neoliberalization has not eradicated poverty across the globe but has instead succeeded at redistributing wealth among a small economic elite.[12] This is a story writ small in "first" suburbs (such as Princeton, after which Ford modeled Haddam), where the concentration of wealth among a privileged few masks alarming trends: during the 1990s, a period of economic growth nationwide, median income stagnated in first suburbs, and in bleak contrast to national trends, the number of high-poverty neighborhoods in many first suburbs actually increased over the 1990s (see note 3). In this sense Haddam, where "people who mold opinion" live in cosseted seclusion, is not only a fitting metaphor for neoliberal policies that create poverty, it is responsible for these policies.

Frank's vision of a "homey connectedness" that he might rely on to build both community and wealth has not been borne out in Haddam (*ID* 93). Instead he finds that "citizens I'd known for a generation and sold homes to, now refused to meet my eyes, just set their gaze at my hairline and keep trudging" (89). In a scene highly evocative of Capra's film, Frank ducks into the local watering hole that has always given him a "sense of safe haven" (*LOL* 170) only to be greeted by a bartender who snarls, "Did you used to live here?"(178). When their testy conversation leads to the contested Bush-Gore election, the bartender bluntly sums up the town's "sinister" mood (183). Counting on his fingers, he notes, "This is your Russian. The next one's your spic. This one's your African. This last one's your Arab or your sand nigger—whichever. You got your choice . . . [f]or what language you want to learn when you vote for fuckin' Gore" (183). The bartender's hateful diatribe not only predicts the fear, loathing, and indiscriminate racial profiling to come as a result of the terrorist attacks but is also indicative of the pervasively angry mood in suburbs where immigrant and poor populations are burgeoning.[13]

Despite the "Pilgrim Village Interpretive Center" and the "Battle of Haddam" reenactors surreally trotting about town and drawing ire from the downtown merchants' association (49), Haddam has hardly become an authentic "community of memory." These "recreated practices of national commemoration," as Boym calls them, have failed to restore in citizens a sense of meaning and continuity (42). Everywhere signs of fakery and impermanence taunt Frank. Having settled into what he thought was the "Permanent Period" (47) of his life, he has happily remarried only to find himself alone after his wife's first husband suddenly returns from the long-thought-dead. His former home, over which he took considerable pride in *The Sportswriter*, has undergone several transformations since he sold it and in its latest incarnation is a garish replica of a Kentucky plantation replete with fluted columns and an electric fence. The maximum-security mini-estate is fittingly dubbed the Not Furlong, suggesting that it, too, will be razed as soon as there is profit to be made and a bigger, grander dream to build (48). Frank's once solid faith in the power of property to establish and secure status is further eroded by the realization that the house he currently owns on the Jersey Shore is one of five still standing, the others on his street having been "blown to shit and smithereens by Poseidon's wrath" (207). As Frank tours farmland in his gas-guzzling Suburban with his business partner, who is intent on getting involved in a get-richer-quicker large-scale development scheme, he expresses his misgivings over his chosen career as a real estate broker, "a profession both spawned by and grown cozy with our present and very odd state of human development" (47). In the previous two novels, Frank proved a master at deflecting guilt; now he must admit, "In other words, I'm implicated. You have a wish? Wait. I'll make it come true (or at least show you my inventory). Up to now, I've thought this basic formula was a good thing. But lately I'm less sure I'm right" (47).

Frank's self-doubt is precipitated, as is so often the case in the male midlife crisis novel, by personal troubles and his own confrontation with mortality. *The Lay of the Land* is indeed an illness story: we learn at the novel's outset that Frank has prostate cancer. Yet according to Ohmann's formula, the familiar trajectory of this narrative is individual recovery in an otherwise unchanged world. Such is not the case in *The Lay of the Land:* Frank's prognosis is decidedly unclear, and the world he inhabits is disorienting and chaotic. The previous two novels assumed, for better or worse, that the suburbs offered residents safety and security. This novel is predicated upon the assumption that life, no matter where it is lived, is full of contingency and discontinuity.

In this manner the novel undercuts the restorative nostalgia Frank found so emotionally potent in *Independence Day*, and which Boym claims is driven by "the anxiety of those who draw attention to historical incongruities between past and present and thus question the wholeness and continuity of the restored tradition" (45). Now, in contrast to the rosy sentimentality with which he portrayed the Fourth of July parade, Frank mocks the incoherence of the Battle of Haddam reenactors "staging assaults and retreats" at the current locations for "Frenchy's Gulf, Benneton, or Hurlburt's Classic Shoes" as well as the replicated Pilgrim village populated by a motley collection of college students posing as "a Negro Pilgrim, a Jewish female pilgrim, a wheelchair-bound Pilgrim, a Japanese Pilgrim with a learning disability and two or three ordinary white kids" who occasionally "step forth . . . to deliver loud declarations about 'the first hard days of 1620' . . . to whoever might be idle enough to stop on the way to the liquor store" (49–50). If the business of restorative nostalgia is to reestablish order, Frank is no longer buying it.

Instead, this novel participates in what Boym calls "reflective nostalgia," which is characterized by the "irrevocability of the past and human finitude" and is therefore "ironic, inconclusive, and fragmentary" (49–50). In a *New York Times* op-ed essay he wrote not long after 9/11 and also in response to the subsequent anthrax scare that further rattled an already traumatized population,[14] Ford urged his fellow suburbanites "to think large and small at once about whom we're connected to and separate from and about what we mean by community. This kind of puzzling can produce a quiet panic, or it can teach us that the knowledge of what confronts us, worries us, scares the wits out of us and makes us sad is the same knowledge we will need to imagine our strength" (A29). Neither the editorial nor the novel suggests that this knowledge has the capacity to return us to a prelapsarian state of comfort and security. Contingency itself becomes the defining feature of Ford's aesthetic, so that personal loss provides the basis for connection with others and "a context where relationships do not always develop by continuity but by contiguity" (Boym 53). In other words, individual experience, which in the first two novels provided the neoliberal argument for personal advancement over the common good, is here reconceived as the first step along a makeshift bridge to a flexible but meaningful sense of collective identity.

After all, it is because he is a cancer survivor (for the moment) that

Frank is so moved by a newspaper article he describes in the novel's prologue, which recounts the story of a nursing professor who has been shot point blank by a disgruntled student. He is stunned to learn that when the assassin asked his victim, "Are you ready to meet your Maker?" she was able to reply, "Yes. Yes, I think I am" (*LOL* 3). Her calm response causes Frank to wonder, "Would I ever say that? . . . It's not a question, let's face it, that suburban life regularly poses to us. Suburban life, in fact, pretty much does the opposite." He then adds forebodingly, confirming what his post-9/11 readers already know, "And yet it might" (4). Though Frank's world may be characterized by uncertainty, he has a new sense of clarity: he endeavors to do all that he can so that he, too, might be ready to "meet his Maker."

As Frank admits, he has spent the majority of his life (and approximately 800 pages in the previous two novels) navigating the familiar course of the suburban protagonist, which is to say keeping "offshore" and "slightly removed from events" (52). He has come to realize that the Clinton presidency did not usher in a "renaissance spirit . . . like a new sun, " and he has grown discontented "getting people into the homes they (and the economy) wanted themselves to be in (at least for a while)" (52). Disappointment and illness, however, have had the salubrious effect of spurring this self-serving everyman toward a new goal: to be a "mensch," or, as Paul Krugman puts it, someone "who takes responsibility for his actions" (A31).

Frank has left Haddam and has for the past eight years lived in Sea-Clift, New Jersey, a zesty stew of a townlette "spiced with Filipinos, Somalians and hard-working Hondurans (who come for the schools) to brew up a tranquil towny heterogeneity that looks modern on paper without feeling much different from the way things have always felt" (*LOL* 267–68). Unlike Haddam, a carefully constructed tableau of homogeneity and continuity, Sea-Clift embodies what might be called the "suburban real"—its population, at once fluid and fragmented, is loosely bound by the shifting sands of contiguity. He has nevertheless remained committed to the friends, neighbors, and strangers he has left behind. Over the course of the Thanksgiving holiday, for instance, in addition to counseling his young business partner, Frank sees to his duties as a Sponsor, since he is part of "a network of mostly central New Jersey citizens—men and women—whose goal is nothing more than to help people" (12). To be a Sponsor, one need have no special expertise; it requires only that Frank be willing to make a phone call, ring a doorbell, or as he had put it at the conclusion of *Independence Day*, "try to add a part of the puzzle" (*ID* 451).[15] He has determined to do "whatever the hell we're all supposed to do to display we're responsible and doing our best to make life better" (*LOL* 253). These efforts are often for naught: his angry rebuttal to the bigotry he encounters at the bar merely lands him in a brawl and gets him unceremoniously bounced from the premises, with no whiff of a promise that he has changed the hearts and minds of the bar's denizens. And despite his good-intentioned if foolhardy decision to intervene when his neighbors are invaded by marauding teenagers with automatic weapons, they are killed, and he is shot in the chest. His good deeds signal neither a return to Capra's Bedford Falls nor the dawn of a new utopia.

Yet Frank's change of heart should not be read cynically. The decidedly unspiritual Frank does not undertake these duties because he is looking for a nice piece of real estate in heaven or for the Tocquevillian reason of "self-interest rightly understood" (Tocqueville 2:122). This is not a narrative that affirms American exceptionalism. Instead, Frank is motivated by simple compassion, something he comes to fully when he is finally forced to reckon with the loss of a son who died nineteen years earlier. In yet another bar at the end of a long day, Frank is perusing a real estate flyer when an item catches his eye about a fellow broker whose son was killed in a drunk driving accident. Unbidden, vicarious grief so overwhelms him that he thinks he is having a heart attack (*LOL* 342–345). Frank has spent the better part of his adult life "sailing alone" as a means of avoiding his pain over his son's death. His visceral response at this juncture illustrates that such traumatic events have the power to weave out of individual suffering shared experience, since as Boym notes, "Voluntary and involuntary recollections of an individual intertwine with collective memories" (50). The basis of such connections may be loss and longing, but the result is a genuine empathy that infuses *The Lay of the Land*—and, I will argue, all of the post-9/11 suburban novels I examine in the subsequent chapters.[16]

In the immediate wake of 9/11, Michael Rothberg posited that the devastation of that day might at least "awaken some people in the United States . . . to the vista of global suffering" ("'There Is No Poetry In This'" 148). Subsequent events undertaken by our government—two wars, the mistreatment of prisoners at Abu Ghraib and Guantanamo, the Patriot Act, unconstitutional anti-immigration legislation, to name a few—suggest that the events of 9/11 awakened only fear, anger, and jingoism. In this context, we might better understand the ethics of the insistently personal perspective of *The Lay of the Land*, which, after all, speaks to and for the majority of voters (and which might also explain Ford's predilection for setting his novels amid hotly contested elections). Boym makes an important distinction between collective and national memory. National memory reads like a "single, teleological plot," whereas collective memory is inconclusive and fragmentary, "offering mere signposts for individual reminiscences that could suggest multiple narratives" (55). Frank's many encounters and quasi-encounters (by way of newspapers and circulars, television snippets and overheard conversations) as well as his random recollections and musings over the course of his weekend odyssey loosely connect his story to multiple perspectives but do not deign to encapsulate the entirety of these experiences in a tidy, cohesive narrative. Frank may be "part of a puzzle" (*ID* 451), but that puzzle is far from solved, since, as Boym notes, "the labor of grief" takes "a lifetime to complete" (55).

Updike concluded his tetralogy by killing off Rabbit; Ford does not give his protagonist this reprieve. Nor does he allow his everyman to "retreat behind the door of the family home," as Bruce Robbins has suggested the post-9/11 novel does (1096). Indeed, Frank willfully resists the temptation to "to go in . . . lock the door, wait this one out," and let his neighbors fend for themselves (459–460). Instead, he is left hanging in midair: Frank is one of several passengers aboard a plane bound for the Mayo Clinic, all of whom have in common a history of illness and an uncertain future.

The Lay of the Land may be pointedly set before the events of 9/11, but it evinces a decidedly post-9/11 sensibility in its emphatic assertion that the world as we once knew it is irrevocably lost: "*Before* is everlastingly gone. There is only everlastingly *after*" (458). What this "*after*" looks like is anybody's guess and asks only one question, according to Ford's protagonist: "Do I see good as even a possibility?" Frank's answer, along with everything else in the novel, is unsure: "I think I do" (476). His response sums up what I've called an aesthetics of contingency, which may be the best he can offer given that the lay of the land is merely shaky ground.

Yet I would argue that this hesitance and Ford's determination to limit his scope to "the human scale upon the land" (485) is also boldly imaginative. In the wake of 9/11 and in the buildup to the Iraqi war, Ford was one of several American authors collected by the Bush administration to contribute to a public relations project for foreign consumption called *Writers on America*. In his piece, Ford quotes the Czech novelist Milan Kundera: "The novelist teaches the reader to comprehend the world as a question. . . . In a [totalitarian] world built on sacrosanct certainties, the novel is dead" ("How Does Being an American Inform What I Write?" n.p.). Still, Ford's very participation in the project suggests a willingness to fold his own work into a teleological "master narrative" meant to advance national interests that may be democratic in name but are often totalitarian in practice.[17] With *The Lay of the Land*, Ford perhaps seeks to redress this misstep by returning his work to the form of a question. In the process, he also reimagines American identity itself as predicated not upon a set of national ideals but, instead, as built and rebuilt by multiple experiences and memories.

Dolores Hayden remarks that suburbia "is the hinge, the connection between past and future, between old inequalities and new possibilities" (245). There is no question that the old inequalities still exist, as *The Lay of the Land* also makes clear. Frank's illness may encourage him to empathize with his fellow sufferers, but his position on a plane bound for the best that US health care has to offer—the Mayo Clinic—is indicative of the privilege he enjoys. But new possibilities are also suggested by an everyman who is incontrovertibly in decline. If Ford's questing protagonist follows the established suburban literary tradition by leading the way for his like-minded readers, he reestablishes the terms of that tradition by no longer pointing in the direction of a better life, as he did in the conclusions of the first two Bascombe novels. Instead, his downward trajectory at the end *of The Lay of the Land* charts a far more nerve-wracking course that directs readers to hope only for a soft landing to cushion their inevitable fall. The novel is undeniably guilty of universalizing Frank's experience: illness, violence, loss, and sorrow can find anyone, after all. In fact, it is in this manner that the novel upsets the familiar dynamics of the suburban subgenre by portraying an everyman who is not isolated in his suffering. By casting Frank as one of many who needs and provides comfort and care, the novel signals a revolutionary path for the new suburban novel to follow in search of common ground.

2

The Assimilated Everyman and the Business of Forgetting

Postwar Living Memorials and the Posttraumatic Suburb in Chang-rae Lee's *Aloft*

In one of two essays to date devoted to Chang-rae Lee's third novel, *Aloft* (2004), Mark Jerng observes that critics have struggled to make sense of the book, both in the context of Lee's earlier work and within the emerging canon of recent American fiction.[1] The conundrum centers on the novel's protagonist: Lee appropriates the voice of a middle-class, middle-aged white male instead of what *New Yorker* critic James Wood identifies as the "solitary," "tormented" Asian American narrators of his previous novels, *Native Speaker* (1996) and *A Gesture Life* (1999) (71). On these grounds, Wood dismisses *Aloft*, asserting that it sinks into "suburban familiarity" that is "clichéd and histrionic" (71).[2] Lee's decision to follow his earlier work, praised for its originality and transnational scope, with a prototypical white male midlife crisis novel is indeed perplexing, especially in the context of the geopolitical implications of the terrorist attacks of September 11, 2001.

It is precisely in this context that the novel, set in the geographical backyard of those attacks, seeks to productively engage its readers. At first blush the novel seems intent on domesticating the crisis, as Richard Gray maintains many post-9/11 novels do. After all, *Aloft* may begin with its protagonist, Jerry Battle, aloft in his own single-engine plane, surveying his Long Island postwar suburb and surrounding area and taking note of the scarred earth where the Twin Towers had once stood. But while the novel initially acknowledges the large-scale catastrophe in the near distance, it quickly sinks into the well-mapped terrain of the postwar suburban novel as it recounts the travails of its amiable but detached protagonist. By novel's end Jerry himself suffers devastating personal loss while flying his plane, so that he lands, presumably once and for all, and retreats into the bosom of his home, seemingly fulfilling Gray's damning accusation that the post-9/11 novel reduces "a turning point in national and international history to little more than a stage in a sentimental education" (30).

My central argument in *American Unexceptionalism* is that the post-9/11 suburban novel's very insistence upon the quotidian and the domestic provides the basis for its unique contribution to the growing corpus of post-9/11 literature. In contrast to those novels that engage directly with the events of that day, such as Don DeLillo's *Falling Man* (2007) and Frederic Beigbeder's *Windows on the World* (2004), *Aloft* and the other novels I examine deal with the crisis circumspectly. As we've seen, Ford obliquely engages the event by setting *The Lay of the Land* in the months before the crisis. *Aloft* is set in the months after 9/11, but the events of that day are mentioned only once, with Jerry's passing reference in the opening scene to the "skyline where the Twin Towers used to be" (20). The novel's reticence on the subject is especially striking given its setting in the postwar Long Island suburbs: of the 2,800 people killed that day, more than 500 were from these towns, leaving the residents left behind to grapple with their loss and grief for years to come (Brodsky n.p.).

Jerry's determination to glide over the implications of large-scale catastrophe in the months following 9/11 calls to mind the government's efforts to restore the nation to a pre-9/11 status quo as quickly as possible. Just days after the attacks, for instance, President Bush told the nation that we were engaged in a "fight for our principles," which would require every citizen's "continued participation and confidence in the American economy" (Joint Session n.p.). Framing the stakes even more explicitly, the president's brother, Florida governor Jeb Bush, admonished Americans to "consider it their patriotic duty to go shopping, go to a restaurant, take a cruise, travel with their family," because "frankly, the terrorists win if Americans don't go back to normalcy" (Foser n.p.). The Bushes' directions to the public baldly illustrate the real threat that 9/11 posed to national interests as far as the power structure was concerned: the devastating interruption to the flow of capital that would persist if the collective sense of anxiety was not quickly alleviated. *Aloft* calls into question such efforts to return to business as usual by advancing an aesthetic of contingency that undermines its protagonist's attempts to restore order. Throughout the novel, but most especially in its final image of Jerry standing in a gaping hole in his own backyard, Lee refuses to provide a tidy resolution. Instead, he leaves his protagonist in a space that just as easily represents either a fresh grave or a fresh start. The novel's insistent uncertainty undercuts the neoliberal values that have come to be synonymous with suburbia—individual mastery, security, the "good life"—and suggests new possibilities for middle-class identity and affiliation in an indeterminate aftermath.

There are plenty of reasons why the suburbs are an appropriate setting for a post-9/11 novel concerned with exploring the contours of its ongoing aftermath. Even before the shattering events of 9/11, the Long Island suburbs depicted in *Aloft* were contending with a crumbling infrastructure and an increasingly vulnerable population.[3] Given all of these changes, Lee's decision to focus on the stock character of the materially comfortable middle-aged, middle-class white suburban male seems an odd choice. Critics have noticed the remarkable resemblance between his protagonist, Jerry Battle, and Ford's Frank Bascombe, an affinity that was a conscious choice on Lee's part.[4] Like Bascombe, Battle was born in the immediate wake of World War II, in 1945. Bascombe, however, represents the canonical White Anglo-Saxon Protestant everyman who has inherited as if by birthright the suburban literary tradition from Cheever and Updike. Jerry, on the other hand, is the blue-collar pretender to that throne. An Italian American whose grandfather changed the family name from Battaglia to Battle, Jerry is a fully assimilated everyman whose family entered the middle class amid the prosperity and suburbanization that followed World War II. Jerry's characterization calls attention to the fact that whiteness and middle-classness are learned behaviors that have underwritten the American success story the suburbs were built to tell.

It might thus be argued that *Aloft* inadvertently works in the manner that Elizabeth Anker describes to reinscribe the prerogatives of white masculinity by staging a familiar drama of beset manhood against the current and specific post-9/11 backdrop.[5] *Aloft* seems to follow Anker's template in the way that Lee registers the wide-ranging distress of the historical present through the all-too-familiar narrative of male midlife crisis. But the novels that Anker uses to make her argument predominantly overlook issues of race and gender in a manner that suggests to Anker "a desire to reverse key historical transitions" (6). As we shall see, *Aloft* engages just these issues in its depiction of Jerry's negligence and casual brutality toward his troubled Korean wife, Daisy. Thus, *Aloft* contradicts the conventional paradigm. Instead of supporting the structures that have supported white male privilege, Lee aims to dismantle them and clear the ground for new community formations.

Timothy Aubry argues that during the 1950s Cheever's high-minded, middlebrow fiction functioned much like the self-help books that were beginning to appear on the market. Cheever taught his white suburban male reader "how to be properly miserable," to cultivate a disaffected stance tempered by "salutary self-irony" that would distinguish him from otherwise indistinguishable white male suburbanites ("Cheever and the Management . . ." n.p.). As we've seen in *The Sportswriter* especially, Frank Bascombe is a master at keeping his ironic distance. *Aloft* offers Jerry as Frank's de facto student: just as Frank in *The Sportswriter* prefers to sail alone, Jerry takes to the sky in his private plane, where from that vantage point he can view the world and still be "completely outside of it, too" (8). But if this novel starts with a protagonist whose disposition imitates the Bascombe we encounter in *The Sportswriter*, it ultimately exposes that model as both a fraud and a failure and holds Jerry accountable for following Bascombe's example.

Jerry Battle's insistent detachment, which, as I suggested in the previous chapter, might arguably have been understood in an earlier era as a mark of his admirable stoicism or as a symptom of his past suffering, is here deemed morally questionable and self-serving. As I will elaborate, only by pointedly looking the other way in the face of both large-scale atrocity and everyday injustice has he secured his privilege. Thus, Lee enlists his emphatically unexceptional suburban antihero to counteract the narrative of American innocence and exceptionalism swiftly marketed by the mass media and the Bush administration immediately after 9/11, in which victims became heroes and disaster was figured as a crucible that once again revealed the indomitable national spirit.

But Lee does not summon the figure of the suburban everyman simply because he is an antihero. Jerry's story in *Aloft* challenges the triumphalist response to our most recent catastrophe by gradually excavating the buried historical trauma that provided the shaky foundation for these postwar suburbs in the first place. By pointedly situating the novel just beyond the Twin Towers' rubble, Lee links the events of 9/11 to Jerry's own long-denied history—a palimpsest of unacknowledged loss and complicity that has until recently supported the entire suburban franchise of safety, comfort, and private property ownership that was meant to fill the void felt by the sixteen million returning World War II soldiers who were originally given the keys to this kingdom. Then as now, government and business interests sought to forestall any interruption to the revitalized economic engine. As we shall see, their efforts in this regard were considerable, evident not only in the carrots provided by the unprecedented Veterans' Bill of Rights that made first-time homeowners of millions of returning white veterans but in "living memorials" that ostensibly honored the dead but, more important, by way of parks, playgrounds, swimming pools, highways, and bridges, pointed toward a seductive future of leisure, ease, and unimpeded upward mobility to a generation only too happy to break from a recent past that included both the war and the Great Depression that preceded it.

In the wake of 9/11, Lee invokes traces of that story not only by setting his novel in the vicinity of the postwar suburb par excellence, Levittown, but in his depiction of three generations of Battle men—Jerry, who shares a birthday with the postwar moment; his father, Hank (The Tank) Battle, who originally moved the family landscaping business to these brand-new suburbs where it flourished, building the living memorials and the privatized, backyard versions that followed; and Jerry's son, Jack, who is currently running that business right into the ground. The Battles themselves well know that their personal fortunes are bound up with the postwar triumphalist narrative. As Jerry explains, his father moved his business to the suburbs and changed the family name from Battaglia to Battle not only to blend in but because it was "squarely patriotic" and would "herald a new and optimistic beginning" (23).[6] But if the family enterprise once thrived by shaping the postwar suburban landscape, Battle Brothers Inc. is on the brink of bankruptcy as the novel opens, thus posing a fresh challenge to the conventional story of the nuclear family living the good life in the suburbs. The novel may begin with Jerry at a safe remove as he soars over the Twin Towers' open grave, but its final image leaves him fully immersed in a crater of his own making, suggesting that the premise of upward mobility upon which these suburbs were built is not just an implausible fiction but a cruel story in dire need of revision.[7]

What Lies Beneath: History, Forgetting, and Living Memorials in the Postwar Suburbs

The representation of postwar suburbia as a wasteland of stultifying conformity, blinding whiteness, and crass materialism is by now familiar enough. The source of anomie at the heart of suburban existence has variously been attributed to the rise of the corporation, rampant consumerism, deadening conformity, the enforced isolation of the detached, single-family home, the anxiety of affluence and its doppelgänger, financial pressure, among other things. This vast body of criticism has combined to create a complex if not particularly flattering portrait of postwar suburban life, yet none has taken particular note of the obvious: these suburbs were originally created for and by the over sixteen million demobilized soldiers of World War II, ostensibly offered to them as a consolation prize for their service and suffering. The impetus driving the massive postwar suburban project, however, was to pave over these soldiers' war experiences as quickly and completely as possible in order to assimilate them into civilian life and make them productive and reproductive members of society.[8] It is this foundational history that *Aloft* nods toward, most especially in its depiction of the family patriarch, Hank (The Tank) Battle-né-Battaglia.

Indeed, Hank is representative of the wave of returning soldiers who may have been greeted as heroes but whose homecoming was also met with trepidation and dread by the federal, state, and local institutions charged with their rehabilitation.[9] Unquestionably, the powers that be were worried about the very real possibility of massive unemployment and the collapse of the wartime economy, but their fears were also shaped by underlying assumptions concerning the character of these particular troops and the social problems that would accompany them home. In his influential treatise *Veteran Comes Back* (1944), sociologist Willard Waller warned of the grave danger that these returning vets posed to society, since, far from being "typical middle-class Americans of the Andy Hardy type," they were part of what he deemed a "blighted generation," having grown up during the Depression and known only poverty and insecurity (248). Their experience during the war did not equip them with skills for civilian life but only stoked the anger already simmering inside of them.

In this regard, Waller might well be describing *Aloft*'s hot-headed patriarch, Hank, who, as a second-generation Italian American growing up during the Depression, was a violent, angry young man, Jerry asserts, "for the usual reasons of privation and poverty and general mistreatment" (289). In contrast to the white Protestant "Andy Hardy" type that Waller outlines, Lee's characterization of a young, scrappy Hank Battaglia calls attention to the tenuous status of immigrants and their children before World War II. David Roediger uses the term "inbetween peoples" to convey the ambiguous position immigrants from Ireland and Eastern and Southern Europe occupied during the first half of the twentieth century: as late as 1937, the scholar John Dollard wrote repeatedly of the immigrant working class as "our temporary Negroes" (Roediger 13).

In the wake of World War II, the challenge was thus considered not a matter of *re*integrating white ethnic enlisted men like Hank into their former lives but of molding them into a new social order that would align with the economic interests of the established order. This was accomplished by way of the GI Bill, or what Karen Brodkin has ironically called "the most massive affirmative action program in American history," since it was "aimed at and disproportionately helped male, Euro-origin GIs" (38). As Brodkin points out, the various benefits provided by the bill—including preferential hiring, small business loans, and, most significantly, low-interest home loans and full educational benefits—were theoretically available to all veterans but in actuality were denied to African Americans and women by way of a variety of unfair practices and loopholes.[10] In contrast, ethnic American males of European origin were now extended membership in the new order, but "as whites, not as new immigrants," as Roediger points out. Indeed, "the new policies merely expanded and clarified the ways state policy could favor whites, raising the stakes for claiming white identity" (230). Roediger outlines the degree to which the provisions of the Federal Housing Authority and the Veterans Administration precluded immigrants from developing their own urban neighborhoods.[11] Immigrants and their offspring were instead steered into participating in the postwar suburban experiment that made them common shareholders in what George Lipsitz has aptly called the "possessive investment in whiteness" (vii).[12]

In truth, the invention of this new social order was a work in progress long before the war ended. Suburban scholar Barbara Kelly points out that as the war was winding down, business and political leaders began strategizing in order to usher in a peacetime economy that would advance their economic interests and prevent the rise of a labor movement similar to the Socialist revolutions that had plagued so much of Europe after World War I (n.p.). They assiduously designed this wished-for future by way of an invented, idealized past that foretold what we would become after the war.[13] Even the war's casualties were enlisted in this project. For instance, *Life* magazine dedicated its July 5, 1943, issue to the war's fallen soldiers, listing the 12,987 servicemen killed in action to date.[14] Following this stark commemoration, however, is an editorial that attempts to make tidy meaning out of horrendous loss: the editorialist determines that "the boys who have gone over the Big Hill" undoubtedly gave their last thoughts to "mom bending over the stove," "the kid brother in the yard," "the movie theater and the baseball diamonds and the cars" so that "he would all in an instant relive that life and know that it was a good life, and if they wanted to call that life 'freedom' that would be Okay with him" ("The American Purpose" 39). In the same spirit that moved President Bush and his cohort to urge citizens to do their patriotic duty by shopping in the immediate aftermath of 9/11, and having concretely defined "freedom" as access to the good life of consumption, the *Life* writer exhorts readers to decide whether these soldiers "died for the fulfillment of a purpose or . . . for the fulfillment of practically nothing." After all, the reader is reminded, "the dead boys will become what we make them" (39). As the editorial makes clear, however, the "dead boys" had already been remade, remembered here as heroic and avid white middle-class consumers whose memory must be honored by "summoning all of the people of the earth to the green pastures of liberty" (39)—vividly imagined in terms of the new roads, private backyards, and sparkling baseball diamonds that would define the coming suburban landscape.[15]

After the war, business and government leaders led by Senator Joseph McCarthy and the developer William Levitt made sure that "the green pastures of liberty" were indeed filled with privately built (but publicly subsidized) single-family housing developments that addressed the desperate need for veteran housing and employment while advancing an ethos of free enterprise, consumption, and upward mobility. As Bill Levitt reasoned, "No man who owns his own home and a lot can be a communist" (Larabee 84). To be sure, factory-produced houses hazily and haphazardly nodded toward America's imagined history by way of the "Cape Cods," "Colonials," and "California Ranchers" that were designed to make "Polish, Italian, Lithuanian, Jewish, and Catholic owners feel that they were claiming a piece of American tradition" (Baxandall and Ewen 131). That these parcels of paradise could be had so cheaply was owing not only to the unprecedented subsidies provided by the VA and the FHA, but to the likes of first- and second-generation immigrants like Hank Battle: distrusted and excluded by labor unions well into the 1930s, these independent laborers willingly worked weekends and charged by the job rather than the hour for Levitt and company.[16]

The original postwar suburbs may have been ethnically diverse but were racially homogenous. This was owing not only to the GI Bill's exclusionary implementation and the FHA's racist lending policies but to the fact that because large-scale communities such as Levittown were privately built, the developers could—and did—enact race-restrictive covenants. Though these covenants were deemed unconstitutional in 1948, the FHA unofficially accepted unwritten agreements and traditions of segregation as late as 1968 (Baxandall and Ewen 175). The Levitts were especially tenacious in maintaining the "caucasian only" clause, maintaining that "most whites prefer not to live in mixed communities. . . . It is not reasonable to expect that any one builder could or should undertake to absorb the entire risk and burden of conducting such a vast social experiment" (Baxandall and Ewen 175). Yet a vast social experiment is exactly what the Levitts undertook; their standardized single-family housing developments had the effect of literally constructing whiteness for these new homeowners. These postwar suburbs were built to help owners forget their ethnic backgrounds and their fraught pasts. The emphasis was on a brand-new future of ease and prosperity. Thus, a 1950 *House Beautiful* article that begins with the challenging headline "How American Is Your Way of Living?" goes on to assert that "the truly American house" reflects "our ideals of the good life" by offering "all the labor-saving devices, the modern equipment, the building techniques and materials" that would enable one to live the "efficient, easy, drudgery-free life that our times and our American genius have made possible" (Bangs 83).[17]

The collective determination to emphasize the future and the living rather than the past and the dead was also concretely expressed by the immensely popular move toward "living memorials" to commemorate the war's dead. Architectural historian Andrew Shanken describes the vociferous debate surrounding the use of living memorials over traditional monuments after World War II, which ultimately "shifted the terms of memorial practice away from what might be thought of as a liturgically based set of rituals, drawing memorialization closer to leisure, recreation, and the desire for cohesive community" (132). Though critics such as Lewis Mumford accused Americans of selfishly serving themselves and not the fallen with "an auditorium or a swimming pool, perfunctorily named a memorial" (107), the bulk of critics and the general public found that traditional memorials were lugubrious and unwanted reminders of death, and agreed instead with the argument advanced in a 1945 issue of *House Beautiful* which pointedly asked, "Do you believe your town can afford to build an imposing monument to World War II while just around the corner children are playing in the streets?" (Darling 42).

Shanken asserts that the primary goal of living memorials was to preserve "social ideals for future generations" (132). More properly, the swimming pools, auditoriums, playgrounds, and baseball diamonds "perfunctorily called memorials" literally constructed the ideal *of* the future by forecasting nothing but clement weather for a nation that placed a premium on physical fitness, family togetherness, and healthy competition.[18] Further, memorial highways and bridges clearly marked for new suburbanites the "American Way," defined by Will Herberg in his influential book *Protestant-Catholic-Jew* (1955) as "'forward looking,' 'optimistic,' and characterized by 'incessant activity' in the ceaseless striving to 'get ahead'" (79). The very term "living memorial" is a misnomer, then, for the bridges, highways, and recreational facilities that were built not to encourage remembrance and reflection but to help Americans move onward and upward.

In this context the architect Philip Johnson, though himself a proponent of the traditional monument, perhaps best captured the essence of the cultural work these living memorials were meant to do when he earnestly proposed a massive mound of dirt as an appropriate monument. Such a mound would "offer a unique opportunity for that most American of modern tools, the bulldozer"(25). The mound of dirt perhaps calls to mind the march over "the Big Hill," while the bulldozer instructs what that journey was for: to bury the past in order pave the way to the bigger, better, brighter future.

As both his nickname and occupation illustrate, *Aloft*'s Hank (The Tank) Battle is the embodiment of Johnson's proposal even as he stands as the primary poster child for the national agenda promoted by Joseph McCarthy and William Levitt, among others. Hank, like the iconic World War II tank, found good work after the war by moving earth to create the playgrounds, baseball diamonds, and swimming pools that "perfunctorily" honored the fallen while cultivating a taste for the good life and the sense of a bright future among postwar suburbanites. As Jerry sums up the company his father built in this new suburbia, it has been a "veritable goldmine" that may have made its business by working in dirt but has until recently thrived on an ethos of heady upward mobility: Battle Brothers Landscaping followed its early clients "to bigger and bigger places right up until they died" (290), since, as Jerry asserts, this is what brought people out to the suburbs in the first place—the "idea about the destiny of the good American life and how each of us had a place in it, guiding it along" (291).

Yet the bulldozer and mound of dirt also tell a haunting counternarrative to this triumphalist story by implying that our national self-image would depend upon quickly burying and forgetting a vexing past of poverty, genocide, and nuclear death in order to smooth the ground for a future of unimpeded prosperity, a pattern of denial that the Battle family has similarly employed in order to preserve their precarious family identity. But atrocities have a tendency of resurfacing. James Berger notes that while our narrative of "national perfection" depends upon suppressing "traumatic events and national crimes" (134), the burden of repression is simply "too heavy for any culture to bear" (135). He traces the cycle of what he calls "apocalyptic purgings, both real and imaginary," that attempt to "distill and redistill the purity of the national moral categories" (135) by repeatedly severing us from a disturbing past that might keep us from realizing our promised destiny.

In the immediate wake of 9/11, the Bush administration and the media engaged in just such an act of "apocalyptic purging" by rushing to make Pearl Harbor that day's historical analog.[19] This comparison attempted to cast Americans once again as unequivocal "good guys" on the global stage and provided the nation carte blanche for avenging that day's heinous crime and remaking the world in our image. So began another page in an ongoing official narrative. The simultaneous resurfacing of the term

"Ground Zero," however, vividly illustrates the pathology that persists when traumatic history goes unacknowledged. Whether intentional or not, the term forever links the destruction and loss of life of September 11, 2001, with the nuclear annihilation of Hiroshima and Nagasaki in August 1945. As Richard Stamelman puts it, "The ruins of the two events lie fused together, their fragments intermingled in the same debris field of history" (14), so that the current event's official narrative was immediately soiled by the unwanted historical memory in which Americans were the perpetrators, not the victims.

The resurfacing of the term "ground zero" also prefigured the nation's asymmetrical and inappropriate response to the 9/11 attacks in the ensuing months and years: recalling the devastating display of might that ended the Pacific war, the US military invaded Iraq with what was billed as a campaign of "Shock and Awe" that would effectively paralyze its demonized, racialized foreign enemy.[20] That this military adventure was undertaken under false pretenses that had absolutely nothing to do with the 9/11 attacks and more to do with the quest to control oil and myriad opportunities for shameless profiteering is by now well established. At the time, however, the invasion of Iraq was met with stunning quiescence—not only on the part of Congress and the national media but by the general populace in America, if not abroad.[21]

Aloft, published just one year after the launch of the Iraq war, addresses a conspicuously silent suburban middle-class readership in the post-9/11 era by recalling its foundational postwar roots. Kelly has pointed out that World War II has come to be known as "the good war" by careful design: the benefits and amenities provided by the GI Bill meant that with no cash investment white veterans were given the keys to houses that the government had regulated, designed, and underwritten (6). In exchange, the government exacted these veterans' loyalty and their pledge not to go digging in their own backyards. Kelly notes, for instance, that "the veterans of World War II are among the most conservative of today's Americans" (6).[22] Remarking upon the apparent irony of such conservative views given that these residents, as World War II veterans, had themselves been beneficiaries of massive government initiatives, Kelly reasons that the subsidies provided by the GI Bill essentially ensured that these homeowners would remain loyal to the government that provided them their house (7). It has become a somewhat stale observation that serious suburban fiction lays bare the seething heart of darkness just below the plush green lawns of its lonely, atomized everymen. In *Aloft* Lee unearths only fragments, but these shards combine to remind us that built into the very foundation of the postwar suburban novel is a history of atrocity, loss, and complicity. If Lee's Battle men are as detached as their literary precursors, Lee now holds them accountable as accessories after the fact for their role in plowing under and paving over this history as part of the lucrative business of forgetting.

Excavating Trauma and Shame in *Aloft*

Aloft explicitly engages the postwar suburbs' founding mythology of victory, virtue, and its attendant promise of an ever brighter future. The novel teems with references to popular representations of wartime valor and sacrifice, ranging from films such as *Saving Private Ryan* (1998) and *The Bridges at Toko-Ri* (1954) to Tom Brokaw's book *The Greatest Generation* (1998). Jerry goes so far as to buy his own single-engine plane to satisfy a childhood fantasy of being an "ace" on the iconic World War II fighter-bomber, the P-47 Thunderbolt.

However, Lee most provocatively engages the postwar ethos that has come to represent the suburbs with the stories he does *not* tell. For instance, the novel does not explicitly mention that Hank (The Tank) Battle is actually a veteran of the war, though distinctly military language accrues to him throughout and he is described as being as "physically solid as the masonry work he and his brothers used to do at the big North Shore mansions," suggesting he was not 4-F (174).[23] This evasion, while seemingly incidental, represents a legacy of denial passed down from father to son to Jerry's son, Jack. The impulse to suppress a disturbing past in order to arrive at a wished-for future also provides the basis for Lee's depiction in *Aloft* of the suburbs as less "living memorials" than mausoleums for the living dead.

The idea that postwar suburbia creates the conditions for living death is, of course, nothing new: zombie films such as *Invasion of the Body Snatchers* (1956) and the *Night of the Living Dead* franchise (1968) luridly make the same case that Cheever, Updike, and Yates make in a more subdued fashion in their depiction of the interchangeable protagonists who sleepwalk through their fiction. As I've suggested, however, Lee moves beyond the familiar critique of the suburbs' numbing conformity and materialism by locating the roots of postwar suburban somnambulism in its traumatic history. In their determination to bury a past of pain, loss, and shame, the constricted characters in *Aloft* also deny themselves the genuine pleasures and satisfactions of lived experience. Instead, family life becomes nothing more than what Jerry deems "the loose association of . . . very separate, unconnected beings, who share only the minimum genetic material and the securely grounded belief that a full belly makes for a carefree, loafing soul" (131). In her seminal work, *Trauma and Recovery* (1992), which delineates the psychological effects of short-lived and sustained traumatic experience, Judith Herman asserts that "the attempt to avoid reliving trauma too often results in a narrowing of consciousness, a withdrawal from engagement with others, and an impoverished life" (42). Lee's characters lead the "anesthetized" existence that Herman describes and which she claims results from the "active process of forgetting"—the repression, dissociation, and denial that are "phenomena of social as well as individual consciousness" and which are the hallmarks of the fictional representation of suburban life (9). In Lee's formulation, the "active process of forgetting"—the deal returning white veterans unwittingly made by accepting the unspoken terms of the GI Bill—is the original sin of omission visited upon generation after generation of Battle men. The unsettling aftershocks rumbling from one Battle to the next delineate the transgenerational effects of trauma, or what psychoanalytical theorists Nicolas Abraham and Maria Torok labeled a "phantom" to describe the ghostly power of a traumatic, shameful, or inadmissible secret that moves across generations (171).

The concept of transmissible trauma as it has been further articulated by theorists such as Shoshana Felman, Dori Laub, and Cathy Caruth has drawn fire for its problematic ethical implications. Critics charge that it promotes a diluted, undifferentiated understanding of trauma's reach, conferring evenly upon witnesses, bystanders, and even perpetrators the mantle of victimhood, along with the sympathy and blamelessness that attends such status.[24] This notion seems particularly repellent when applied to the privileged white middle-class males who populate postwar suburban fiction. But Lee is not interested in tracing an inheritance of loss or the heavy burden of guilt as it moves from one beleaguered everyman to the next. In *Aloft* the transgenerational phantom is no free-floating force that overtakes its victims. Instead, it is a carefully preserved legacy of complicity that has defined not just the Battle family dynamics but its long-successful business model: to wit, each principal of Battle Bros. Inc. has learned at his father's knee how to profitably cultivate a landscape designed to promote numbing forgetfulness.

Lee articulates these terms at the novel's outset, as he offers his readers an aerial view from the tiny cockpit of Jerry Battle's plane. There is little doubt that the plane is indicative of upward mobility taken to dizzying heights. Yet Jerry's description of the landscape he helped shape—the "trees, ideally formed and arranged" and "the simple, square houses set snugly in rows" like so many gravestones—is oddly funereal, as if he himself has already gone over the "Big Hill": "From up here," he observes, "everything looks perfect" (3). As the story also makes perfectly clear, while Jerry may be effectively dead, he is hardly a victim. As he buzzes over the gaping absence of the Twin Towers, the novel invokes the traumatic events of September 11, so that Jerry's plane is figured as an instrument of death that he himself steers—though unlike the pilots of that day, he is driven not by fanaticism but by his determination to distance himself from his messy and complicated history.

Lee likewise holds Hank (The Tank) accountable for preparing the ground for his own living death. Hank has always taken pride in his part in "guiding" the "destiny of the good American life" (291), and now he has finally earned the best of what that "good life" has to offer: a room in the Ivy Acres Nursing Home, where Jerry, at least, is assured his father will be offered the "ultimate luxuries of Ease and Convenience" and will "live out the rest of his days in complete security and comfort and without a worldly care" (7). Though Hank himself complains bitterly that this is hardly what he worked for all his "stinking life" (6), Lee offers the nursing home as the ghastly logical conclusion of a utopian vision founded upon the sequestering of death and the sanitization of suffering that Hank himself has been instrumental in realizing.

Finally, Jerry's son, Jack, the latest Battle to take over the family business, has likewise built his own tomb—a McMansion in a fortress-like gated community, tricked out with personal entertainment systems for both of his children, his-and-her bathrooms in the master suite, and an airtight den where he can enjoy his cigars in peace. The house that Jack built is a "truly American house" that reflects the "ideals of the good life,"which is to say that it encrypts each family member in the most luxurious mausoleum that money can buy (Bangs 83).

By the time the time the novel opens, however, events have conspired to disturb the Battles from their self-inflicted cryogenic slumbers. Hank, for instance, is beset with the early symptoms of dementia, so that "best forgotten" memories keep "crowding" his brain unbidden (155). Jack, in the meantime, has so overexpanded the family landscaping business that he is at risk of losing not only his mausoleum-like home but also the family landscaping business that has thrived for three generations building so-called living memorials.

The catalyst that rouses Jerry from his burial chamber is his daughter, Theresa, a Stanford PhD who has come from California for a visit with her fiancé, Paul, and brings with her news that she has non-Hodgkins lymphoma, she's pregnant, and she intends to keep the baby. Jerry, who has absorbed some of his daughter's academic jargon, throws up his hands and proclaims, "Jerry Battle hereby declines the Real"(230). The Real, as Jerry understands it, might best be described by what Slavoj Žižek calls "real reality," or the "destructive Void" that has the capacity to unsettle Western citizens' complacent acceptance of a "Virtual Reality" that Žižek likens to the ersatz suburban setting of the 1998 film *The Truman Show* (12–15). Theresa's problematic pregnancy, endangered by a (medical) history that will ultimately kill her, is the embodiment of just such a "destructive Void, " and her condition impels Jerry to begin sifting through the layers of unacknowledged loss, complicity, and shame that he, his father, and his son have so zealously kept buried in their psychic crypts.

There is Jerry's brother, Bobby Battle, who was killed in the Vietnam War. He had enlisted on a whim because his father, Hank, committed to the "active process of forgetting" his own war experiences, told him it would be an opportunity to "take in the sights of Southeast Asia" (149). After Bobby's death, Hank removes himself to the basement, where he sets to work on his 1/175-scale USS *Arizona* (112), a project he works on for the next three years. Hank's retreat to his bunker and his painstaking effort to rebuild the battleship sunk at Pearl Harbor constitute an attempt not only to deny his own loss but to justify it by "redistill[ing] the purity of the national moral categories," as Berger puts it (135). Hank literally seals off Bobby's memory by locking the door to his untouched bedroom until a roof leak causes so much mold, stench, and rot that he has to strip it down to the studs. All that Hank salvages are his son's baseball trophies, which he soaks in bleach in order to restore the pristine "American Golden Boy-hood" for which soldiers such as Bobby supposedly went over the "Big Hill" in the first place (*Aloft* 154). Hank's effort to rework and cleanse history is a sisyphean exercise, however. Like the Vietnam War itself, Bobby's death remains unresolved: he hovers over the text as "Bobby Ongoing," since only his helmet and a bloody boot were ever recovered, fragments that psychically compete with the polished baseball trophies that Hank keeps on display in his room in the nursing home (147). Wolfgang Schivelbusch deems that "it is possible that the destruction of September 11 uncovered the suppressed remains of Vietnam" (293); the memory of Bobby similarly resurfaces. And though Jerry picks at the unfinished business of his brother's life and death, it is a scab that refuses to heal: the story, if not its individual characters, is committed to an aesthetics of contingency that resists the urge to offer the comfort of closure.

More central to the narrative but just as spectral is Daisy, Jerry's late wife and the mother of his children. We learn little about this cipher other than that she was a Korean immigrant with a "hardscrabble past" whose broken English spared Jerry from "in-depth and nuanced discussions" (*Aloft* 119). Jerry does, however, give a fairly detailed account of Daisy's erratic conduct, describing "DSM-certified" symptoms that would manifest themselves with sleepless nights spent feverishly redecorating their ranch-style home; naked expeditions to the local playground; and drunken midnight dips in the backyard pool despite being unable to swim—compulsive, risky behaviors indicative of someone suffering posttraumatic stress disorder (PTSD).[25] Her obsession with her ranch house and her forays to the playground and the swimming pool can also be construed as desperate attempts to find solace in the living memorials that are supposed to deliver the good life and aid in "the active process of forgetting."

Undoubtedly, Daisy's inability to successfully bury her past is consistent with behaviors associated with trauma victims, who, Judith Herman observes, "wish to forget but cannot (8)."[26] The novel itself, however, fully suppresses the details of Daisy's traumatic past: whatever haunts her remains unspoken. This conspicuous silence raises the moral stakes behind Lee's curious decision to lend his narrative voice to a white middle-class male. Jerng notes that critics have alternately read Jerry as a "white suburban subject who can speak to universal themes," and an "ethnicized" character whose working-class Italian American origins align him with the Korean American males of Lee's earlier novels who likewise struggle with "the common problems of cultural identity and belonging" (189). Lee may indeed be drawing a comparison between Jerry and his Korean American characters, but he does not imply that their experiences are equivalent. Instead, Lee's portrayal of Jerry's suffering wife, Daisy, highlights the difference between them. Jerry can toggle easily between the ethnicized sense of self he has inherited and the universal claims afforded a white suburban subject, since both harmoniously attest to the validity of the national narrative's core promise of individual opportunity and advancement. As Jerry describes his felicitous background,

> If you took an accounting of all who proceed us, . . . you'd have some kind of portfolio of golden twentieth-century self-made American living, all those spic-and-span houses and Gunite pools . . . the double wall ovens set on timers to bring the roast rosemary chicken and casserole of sweet sausage lasagna to just the right crisp on top as Dad pulled the white Lincoln up the driveway, their contribution to our Great Society being the straight full trickle-down to my generation of Battaglias and Battles and Battapaglia's and the rest of us with the sweetheart deal of a Set-It-and-Forget It existence. (*Aloft* 289)

Daisy, on the other hand, represents what Min Song calls "The Strange": that is, a "foreigner, nonconformist, or racial other" who bears "the material traces of a history that exists in contradiction to the state's own self-serving stories" (*Strange Future* 3). Jerry's wooing of Daisy and his subsequent efforts to separate her from a disturbing past he'd rather know nothing about mimics the assimilation process itself; their unhappy union illustrates how perverse and nullifying this process can be. Jerry does everything he can to silence Daisy. He strips her of phone privileges so she can't call relatives in Korea, and when her behavior becomes increasingly troublesome, he takes his father's advice "to be a little brutal" (*Aloft* 104). Hank further advises that Jerry deny Daisy "any money or attention. . . . Don't let her out of the house for a week. Then when she's down in the dumps bring her some diamond earrings . . . And if that doesn't work, call Dr. Derricone," a crusty general practitioner who promptly prescribes Valium (104). Hank's proffered tactics of bullying, withholding, bribing, and medicating follow the classic pattern of an abusive relationship. These tactics also crudely replicate the conflicting courses of treatment accorded World War II soldiers suffering from PTSD, who were variously shamed, denied compensation, drugged, and bribed to forget.[27]

All of these courses of action, by turns abusive and obtuse, are forms of discipline meant to show Daisy her particular place in guiding the "destiny of the good American life" (219). In her frenetic efforts to embody the ideal 1950s homemaker, Daisy appears to occupy the position Betty Friedan describes in her groundbreaking book, *The Feminine Mystique* (1963). Friedan establishes the various ways that middle-class women in the postwar era were coerced into fully devoting themselves to their roles as mothers and housewives: in both their reproductive capacity and in their role as consumers, women were charged with the impossible task of satisfying the postwar capitalist economy's bottomless hunger for growth. But Daisy and Jerry's marriage does not play out against the backdrop of 1950s conformity. Instead, their union spans the late 1960s through the mid-1970s—a tumultuous period marked not only by the Vietnam War that claimed Bobby but by the women's and civil rights movements—events Jerry does not mention and needn't, since it is initially his good fortune to be married to an "old-fashioned girl" whose predilection for orderly housekeeping and pleasing her man he credits to her being not "so long removed from the old country" (101). Jerry's reductive description of Daisy's ostensibly culturally determined attributes damningly indicates that as far as he is concerned, Daisy is herself a commodity—a foreign import. When she breaks down, Hank recommends special handling: "If [Daisy] were a plain sedan like your mother you wouldn't have to worry. . . . But with a sleek machine, you've got to tool a governer [*sic*] onto the sucker, do something to cut her fuel" (105). Hank's advice, delivered in 1975 after a period of upheaval that profoundly challenged white male privilege, crudely anticipates the strategy behind a particularly savvy strand of multiculturalism that domesticates difference by reducing it to a collection of dehistoricized, depoliticized goods and artifacts. Vijay Prashad concludes that "consumerism seems to be the main drive for this kind of multiculturalism," which simultaneously exploits and contains racial ethnic identity in service to patriarchy (112). Whether Daisy is serving up delectable "Oriental-style dishes" (*Aloft* 101) poolside or modeling a fetching new outfit that Jerry declares makes her "good enough to eat," she obliges rather than threatens the prerogatives of white privilege (114).

That Daisy ultimately drowns in the backyard swimming pool, the pièce de résistance of "living memorials" and the cornerstone of the Battle family business of forgetting, clearly implicates Jerry in her death (8). By cutting Daisy off from her family in Korea, by avoiding "in-depth and nuanced conversations," and by ignoring her assorted cries for help, Jerry betrays the degree to which he is personally invested in washing Daisy clean of her inconvenient history. Ironically, in his effort to cleanse Daisy of a past that sullies the pristine national narrative, Jerry not only denies but repeats the pattern of abuse, subjugation, exploitation, and brutality that has historically guaranteed white male hegemony at the expense of racialized, sexualized others. Further, Jerry's willful ignorance effectively pushes Daisy to her death, since, as Dori Laub insists, the inability to give voice to one's traumatic past "is perhaps the true meaning of annihilation, for when one's history is abolished, one's identity ceases to exist, as well" (Felman and Laub, 82). According to Laub's logic, the person who refuses to serve as a witness becomes a perpetrator after the fact, since "not knowing is an active process of destruction" ("Not knowing is an active process . . . " n.p.).

Jerry likewise damages his children by cutting them off from their own traumatic history; after Daisy's death, he immediately deploys one of his crews to "bulldoze[ ] over the offending site and roll[ ] out perfect new sod," so that Theresa and Jack can "at least play without a care or a thought" over what had once been the swimming pool in which their mother died (*Aloft* 229). Jerry may be motivated by his desire to protect his children, but his execution of what his daughter later identifies as "the world speed record for goodbyes" instead consigns them, most especially Jack, to their own inner prisons of unassimilated loss, grief, and shame (321).

For as Theresa reveals as the novel moves toward its harrowing conclusion, Jack has recently confided that he actually saw Daisy right before she died, having come home early from camp that day to discover his mother, naked, inebriated, and poised at the edge of the diving board. Jack remembers that all of Daisy's floats had been cleared from the pool and lined up along the edge like "the audience" (320), assembled by Daisy presumably, in what Laub calls "a creative act of maintaining and establishing an internal witness" to substitute "for the lack of witnessing in real life" ("Truth and Testmony" 71). But the cartoonishly macabre tableau that Daisy arranges does not provide her with the recognition, sense of safety, or connection she needs. Instead, these "witnesses" offer damning testimony to the flimsy support system offered up by what her academic daughter, Theresa, might call the "suburban imaginary," which may have kept her temporarily afloat, but ultimately could not sustain her.

Given that Jack was only a small child at the time, it is certainly understandable that he would opt to "decline the Real" by fleeing undetected and spending the next several hours on a swing set at the playground (*Aloft* 320). Jack's escape to the swings, however, augurs a lifetime of ceaseless activity in service to the upward mobility that ultimately gets him nowhere. Lee uses the swing set in much the same manner that he does Daisy's pool floats and the plane that Jerry purchased to fulfill an unrealized childhood fantasy. These toys are diminutive versions of postwar living memorials, likewise meant to obfuscate the past, compensate for lack, and inculcate the ideal of upward mobility. Lee's representation makes clear that such a goal is pure folly: Daisy's floats could not make her forget the unspoken trauma of her past or make up for her inability to swim; the rocking motion of the swings could neither blot out what Jack had witnessed nor provide the comfort and security of his missing mother.

Similarly, Jerry's plane, which has provided him the necessary distance to afford him a rosy view of his life and allow him to evade responsibility, is doomed to come crashing down. The novel corroborates Caruth's assertion that avoiding the past does not point toward a wished-for future but instead toward "its inadvertent and unwished-for repetition" (*Unclaimed Experience* 2). Jerry and Theresa are enjoying a rare father/daughter excursion on his plane when she shares with him Jack's recent revelation and the confusion, grief, guilt, and bitterness that both she and her brother felt after their mother's death. Moments later, they encounter a freak storm and Theresa's placenta ruptures. Jerry manages an emergency landing, but it is too late: like Daisy, who had flown "like a seabird straight down to the bottom" of the pool (*Aloft* 124), Theresa is dead by the time they arrive on the ground.

Jerry may have made every effort to save his mixed-race daughter, but his failure, however unintentional, is of a piece with the denial and complicity that inculpate him in Daisy's death. Earlier in the novel, Jerry muses that his "particularly handsome and even stunning" mixed-race clan would make fitting subjects for a "fashion magazine spread titled something like 'The Spoils of Battle,'" comely evidence marshaled to attest to the benevolence and inclusiveness that characterizes the so-called American way (69). As Jerry's suggested caption inadvertently indicates, however, the abundance that he and his family enjoy is the direct result of US military action abroad. The real spoils of battle—Daisy, who represents the untold victims of American foreign policy—has been carefully edited out of the picture-perfect story of American exceptionalism that three generations of Battle men have been enlisted to tell.

In this sense, *Aloft* appears to belong to the body of literature that Sally Bachner examines: American fiction written from the 1960s onward that demonstrates a fascination with violence that it nevertheless claims is unspeakable. As Bachner argues, what we label unspeakable "is not really unspeakable. It is merely that about which we prefer not to speak" since its articulation might confirm "the suspicion that the violence and suffering that takes place elsewhere is the product of the very economic and political practices that guarantee U. S. prosperity and security" (8, 5). The fiction that concerns Bachner (by Pynchon, Roth, DeLillo, and others) both expresses and alleviates the anxieties of prosperous Americans by depicting political violence as something that occurs "both outside the physical boundaries of the nation and to other people" (10). Lee's novel concerns itself with just such materially comfortable Americans who would rather not know about the suffering that happens beyond their suburban borders. *Aloft*, however, which pointedly takes place in the wake of 9/11, when deadly political violence encroached our boundaries for the first time since Pearl Harbor, suggests that the material and psychic consequences of US military and economic policies abroad can no longer be denied. Jerry's crash landing locates him in what Don DeLillo calls "the Ruins of the Future" in an essay that grapples with a post-9/11 landscape irrevocably scarred by "a narrative that has been developing over years" (33). Just as Lee's novel invokes the ruins of the Twin Towers in its opening pages, so, too, it implicitly engages the catastrophic events of that day and the people "falling from the towers hand in hand" in its penultimate chapter as Jerry grabs hold of his daughter's hand and clamps his eyes shut in order to prepare for the terrible unknown that awaits them on the ground (DeLillo 39).

Images of Home in the Post-9/11 Suburban Landscape

Certainly Gray might fault *Aloft* for its reduction of a national tragedy to a story of personal loss that once again seems to cast the white suburban male as the victim of events beyond his control. But the novel dredges up the postwar suburb's buried traumatic history and connects it to the recent catastrophe in order to redefine the suburban ethos altogether. If Lee locates the source of his prototypical everyman's guilt in his willful determination not to know, after his crash landing Jerry is forced to confront the full weight of that long-denied knowledge.

Theresa's role from the start has been to awaken Jerry from his dreamlike detachment, and with her death she indeed forces him to confront the Real he has been so intent on denying. But Jerry's encounter with the "destructive Void" is more than a matter of knowing loss: the novel advances this knowledge as a moral burden (Žižek 12). We can perhaps begin to grasp the change that Theresa inspires in Jerry by looking to Cathy Caruth's discussion of Lacan's analysis of a dream first interpreted by Freud. Freud describes a father who had spent days beside his dying son's bed. After his son's death, the father lay down in the next room and dreamed that his son was once again alive and standing beside him, imploring him to wake up because he was on fire. When his father awoke, he saw that a candle had actually fallen and lit the wrapping on his son's arm that might well have set the entire house aflame (*Unclaimed Experience* 93). Caruth notes that if Freud's central question in interpreting this dream had originally been "*What does it mean to sleep?* Lacan discovers at the heart of this question another one, perhaps even more urgent: *What does it mean to awaken?*" (99). The moment of awakening, after all, is infused with the father's horrible realization, once again, that his child is dead, but also with the awareness that he is indebted to that child for saving his life. Caruth explains that the father's story is thus that of "a survival inherently and constitutively bound up" with his dead child's entreaty: "Lacan resituates the psyche's relation to the real not as a simple matter of seeing and knowing the nature of empirical events . . . but as the story of an urgent responsibility, or what Lacan defines, in this conjunction, as an *ethical* relation to the real"(102; emphasis original).

Bachner astutely unearths the problematic logic that guides Caruth's account of the dream's meaning. Caruth asks readers to assume the position of a parent who has lost a child so that we might better understand the terms of our own ethical relation to the real. But as Bachner points out, that burden "entails waking up too late, awakening to a corpse" (22). In other words, Caruth does not relate the poignant story of a father losing his son to exhort us to "act to prevent the death of strangers as if they were our own children," since these deaths can neither be anticipated nor prevented (22). Instead, Bachner argues, Caruth's translation of the story casts us as "*survivors*" who "do not need to do anything: merely by being human subjects we both fail and succeed (by failing) in our encounter with the real, a real that is paradigmatically located in the death of our own child" (23; emphasis original). Caruth thus reiterates the philosophy of postwar advocates for so-called living memorials and anticipates the Bush administration's admonition to "go back to normalcy" by suggesting that our sole duty as survivors is to move past the traumatic event and get on with the business of life.

Given that *Aloft* similarly narrates the story of a father who is called back to life by a child who dies, we might determine that the novel likewise does so to excuse its privileged readers from any moral obligation to respond to circumstances beyond their control. But Theresa's death awakens Jerry to the fact that he is responsible for much more than his own survival; he is ethically bound to do what he can to alleviate others' misery. Indeed, immediately before the plane hits turbulence and her placenta ruptures, Theresa makes an explicit appeal to her father: she asks that he invite his father, recently escaped from the nursing home, and Jack and his family, whose financial woes will force them to move, to come live with him. Jerry protests, but when Theresa searches his eyes, looking "for the glimmer of a character somehow more wise and generous and self-sacrificing" than she has ever known him to be, he begins to come to terms with the consequences of his history of denial and detachment and is swayed, concluding in disbelief that "the Real" is now embodied in himself (316).

Overturning the master narrative of production and reproduction written into the suburban single-family house, Jerry follows his late daughter's directive to invite his extended family to come live with him—his father, his son and his wife and two children, as well as his son-in-law and his new baby grandson, who was born prematurely but survived the crash. This expanded household, a Rube Goldberg–style shelter hastily assembled to accommodate his extended, mixed-race, multigenerational family, is messy, crowded, and distressed but also vital and dynamic. The house advances a vision of community that is provisional in every sense of the word: the makeshift structure may be a quick fix, but in its recognition that life itself is provisional, it reimagines the suburb as a potential site of renewed social connection that addresses the varied needs of its diverse, changing population.

By suggesting new possibilities, the crowded house also represents a radical departure from the sterile, deadening portrayal of suburbia that Lee offers in his two earlier novels. In particular, he revises the devastating narrative of *Native Speaker*, in which the protagonist's small, mixed-race child is smothered to death by a group of white children while visiting his grandfather in the suburbs. In contrast, in the conclusion to *Aloft*, Lee introduces a mixed-race child whose violent *birth* suggests the transformative power of the collective memory of loss to redefine the contours of community. The baby is quite literally a living memorial, his very being inscribed by trauma. Unlike the living memorials of the postwar era, however, which were designed to obscure troubling elements of the past in order to promote a national mythology of victory and virtue, the baby, christened Barthes Tae-Jon Battle, implicitly bears witness not only to his own loss but to the suppressed history of grief, trauma, guilt, and atrocity that he carries within him.

The baby's first name, Barthes, may offer literary-minded readers the easy pleasure of associating him with his namesake's famous essay, "The Death of The Author," which renounces the validity of a master narrative. More provocatively, however, the middle name Tae-Jon may finally offer oblique testimony to the source of Daisy's unspoken suffering as well as to an unacknowledged page in the official US history of the "forgotten war" in Korea. In sharp contrast to the heroism and sacrifice depicted in *The Bridges at Toko-Ri*, historian Bruce Cumings unearths the disturbing details of the Taejon massacre, which took place at the start of the Korean War and which he calls "one of the most astonishing cover-ups in postwar U.S. history" (174). Cumings recounts the murky history of at least four thousand people who were butchered by ROK (South Korean) police under the direct supervision of US advisers and then layered "like sardines" in trenches that local citizens were forced to dig (175).[28]

The Taejon massacre is thus another piece of the baby's embodied memory and part of the mass grave that the postwar suburbs were meant to pave over—one more fragment that the novel delicately excavates in order to expose the haunting counternarrative to the state's official history, the denial of which, the novel implies, has landed us in "the ruins of the future." Yet the birth of a child also suggests that these newly exposed ruins should not be construed apocalyptically. As Svetlana Boym explains, the "shattered fragments, ellipses and scenes of the horrors of war" (52) are the "common landmarks of everyday life" (53) that make up collective memory, which she likens to "a playground, not a graveyard of individual recollections" (54). In keeping with Boym's rubric, Lee provides his readers with only scant hints of his characters' traumatic pasts in order to delineate a narrative ethics that resists the balm of closure that a full accounting might offer. Indeed, the baby represents a narrative that is just beginning: while he may be a repository for bits and pieces of his forebears' stories, his own is as yet unwritten, so that he does not offer readers resolution but only possibility. As much as the birth of a child signals hope, the baby should therefore not be misunderstood as providing healing closure. As Jerry observes, the baby looks nothing like his lost mother, Theresa (*Aloft* 333). The baby is a stranger, in other words, whose quotidian demands for attention, care, and compassion define in concrete terms for Jerry and the entire household their ethical relation to "the Real."

In this sense, the vision of community that the extended family advances also runs the risk of participating in precisely the sort of restorative nostalgia that drove the original postwar suburban project in the first place by feeding our collective longing for the comfort and security of an imagined home. The original suburbs have been characterized by exclusion, and it is no wonder: Boym points out that restorative nostalgia provides the basis for the them-vs.-us thinking that concludes that the home is "under siege" and requires "defense against the plotting enemy" (43)—the kind of thinking, in other words, that so quickly came to dominate post-9/11 discourse. In this context, we can appreciate the novel's insistently personal perspective and Lee's decision not to engage the events of that day directly: the novel does not ask its readers to choose sides in a hotly contested political climate but to rethink the ways that we are connected to one another.

This is not to say that the novel corroborates the notion that trauma is unspeakable. Instead, it identifies in no uncertain terms the devastating consequences of a narrative that has sought to excise from its script of the American "good life" the pain, suffering, exploitation, and death that have underwritten that story. The flattering portrait of the Battle clan attests to the degree to which affluent Americans have been successful at keeping such unpleasant evidence at a safe remove, so that the world looks, as it does to Jerry from the splendid isolation of his private plane, "pretty magnificent" (1). The deadly events of 9/11, however, have brought that devastating evidence home.

This becomes especially clear in the novel's final scene, as Jerry climbs down into the hole he has just dug in his own backyard as part of the ongoing construction for the radically reimagined extended family home. As it happens, this is the location of the swimming pool in which Daisy had drowned. Now, inside the trench, he surveys what he deems an "archeological" excavation of rusted toys, rotting sneakers, and chipped pool tiles, "like some ghostly ruin of Pompeii" (342). The reference to Pompeii, of course, has its echo in the ruins of the Twin Towers collapse, and runs like a bridge across centuries and continents of catastrophic loss and heinous atrocity.

Throughout the novel, Jerry has gingerly excavated losses that dimly link the historical traumas of World War II, the Korean War, the Vietnam War, and the September 11 attacks. Now, as he stands in the gravelike hole sifting through the everyday artifacts of an irrecoverable past, he reminds the reader that these large-scale events are, at their core, the stuff of intensely private experiences of pain, guilt, and longing. DeLillo similarly recalls the flotsam and jetsam that littered lower Manhattan in the days after September 11—the photographs of missing persons, the improvised memorials, the lost shoes, cell phones, and handkerchiefs, "the graffiti of love and peace"—devastatingly personal expressions of grief that confirmed that "many things are over. The narrative ends in the rubble" (35). But these assorted fragments also served to admonish us that "it is left to us to create the counter-narrative" (35). Ford's *The Lay of the Land* may have prepared the ground, but Lee's novel completely overturns the suburban narrative of the detached everyman to posit just such a counternarrative. In its modest conceptualization, that story is a work in progress that holds us all in equal relation to "the Real" and equally responsible for those within and beyond our borders.

3

"How to Live?"

The Case for Failure in Jonathan Franzen's *Freedom*

The Predicament of Success

The name of the chapter that introduces Chip Lambert, the central character of Jonathan Franzen's 2001 breakout novel, *The Corrections*, could not be more apt: "The Failure." Chip, a straight white male and the middle child of middle-class parents from a midwestern suburb, has been situated comfortably for much of his life in society's center. But as the chapter opens we learn that he has lost his job and his girlfriend, he's flat broke and several months behind on his rent, so that he barely subsists on the margins of a society where things might be "getting better and better for women and people of color, and gay men and lesbians," but he has "*nothing*" despite "the longest sustained economic boom in American history" (44, 91; emphasis original). The chapter proceeds to describe with gusto the excruciating details of Chip's debasement and his special talent for self-sabotage. We learn of the torrid, drug-induced bender with a coed that gets him ignominiously fired from his tenure-track job; the semen-stained chaise that he sniffs for weeks afterward in search of her scent; and the whole salmon he stuffs down his pants in an upscale market so that he will have something to serve his visiting parents for lunch, to name just a few of the highlights of his fall from grace. Chip Lambert does not just fail, in other words. He fails spectacularly.

As I discuss in my introduction, *The Corrections* is one of several pre-9/11 male-authored suburban novels that engages in the strategy outlined by scholars such as Kathleen Fitzpatrick, Hamilton Carroll, and Sally Robinson who argue that the white male's sense of personal injury is part of a distasteful and disingenuous strategy to reclaim for himself the rights and recognition that he feels have been usurped from him by formerly marginalized groups. George Yudice sees this as the process of reidentification, wherein the straight white male punishes himself for his share in an oppressive patriarchal culture. The powerlessness that accrues to him as he acknowledges both his culpability and the decline of that culture thus gives him access to his own version of the empowering "rhetoric of oppression" enjoyed by other marginalized groups (271). Accordingly, Chip is a virtual glutton for punishment. He deftly manages the stakes of his own failure, to paraphrase Carroll, so that he miraculously emerges by novel's end as its hero, duly chastened and fully redeemed.

But if Franzen launched his career by depicting straight white male characters who flail at the edges of mainstream society, this became a tough act to pull off after the overwhelming success of *The Corrections*, when Franzen found himself at the front and center of mainstream culture.[1] Even before the release of Franzen's next novel, *Freedom*, President Obama caused an outright feeding frenzy by accepting an advance copy for his vacation reading, and Franzen's former nemesis, Oprah Winfrey, announced with much fanfare that she had selected the novel for her final televised book club. And if these endorsements weren't enough to suggest that with his latest novel Franzen has achieved the sort of cultural status he himself had once been convinced was no longer possible for a straight white liberal male novelist,[2] his bespectacled, befuddled image landed on the cover of *Time*, emblazoned with the triumphant headline "Great American Novelist." Yet the accompanying cover copy, taken from Lev Grossman's feature story inside the magazine, is careful to qualify Franzen's "greatness": "He's not the richest or the most famous. His characters don't solve mysteries, have magical powers or live in the future. But in his new novel, *Freedom*, Jonathan Franzen shows us the way we live now" (n.p.). Franzen's talent and the novel's putative universal appeal inhere in both the author's and his characters' *un*exceptional status as not too rich, not too famous, not at all special everymen. In this manner, the feature story manages the stakes of success. These privileged white males, after all, are no different from any of us.

As these pages have attempted to demonstrate and the runaway success of *Freedom* clearly indicates, the male-authored novel dramatizing white middle-class experience has enjoyed renewed cultural vitality in the years following the events of 9/11. The reception of *Freedom*, however, confounds my argument that the new suburban novel actually works to undermine the universal claims of white middle-class heteronormative experience: its many reviews put on full display the assumptions of what Ohmann describes as the "common class" (209) of agents, editors, reviewers, readers, and writers whose experiences overlap enough to allow Grossman to confidently assert, for instance, that Franzen's novel about a white upper-middle-class family is not about a "subculture; it's about the culture"(48). To be sure, as with his previous novels, Franzen uses what Grossman calls a "wide-angle lens" to offer a sweeping picture of the State of the Union since 9/11, thus parting ways with the other novelists I've discussed who only obliquely or metaphorically reference the events of that day. But if *Freedom* roils with the tension, anger, and malaise brought on by the fear- and war-mongering that followed the events of 9/11 as well as an economy that has steadily worsened since, what has most impressed *Freedom*'s critics is not the novel's trenchant observations concerning national or world affairs but its sympathetic depiction of characters who are "analogous to us," as Ohmann would have it. The author Curtis Sittenfield, for instance, notes with approval that *Freedom* is "an ethnography of a particular marriage; a meditation on the disappointments and compromises of approaching and then inhabiting middle age; and a long, juicy, scathing, funny and poignant indictment of contemporary American life" (n.p.). That is, *Freedom* is at heart a personal "illness story" in which illness is once again a matter of "malaise" and "neurosis" (Ohmann 212): the novel centers on the romantic and existential struggles of a white middle-class protagonist so immediately recognizable that he could be someone we might "even run into someday at the grocery store," as Sam Anderson puts it in his *New York Magazine* review (n.p.).

Which once again raises the question: how are we to account for the particular appeal of this particular novel at this particular time? I've argued that writers returning to the suburbs have sought to reformulate an aesthetic that better responds to the social issues that challenge the shifting suburban terrain. Franzen writes a somewhat different equation in *Freedom*. His novel does not indicate that the suburbs have become more worldly; instead, the repellant values once associated exclusively with homogenizing suburban culture—consumerism, possessive individualism sanctified by the cult of the nuclear family, the fetishization of private property—have infected the culture at large.

Consider that *Freedom* centers on a straight white liberal male, Walter Berglund, and his family, who must cope with the requisite banal suburban challenges: pesky neighbors, marital strife, generational rifts, career struggles, and the all-encompassing old ennui. And just like their literary brethren, they console themselves with home-improvement and self-improvement projects, extramarital affairs, psychotherapy, and self-medication. But as it happens, the Berglunds are not properly suburban.[3] In the novel's overture we learn that Walter and his wife, Patty, had been urban pioneers who in the early 1980s bought a home in a rundown section of Saint Paul in order to "relearn certain skills that [their] own parents had fled to the suburbs specifically to unlearn" (4). Over the next two decades, however, Walter and Patty painstakingly renovate not only their ramshackle Victorian house but the neighborhood itself so that it becomes an exemplar of the suburbs they had sought to flee—an exclusively upper-middle-class enclave of bourgeois tastes, family values, and self-satisfaction that has been wiped clean of the "drunks," "panhandlers," "feral cats," and people "of color" who had once been at home here (4). In the opening pages of *Freedom*, Franzen offers the sanitized, gentrified inner-city neighborhood along Summit Avenue as grounds for skewering residents who are caricatures of loathsome suburbanites: striving, hypocritical "super-guilty sort of liberals," the likes of whom may once have been "active with the SDS" but were now "very active in the craze for Beaujolais nouveau" and in whom, "if you were to scratch below the nicey-nice surface, you might be surprised to find something rather hard and selfish and competitive and Reaganite" (8). Unquestionably, this first chapter offers an intentionally reductive portrait of characters that the novel will subsequently complicate. But the prelude's withering satire is also only the opening salvo in the novel's full-scale attack on the mythos of upward mobility that has for the past several decades fueled middle-class aspirations and valorized individual rights over the pursuit of the common good.

As we've seen, Ford, Lee, and Ferris, whom I discuss in my introduction, have likewise suggested that the premise of upward mobility underwriting the postwar suburban ideal is not sustainable. In *Freedom* Franzen amplifies their concern to a fever pitch with a narrative that roams from the gentrified midwestern city of Saint Paul to the coal-rich mountains of West Virginia to the Green Zone of Iraq and back in order to chart the devastating environmental and social effects of suburban sprawl, which the narrative figures as both a material fact and an insidious state of mind. In what is by now a gesture familiar enough to risk being hackneyed, Franzen wags a finger at the gas-guzzling SUVs, the proliferating McMansions, and the big-box stores that peddle big-screen televisions in order to excoriate the peculiarly American desire to "supersize" it: ours, after all, is an economy that depends upon growth.

Far more haunting, however, is the novel's account of what has been excised from the success story suburbanization has been written to tell: not just "feral cats" and "drunks" but the urban and rural poor; young soldiers and anonymous victims of foreign wars; swaths of countryside; and whole species that have been displaced, disrupted, or destroyed by the engine of progress. The novel calls attention to these accumulating, irrevocable losses that litter the sprawling path of the American Way in order to overturn its cynical promise of an ever brighter future.

Freedom's bristling negativity appears inconsonant with its mainstream triumph and Franzen's own newfound faith in the novel's special ability to do "socially useful things" (Grossman 48). Of course, pessimism is nothing new either for Franzen or in literary and pop-cultural representations of suburban landscapes in general. By now the notion that suburbia is a repository for our worst nightmares has been well rehearsed. In his examination of postwar suburban fiction and films, Robert Beuka observes that "the suburb has come to reflect the phobias and insecurities of American culture"(19). But as Bernice Murphy points out in her study of the "Suburban Gothic" subgenre in fiction, film, and television over the past sixty years, in these works, "one is almost always in more danger from the people in the house next door, or one's own family, than from an external threat" (2). The danger, in other words, is contained within. Thus, postwar representations of suburbia ranging from John Keats's scabrous satire *The Crack in the Picture Window* (1956) to Alan Ball's film *American Beauty* (2000) may send up the suburb and its odious inhabitants, but they simultaneously suggest that there is a thriving culture elsewhere to which we who know better can and should relocate. In contrast, *Freedom* presents us with characters uncomfortably "analogous to us" who bumble, stumble, and fall in an environment from which there is no escape: the inner-city neighborhood in Saint Paul, an isolated lakeside retreat, the suburbs of New York, and the hills of West Virginia are all equally susceptible to the terrible temptations and devastating effects of pursuing the suburban-style good life.

Given that Walter clearly articulates the author's own political and environmental concerns, it might initially appear that *Freedom* seeks to reclaim moral authority for the straight white liberal male. Indeed, the post-9/11 setting offers rich material for a social malcontent like Franzen to expound upon from his soapbox; we can imagine that one of *Freedom*'s central characters, the punk rock musician Richard Katz, speaks for the author himself when he muses that his best work has "coincided with Reagan I, Reagan II, and Bush I; . . . Now came Bush II, the worst regime of all . . ." (193). *Freedom* indeed trains its satiric eye on the antics of the Bush administration and its billionaire cronies in its portrayal of a political system contaminated by shameless opportunism and profiteering: unlike Franzen's earlier novels, which depict characters swept up in the vortex of a heedless and impersonal capitalism, the dark force at work in *Freedom* is explicitly associated with human actors motivated by personal interests.

But it is in the novel's very determination to attach names and faces to the invisible hand of capital that *Freedom* reserves its harshest judgment, not for the shady characters who operate at the narrative's margins but for the putatively well-meaning but complicit white liberal male protagonist at its center. Walter, a committed environmentalist, knowingly if counterintuitively throws in his lot with the unscrupulous energy magnate Vin Haven, in order to create a sanctuary for an endangered bird beloved by both him and Haven. As we shall see, Walter is not a victim of Haven's duplicitousness but of his own self-serving delusions: though he secures a small parcel of land for the sanctuary, it is won at great cost: Haven's conglomerate plans to destroy far more land than it will preserve in order to extract coal via the environmentally unsound practice of mountaintop removal (MTR). The consequences of Walter's dealings with Haven are disastrous, eventuating in the destruction of pristine West Virginia countryside, the eviction of people from their homes and land, and, at least indirectly, the car crash that kills Walter's young Indian lover and his partner in the park enterprise, Lalitha. As is the case in Franzen's first three novels, *Freedom* dramatizes the misguided attempt of its compromised white liberal male to game the system. But while the beleaguered protagonists of Franzen's earlier works largely fail in their efforts, Walter must cope with the devastating and irrevocable effects of his pyrrhic victory.

It is by way of Walter's dubious personal success, however, that we can better appreciate precisely what the novel has to say about "the way we live now." As I discussed in the first chapter and David Harvey has so clearly outlined, one of the groups to mobilize alongside the various protest movements of the 1960s and '70s were the very wealthy, who were able to wed capitalist class interests to the basic values of human dignity and individual freedom that informed the demands of disenfranchised minorities, protesting students, globally minded humanitarians, and environmentalists.[4] As we've seen, the emphasis on personal property ownership made neoliberal ideals especially appealing to a rising middle class of white suburban homeowners; what Franzen's novel also makes clear, however, is the degree to which these ideals subsumed the larger aims of various activist groups, whose calls for recognition, rights, resources, and justice quickly came to be translated into universal access to the goods, services, and property that are the hallmarks of middle-class membership. As Harvey additionally points out, the premium placed on individual rights unsettles the grounds for social justice, since its pursuit demands "a willingness to submerge individual wants, needs, and desires in the cause of some more general struggle for, say, social equality or environmental justice" (41).

This is precisely the insight that informs Franzen's exploration of the relationship between privilege and justice in *Freedom*. Indeed, the crisis upon which the novel arguably turns is the violent death of Walter's lover, Lalitha. Like Theresa in *Aloft*, Lalitha is an Ivy League–educated woman of color who validates the aims of a liberal democracy that maintains that every individual should be able to succeed regardless of race, gender, or sexual orientation.[5] The car crash that kills her—perhaps a terrible accident or perhaps, Walter imagines afterwards, the result of racist maliciousness—suggests that the ethos of inclusion has failed to deliver on its promise. More provocatively, however, the accident might never have happened had Walter honored Lalitha's wish that he accompany her to launch their social justice project instead of pursuing his own agenda to visit with friends and family. Walter may not be directly responsible for Lalitha's death, but the novel implicates him for his self-serving myopia and makes clear the consequences of the failure to defer one's individual desires in favor of the greater good. As we shall see, Lalitha is committed to a vision of global and environmental justice that is at odds with American economic interests even as she enlists those interests to help her develop her project. Her death therefore not only damningly demonstrates that such a partnership is untenable but indicates, in the same way that Theresa's death does in *Aloft*, that the violence committed beyond our borders to secure American prosperity and liberty has come home to roost.

In its unremittingly grim account of the terrible personal, geopolitical, and environmental costs of an ethos predicated on the quintessentially "suburban" values of autonomy and upward mobility, *Freedom* testifies to the damning failure of success. But it also radically locates in ruin, loss, and despondency the basis for an aesthetic whose "social usefulness" resides in its unwillingness to contribute to the happily-ever-after fairy tale of the elusive American Dream. *Freedom* depicts characters who must accept that their dreams have been irrevocably dashed. Their circumstances do not demand from them the fortitude to strike off alone in pursuit of their aspirations but call instead for a willingness to compromise, cooperate, and sacrifice in order to imagine new ways of being together in a fragile world.

For the Sake of the Kids

Failure, loss, and despondency are hardly strangers to the white male protagonists who populate either *The Corrections* or Franzen's earlier two novels, *The Twenty-Seventh City* (1982) and *Strong Motion* (1992). But Lalitha's death in *Freedom* is so shocking and her character so sympathetic that we might read her as little more than a sacrificial lamb who elicits from Walter the regret and grief required for his moral redemption—as Elizabeth Anker argues, the raison d'être of the post-9/11 male midlife crisis novel. But Lalitha's characterization does more than admonish and ultimately forgive Walter for the self-interest, hypocrisy, and benign neglect that undergird his liberalism. For Lalitha is distinguished in this novel not just because she is a woman of color but because she emphatically refuses to adhere to the heteronormative imperative to reproduce—as she tells Walter of her decision to have tubal ligation at the age of twenty-five: "I'm a freak . . . I'm the girl who doesn't want a baby. That's my mission in the world" (496). When Walter suggests that she hold off having the procedure in case she changes her mind at some future date, Lalitha feistily declares, ". . . *fuck* my future self! If it wants to reproduce, then I already have no respect for it!" (308; emphasis original).

Lalitha's stubborn determination not to have a baby echoes Lee Edelman's similar rejection of the fetishized Child and what he calls reproductive futurism in his polemical treatise *No Future: Queer Theory and the Death Drive*, in which he issues his own call to arms to "fuck the social order and the Child in whose name we're collectively terrorized" (29). For Edelman, the imaginary Child represents the very "telos of the social order and . . . the one for whom that order is held in perpetual trust" (11). Edelman offers as a challenge to the existing social order a queer antisocial aesthetic that he outlines in Lacanian terms. The queer, he explains, negates sexuality, identifying it not as a life force that connects pleasure to meaning, identity, and futurity but as an expression of the death drive that shatters the self along with its sense of mastery, coherence, and continuity. Thus, if the image of the Child guarantees the perpetuation of the existing social order by smoothly advancing the chain of inheritance from one generation to the next into an always deferred future, Edelman locates in the figure of the queer the social order's "traumatic encounter with its own inescapable failure" (26). In Edelman's conception, queerness is a mantle one chooses to wear in order to heroically assume an "oppositional political stance" that has the unique ability to rupture the hegemony of hope that the Child represents by countering its lie of a brighter future with the only guarantee there is: our own mortality (27). Edelman is careful to stress that the figure of the Child he invokes is an abstraction, apart from any historical or actual child. But as *Freedom*'s engagement with reproductive issues makes clear, the role the child plays in securing the future is anything but an abstraction.

Indeed, this insight drove postwar suburbanization. As we saw in the previous chapter, mass-produced housing developments answered the problem of maintaining wartime production levels by promoting a way of life built around property ownership, consumption, and recreation. As perhaps goes without saying, however, at the center of the lifestyle suburbanization sought to promulgate—its raison d'être—were children, lots of children. Along with production levels, reproduction rates were and are considered crucial to the nation's future economic health. During the Great Depression and World War II, birthrates had declined by 17 percent, as couples delayed or declined having children due to poor economic conditions. After the war, however, fertility rates soared: from 1946 to 1964 the national average went from its low during the Depression of just over 2 children per woman to over 3.5 children per woman (Mather). The Baby Boom has largely been seen as an optimistic response to improved economic conditions. But suburbanization not only encouraged this response, it sacralized it. Andrew Shanken, for instance, notes that the proponents of so-called living memorials to honor World War II veterans—the playgrounds, parks, Little League baseball fields, and swimming pools I discussed in the previous chapter—promoted their use and the lifestyle they embodied as the equivalent of a patriotic duty (Shanken 133). As the child-centric nature of these facilities also suggests, that duty included giving birth to the children who would fill these playgrounds, parks, and pools. The familiar justification that one moved to the suburbs "for the sake of the kids" indicates the degree to which the pursuit of the "good life" was also conceived of as a personal sacrifice that contributed to the greater good.[6]

Betty Friedan has famously savaged the postwar cult of the nuclear family in her seminal work, *The Feminine Mystique* (1962), which excoriates what she calls the "comfortable concentration camps" of the suburbs that reduced women to baby-making machines (282). But if Friedan's book contributed to the subsequent women's liberation movement of the late 1960s and 1970s that freed women from the imperative to have and raise children, Franzen's novel, which opens in the mid-1980s, contends that all of those protests led straight back to the fetishization of the child and a set of "contemporary questions like, what about those cloth diapers? Worth the bother?" (4). The gentrified urban landscape that Franzen depicts in the opening pages of *Freedom* reveals a world as single-mindedly devoted to the vicissitudes of child-rearing and homemaking as any postwar suburban development.

In her book *The Queen of America Goes to Washington City* (1997), Lauren Berlant explores the valorization of domestic life over public engagement during these same Reagan years, arguing that "in the process of collapsing the political and the personal into a world of public intimacy, a nation made for adult citizens has been replaced by one imagined for fetuses and children" (1). Berlant offers a nuanced and thorough account of the conservative coalition's investment in the rhetoric of what she calls a "familial politics of the national future" (1). I'd suggest as well that there was a concrete reason that the Reagan administration advanced children (and even better, not-yet-born children) as the ideal citizens to promote its neoliberal agenda and secure it for the future, since it would take more children to lift the nation out of the previous decade's economic slump. After all, when Reagan took office in 1982, fertility rates were even lower than they had been at the height of the Great Depression, at an average of less than 2 children per woman. Although demographers similarly attribute the low birthrates of the 1970s to the decade's dismal economic conditions, the steady decline of birthrates from a high in 1960 of 3.65 children per woman to less than half of that by 1980 also coincided with the rise of the women's rights movement. We might therefore understand the administration's obsession with so-called family values as part of a practical plan to encourage women to get back to the economically important business of making babies.

Lalitha's refusal to participate in these fertility rites, however, is not a personal act of defiance against those who seek jurisdiction over her body but is instead a testament to the passionate commitment she shares with Walter to address the arcane issue of population control. To be sure, as squeamish as Walter and Lalitha both are about promoting MTR on behalf of the coal scion, Vin Haven, they've seized the opportunity not only to create a bird sanctuary but to fund a campaign to raise public awareness about the disastrous effects of population growth—hardly an easy sale in a culture that has embraced a distinctly suburban ethos that centers on the supposed needs of children to justify bigger houses, bigger cars, and safer streets.

The novel's engagement with the topic of overpopulation is thus both anachronistic and provocative. In the 1960s and 1970s the issue galvanized political and popular discourse: global population, after all, had ballooned from 2 billion in 1930 to 3 billion by 1960, and demographers, environmentalists, and policy makers predicted that even minimal growth rates over the next several years would be exponentially disastrous, leading to mass starvation and misery.[7] Since then, of course, concern over population growth has actually reversed, at least in developed nations where birthrates continue to decline, despite the fact that by 1999 the population worldwide had doubled to 6 billion and is projected to reach 9.5 billion by 2050.[8] Across Europe, for instance, dramatically declining birth rates have so alarmed policy makers that they are not only considering but implementing a variety of public relations campaigns and incentive programs to promote higher birth rates.[9] As it should, then, the conversation concerning demographic trends has adapted accordingly to address the long-term implications of both declining and rising birth rates across the globe. As Ursula Heise points out, while the mass hysteria of the 1960s and 1970s over an apocalyptic population explosion may have receded, discussion now astutely focuses on distributive justice, gender inequality, reproductive health, access to education, and uneven resource consumption patterns (69–70).

Still, as heartening as the tenor of these discussions among concerned professionals may be, Walter is correct in noting that overpopulation is simply no longer "part of the national conversation," and it is perhaps no coincidence that concern over population growth in this country diminished just as neoliberal ideology was beginning to tighten its grip on the collective imagination (382). As Walter's best friend, fierce rival, and former college roommate, Richard Katz, puts it, "The real reason you can't get any cultural traction with overpopulation is that talking about fewer babies means talking about limits to growth. Right? And growth isn't some side issue in free-market ideology. It's the entire essence. . . . If you want to be heard in the capitalist media, and communicate in a capitalist culture, overpopulation can't make any sense. It's literally nonsense" (383).

It is indeed a simple equation that explains why the issue of population control is, as Walter puts it, "a downer": economic growth depends on population growth (382). Free-market enthusiast Joel Kotkin, for instance, remains bullish on America's future because unlike other industrialized nations, our population is surging. Kotkin maintains that the United States' climbing fertility rate will be the driving force behind the nation's economic resilience in the decades ahead, and he offers a fresh spin on Margaret Thatcher's infamous claim that there is no such thing as society in his proclamation that "the road to the American future will be primarily laid not by the central state but by families, individuals and communities" ("The Kids Will Be Alright" n.p.).[10] If, in a scene set during their early-'80s college days, a young Richard Katz could hope that Margaret Thatcher represented "the excesses of capitalism" that would "inevitably lead to its self-destruction" (101), a quarter century later, Kotkin's reiteration of her central tenet and his unabashed faith in the value of growth illustrate the degree to which neoliberal imperatives have indeed so thoroughly saturated the social fabric as to be common sense. As Edelman explains, both the left and the right are equally invested in the image of the child, since "we are no more able to conceive of a politics without a fantasy of the future than we are able to conceive of a future without the figure of the Child"(11). Thus, a present-day Walter complains that even the "NPR news unit, once upon a time fairly liberal, had become just another voice of center-right free-market ideology, describing even the slightest *slowing* of the nation's economic growth rate as 'bad news'" (314; emphasis original).

It is to both Walter's and Lalitha's credit that they are determined to revive a social issue that has lost all traction in the popular imagination. As the novel makes clear, however, while Walter and Lalitha are united in their dedication to the cause, their underlying motivations diverge. For her part, reversing population growth had been Lalitha's goal since taking a formative trip as a teenager to West Bengal, where she witnessed overcrowding, poverty, and suffering that "pushed her, on her return to the States, into vegetarianism and environmental studies, with a focus, in college, on women's issues in developing nations" (334–35). Thus, while Lalitha's passionate interest in population and sustainability issues may lead her to assume what Edelman calls the "*structural position* of queerness," her preternatural ability to connect with others and her earnest desire for global social justice reveal the limits of Edelman's thesis, committed as it is to an apolitical poetics of disavowal and disengagement (27; emphasis original). After all, the embrace of queer negativity, Edelman insists, "can have no justification if justification requires it to reinforce some positive social value" (6). As such, Edelman's antisocial aesthetic is more properly embodied by Lalitha's dour, misanthropic boss and lover, Walter. Indeed, if we are to find fault with Lalitha at all, it is for her uncritical allegiance to him, since her own appealing characterization exposes the self-involvement of Walter's own breach with the existing social order.

To be sure, like Lalitha, Walter has also been obsessed with the issue of overpopulation dating back to his college days in the late 1970s. But while his unrelenting zeal for an unpopular cause might appear to put him far afield of the ideological mainstream, Walter betrays the degree to which he, too, is motivated by the individualistic impulses that drive the neoliberal agenda when he explains to Richard his odd decision to work for billionaire Vin Haven:

> Billionaires . . . tend to care. They've got a stake in keeping the planet not entirely fucked, because they and their heirs are going to be the ones with enough money to enjoy the planet . . . Self-interest, yeah, but a total win-win. In terms of locking up habitat to save it from development, it's a lot easier to turn a few billionaires than to educate American voters who are perfectly happy with their cable and their Xboxes and their broadband (226).

When Richard ironically points out that Walter no doubt doesn't want "three hundred million Americans running around your wilderness areas anyway," Walter avers, "Exactly. It wouldn't be wilderness anymore" (226). Walter's jealous sense that he must preserve "his" wilderness from the masses is exactly in keeping with the "peculiarly bourgeois form of antimodernism" that William Cronon describes in his seminal essay, "The Trouble With Wilderness": the nostalgic notion of an untouched natural landscape that is "very much the fantasy of people who have never themselves had to work the land to make a living . . . for the romantic ideology of wilderness leaves precisely nowhere for human beings to actually make their living from the land" (80). It isn't just that Walter's insistence that wilderness ought to be "entirely free of human taint" is repugnantly elitist, though it certainly is that (302): in his determination to clear a parcel of West Virginia backcountry of the inconvenient inhabitants who have subsisted there for generations, Walter is enraged by the "stupid" "poor white unreason and resentments" of its stubborn holdouts, whose "negligible skills" did not extend "beyond hunting, engine repair, vegetable growing, herb gathering, and welfare-check cashing" (316–17). More disturbingly, Walter's determination to empty the land of the influence of humans who have occupied it for generations recalls the removal of Native Americans to reservations in the nineteenth century immediately preceding the movement to create national parks. Seen in this light, Walter's hubristic desire to return his warbler park to its mythical virgin state represents a criminal evasion of history that smacks of cultural imperialism.

Finally, though, the glorifying of pristine, cordoned-off wilderness also enables an escape from genuine accountability. As Cronon points out, by confining nature to designated areas, no matter how grand in scale, we exempt ourselves from caring for the environment we actually inhabit. Cronon might well be describing Walter when he asserts that "to the extent that we live in an urban-industrial civilization but at the same time pretend to ourselves that our real home is in the wilderness, . . . we give ourselves permission to evade responsibility for the lives we actually lead" (81). Because for all of Walter's indignation, both his preservationist efforts and his nascent antigrowth initiative are not, like Lalitha's, rooted in a concern over environmental justice or women's reproductive rights but are outgrowths of his own misanthropy and bourgeois sense of entitlement. Walter fumes about the rampant individualism that fuels his compatriots' SUVs and provides the raw material for their McMansions, but in a rare moment of self-awareness he confronts his shame over his desire for Lalitha: "he saw himself . . . as another overconsuming white American male who felt entitled to more and more and more: saw the romantic imperialism of his falling for someone fresh and Asian, having exhausted domestic supplies. . . . How to live?" (338–339). This question runs like a refrain throughout the novel whenever Walter confronts a moment of moral indecision: cloth or disposable diapers (4)? What to order from the menu when all of the choices are environmentally suspect? "Fuck it . . . the rib eye" (325). It is an empty question, in other words—the handwringing we might expect from a milquetoast who for all of his self-righteousness refuses to make the hard choice.

To be fair, Walter's interest in wildlife and his concern over the long-term effects of population growth are not the by-products of some puerile understanding that nature exists to be his own private playground; Walter is cut from more substantial cloth than the sniveling weekend warrior Delaney Mossbacher of T. S. Boyle's *The Tortilla Curtain;* it is his fervent wish to leave as a legacy "something to help a couple of ecosystems make it past the pinch point"(343). But while Walter's conservation efforts may be deeply felt, they nevertheless spring from the same tradition as does the mainstream environmental movement (which counts Walter's former employer, the Nature Conservancy, among its ranks), which has its roots in the nineteenth-century celebration of wilderness by men of elite class backgrounds such as Theodore Roosevelt—the first conservation president and champion of the national parks movement. Cronon notes the irony in the fact that "the very men who most benefited from urban-industrial capitalism were among those who believed they must escape its debilitating effects" (78).

Vin Haven is, of course, a latter-day version of these industrialists—"the sort of nature lover who happily blasted cinnamon teal out of the sky but also spent hours raptly monitoring, via closed-circuit spycam, the developments of baby barn owls in a nest box on his property" (317). Haven's ranch reminds us that the civilization/nature dichotomy is inherently false: his "habitat for game birds" is as manufactured as any urban center. And Haven himself is just one more in a line of wealthy white men who have "projected their leisure-time frontier fantasies onto the American landscape and so created wilderness in their own image" (Cronon 79). Walter's relationship with the aptly named Haven traces the evolution of the mainstream environmental movement from its nineteenth-century origins to its present manifestation.

As Adam Rome outlines in *The Bulldozer and the Countryside: Suburban Sprawl and the Rise of American Environmentalism,* in the postwar era environmental efforts once championed by elite urban industrialists were taken up by newly affluent suburbanites who witnessed firsthand the environmental devastation of suburban sprawl since "the bulldozer was never far from the living room" (6). If one of the amenities postwar suburbia offered its residents was the ability to live closer to nature, suburbanites quickly discovered that "the destruction of nearby open spaces robbed children of beloved places to play—and the losses hit home more vitally that the threats to far-off sites . . . ever could" (8). Rome describes the first suburban environmental activists as mothers who made three kinds of arguments to launch what came to be known as the Open Space Movement: the first argument made a case for "conservation"; the second focused on "amenity"; and a third dealt with "outdoor recreation" (123). In other words, suburban environmentalism was driven by consumers who felt that one of their most precious commodities was being compromised by irresponsible producers.

The original activists in the Open Space Movement may have been suburban housewives, but by the 1970s affluent white males found their way to the cause. As Andrew Ross explains in his essay "The Great White Dude," amid the organizing of women, people of color, and gays and lesbians, "angry white men" found "an accommodating haven under the big tent of environmentalist science" where they would not be "automatically required to address questions about race, class, gender and sexuality" (174). Perhaps this explains the bizarre inadequacy of Walter's response to racist slurs against Lalitha. When a hillbilly bigot sidles up to Walter in a restaurant men's room and sneers, "Like the dark meat, do you? . . . I seen what you doing with that nigger girl," Walter's response is almost as offensive as the comment itself: "She's Asian," he replies and skulks off before a fight can ensue (330). Confronted by the bigot once more, he says simply, "Not interested" (331). On the one hand, we might read this disquieting episode as another indictment of liberal multicultural discourse in general: Walter's initial inappropriate response participates in the same questionable rhetoric that Vijay Prashad critiques in his book *The Karma of Brown Folk* (2000), which begins by quoting W. E. B. Dubois's famous question to his fellow blacks—"How does it feel to be a problem?"—in order to pose a variation of the same to Asian and South Asian Americans: "how does it feel to be a solution?" (viii). Prashad offers these twinned questions to expose the insidious violence enacted by multiculturalism and its attendant model minority myth, which he argues have been deployed by the powers that be to divide minorities by inculcating the ethos of possessive individualism as the predominant value of a pluralistic society. Walter's unwillingness to take a punch on Lalitha's behalf caustically demonstrates that the liberal multicultural agenda is "not interested" in the pursuit of genuine social justice if it involves self-sacrifice.[11]

But I'd like to further suggest that this odd episode—which transpires on the evening that Walter and Lalitha are celebrating their dubious "success" in West Virginia—also illustrates the inadequacy with which the mainstream environmental movement has, like Walter, dealt with "questions about race, class, gender and sexuality" in its single-minded pursuit of its conservation agenda (Ross 174). This is certainly the argument that the environmental justice movement has made. Originally launched in the early 1980s by low-income urban women of color who used grassroots activism to combat the uneven distribution of environmental hazards such as toxic waste, the movement's advocates object to the myopia of mainstream environmental groups whose privileged perspective has been largely blind to the environmental struggles of poor urban and rural populations (Di Chiro 310)—a dynamic baldly drawn by Walter's arrogant outburst against a (female) protestor blocking his entrance to the West

Virginia site: "I *own* this fucking land!" he screams at her, "Do you understand that? *I own everything you can see here!*" (363; emphasis original).[12]

Walter's assertion of his property rights reflects what Rome sees as the "limited aims" of a sensibility that originally manifested itself as the will of privileged homeowners to defend their own quality of life (13). Indeed, Walter reveals the affluent suburban roots of his environmentalism when he advocates for the name Free Space for his fledgling movement, which recalls the efforts of postwar suburbanites on behalf of the Open Space Movement. When his daughter complains that the name summons visions of a free parking space—a boon to any suburban car owner—Walter determines that that is so much the better, since "We all know what it's like to have trouble finding a parking place. Fewer people on the planet, better parking opportunities?" (365). In this instance, Walter inadvertently makes clear that his social activism does not extend much beyond the perimeters of his own self-interest.

The philosophical rift between environmental justice activists and mainstream environmentalists like Walter may have grown alongside the various battle lines drawn between marginalized groups and privileged straight white males in the 1980s and '90s, but if its terms are familiar, they are hardly banal. If anything, the debate has only grown more intense as the issues surrounding climate change and sustainability complicate and raise the environmental stakes. In her discussion of the complex relationship between environmentalism, cultural difference, and globalization, Heise outlines Ulrich Beck's argument in *Risikogesellschaft* (1986) that technological development has evolved to the point where society is no longer able to "protect itself against the unintended 'side effects' of its own technologies, which, formerly latent and invisible, are now emerging into full public view" (147). Beck argues that for all of their efforts to insulate themselves from the deleterious effects of modernization, including foisting the burden upon less empowered populations, the socially privileged have only delayed harm; they have not prevented it. "Poverty is hierarchical, smog is democratic," Beck maintains (cited in Heise 147). Heise is careful to note the nuances of Beck's argument, stressing that he does not mean to claim that the materially disadvantaged and the socially privileged are equally exposed to the risk of environmental disaster—on the contrary. Beck goes on to say that "the globality of risk does not mean global equality of risk. The opposite is true," so that he contradictorily offers this dictum: "*pollution follows the poor*" (Beck 5; emphasis original). This is because what he calls "risk society" is not fully established but emergent. "One thing is clear," Beck maintains. "Endemic uncertainty is what will mark the lifework and the basic existence of most people—including the apparently affluent middle classes—in the years that lie ahead" (12).

Beck's description of a worldview necessarily shaped by unpredictability articulates the aesthetics of contingency that I've argued thrums like a bass line throughout the novels of Ford and Lee. Franzen's novel, however, wears its poetics of precariousness on its sleeve to the point of being shrill. Throughout the novel, as Walter angrily wends his way through highway traffic, argues with his wife, or blows off steam as he sends Lalitha to deal with protestors, he enumerates the statistics that are evidence of the planet's impending collapse. These, for instance, are a day's worth of calculations: "Net population gain: 60,000. New acres of American sprawl: 1,000. Birds killed by domestic and feral cats in the United States: 500,000. Barrels of oil burned worldwide: 12,000,000. Metric tons of carbon dioxide dumped into the atmosphere: 11,000,000. Sharks murdered for their fins and left floating finless in the water: 150,000" (364). Walter's recitations are mantras he uses to quiet his mind, since there are "days so bad that only their worsening, only an outright descent into an outright orgy of badness, can redeem them" (364).

Such passages abound, evidence of Walter's petulance and privilege: it is a fortunate person indeed who can luxuriate in "an orgy of badness" in the privacy of his car, his hotel room, or the fashionable DC townhouse he bought for a pittance from his benefactor, Haven. But while these doomsday reveries may give expression to the "Nice Man's Anger" (290), they also function to enunciate the stakes of the novel's bulky theme: the "side effects" of freedom, or what Beck calls the "various unintended consequences of radicalized modernization" (4) that Walter frets have not "quite reached the point" of being "undeniable" (382). On September 11, 2001, those unintended consequences indeed reached their breaking point in a moment that made painfully clear that Americans were now fledgling citizens in a "world risk society." Walter's ranting perhaps seeks to keep in play the sense of contingency that we are inclined to suppress.

Critics have generally attributed these frequent textual interruptions to the author himself, who, like Walter, is a committed and knowledgeable environmentalist and bird lover. But if Franzen has inserted his agenda into the text in order to elicit horror and inspire action among his readers, his frequent tirades have largely been dismissed by critics as self-important and hyperbolic hectoring. Margaret Hunt Gram argues that the ineffectiveness of the novel's frequent vitriolic parabases is perhaps indicative of the bourgeois novel's limits in general. After all, the middle-class novel may critique and instruct its readers, but it does so by example, offering characters who resemble us and with whom we closely identify. We may recognize Walter's road rage and even understand his inability to stand up to the belligerent racist in Lalitha's defense, but we do not necessarily appreciate being lectured. The form simply does not lend itself to leading readers to think abstractly about the aggregate. I would further add that the majority of these hyperbolic diatribes pointedly locate the problem where the majority of Franzen's upper-middle-class readers are not. As *Washington Post* critic Ron Charles puts it, "In the unlikely event that some strip-mining, ocean-dumping, panda-hunting rube stumbles onto this novel, he'll get his comeuppance for sure, but everybody else will probably use these cranky public service announcements as a chance to stretch their legs("Jonathan Franzen's New Novel, *Freedom*" n.p.)" In other words, these textual interruptions actually let readers off the hook.

Especially since "everybody else," or the bulk of Franzen's readers, also do not count themselves among the rural, urban, or global poor, which is where Walter locates the brunt of the population problem. In an uncharacteristically level-headed manner, he lays out the issue for Katz by pointing out that "having large families tracks inversely with economic status, and so does the age at which girls start having babies. . . . You can cut the growth rate in half just by doubling the average age of first-time mothers from eighteen to thirty-five" (382). Walter identifies his public relations problem as twofold: how to get around the charge of elitism that comes with trying to "tell poor people and uneducated people not to have so many babies" (382), and how to persuade people to sacrifice their personal liberties when "if you don't have money, you cling to your freedoms all the more angrily . . . even if you can't afford to feed your kids, even if your kids are getting shot down by maniacs with assault rifles" (383). When Katz counters that the real problem with Walter's antigrowth agenda is not the impingement of personal liberties but the imperatives of free-market capitalism, Walter demurs, once again intimating that the problem rests with the lower classes when he insists that "the conversation about rights in this country isn't rational. It's taking place on the level of emotion and class resentment" (384). Given that the novel predates the Occupy Wall Street movement when Walter might be able to claim membership among the 99 percent, we can assume that Walter considers himself, as a member of the upper middle class, a direct object of such class resentment.

Despite the many opportunities that Walter takes throughout to rail against suburban sprawl, McMansions, SUVs, Xboxes, and all manner of goods associated with the escalating consumption of his middle-class peers, at this crucial juncture, when his calm demeanor suggests that it might indeed be the author himself who has assumed the stage, he not only releases his liberal middle-class readers of any accountability, he shamelessly panders to them. Indeed, if past, current, and impending crises are in any way an upper-middle-class problem, the novel suggests, it is only because it falls to them and now their children to educate their less reasonable compatriots. "Positive social change works from the top down," he says.

> The surgeon general issues his report, educated people read it, bright kids start to realize that smoking is stupid, not cool, and national smoking rates go down. Or Rosa Parks sits down on her bus, college students hear about it, they march in Washington, they take buses to the South, and suddenly there's a national civil rights movement. We're now at the point where any reasonably educated person can understand the problem with population growth. So the next step is to make it cool for college kids to care about the issue (384).

Leaving aside the offensive assumption that it was (white) college students who led the civil rights movement, in a novel shot through with cynicism and negativity, Walter's uncharacteristically hopeful plan to enlist college students to steer public opinion on the issue of population control nostalgically participates in a version of what Stephen Schryer calls the "new-class fantasy" of intellectuals who had entered mainstream society in the wake of World War II with teaching positions at universities newly charged with educating a massively expanding middle class (6). These professional intellectuals, Schryer explains, who considered themselves above the "purely pecuniary motives of the capital-owning bourgeoisie" (2), would "shape the culture by example rather than through specific social reforms" (6). Walter's faith in college students' ability to lead by example presupposes that these students have themselves been led by the example of those who have gone before them—namely upper-middle-class progressives like Walter, who himself has two college-age children. If the underdeveloped character Jessica, Walter's daughter and a member of the Free Space planning committee, is an inchoate realization of the new-class fantasy, his son Joey exposes the fallacy at its core: namely, that this new class of "university-educated knowledge workers" has somehow transcended the demands of mainstream capitalist culture (Schryer 2).[13]

Anker argues that the post-9/11 novel is usually an Oedipal narrative that dramatizes the "perceived menace to paternity . . . and corresponding onus to secure the threatened patrilineal bequest, thus figuring the sanctity of the father-son bond as the essence of what 9/11 jeopardized" (2). *Freedom* likewise delineates an Oedipal struggle, but the dynamics are somewhat different from those that Anker delineates: Walter's relationship with his son has always been characterized by conflict that the events of 9/11 and their aftermath bring to a head. Joey, a precocious capitalist and as callow as his father is sincere, is a freshman at the University of Virginia when the Twin Towers are struck—an event that initially affronts him as a blight on what should have been his golden college days. Ultimately, however, Joey finds his way to the center of power, impressing a wealthy political insider and thus securing a lucrative position with a bogus subcontractor—a job he hopes will get him "rich enough and tough enough fast enough" that he will "never again have to take shit from his dad" (412). For his part, upon hearing of Joey's involvement with a company that sells parts to outfit army trucks in Iraq, Walter lashes out that it "*physically disgust*[s] him to have raised a son so selfish and unthinking that he was willing to connive with monsters trashing the country for their personal enrichment" (427; emphasis original).

Yet despite the rancor between father and son, and despite Walter's angry accusation that "Middle Eastern kids the same age as you are getting their heads and their legs blown off so you can make a ton of money," it is to his father that Joey turns when he realizes that he has indeed been involved in a scam that could bring serious harm to soldiers relying upon spare parts that are useless junk (428). This confession, far from eliciting anger from his father, forces Walter to admit "the degree of his own implication," since the same company paying Joey, LBI, is the same that has hired Walter's displaced West Virginians at its newly opened body-armor plant (501). Thus, although the novel seizes the post-9/11 moment to repair the ruptured relationship between father and son, it does so not to reassert white male privilege but to deconstruct it: in the case of Walter and Joey, the "patrilineal bequest" is not a beacon for the future but, to borrow Edelman's terms, a "traumatic encounter with its own inescapable failure" (26). Because as supposedly different as their temperaments and politics may be, Walter and Joey are united by a shared delusion of self-mastery that is subsequently shattered. Both men, as it turns out, represent what Pierre Bourdieu has called the dominated segment of the dominant class. As does *Aloft*, *Freedom* follows the line from one generation to the next in order to challenge the legacy of entitlement that has provided the basis for white middle-class male identity. Both novels determine that their hapless everymen have acted according to a script written *for* them, not *by* them. Unlike *Aloft*, however, which suggests that the master narrative passed from father to son can be reconstituted through the experience of loss and the acknowledgment of accountability, *Freedom* may repair the father-son relationship, but it does so by breaking the rule of succession that transports a nostalgic version of the past into the future. Walter and Joey reverse the established order: it is the son who provides the seed money for his father's antigrowth initiative with tainted profits from a conglomerate that feeds on growth. It is an unsavory past that father and son now work to forestall.

As it happens, Walter's fraught reconciliation with Joey immediately precedes the discovery that his wife, Patty, has had an affair with his best friend, Katz. This revelation further cements Walter's sense that he has been duped by a master narrative in which he has played only a minor supporting role. Thus, we might applaud the audacity with which Walter finally seizes control of his story, not so much stepping out of the middle-class mainstream as experiencing a psychotic break from it. First, he unceremoniously and decisively evicts Patty after twenty mediocre years of marriage—a tidy if fairly standard rejection of the marriage plot that once defined the bourgeois novel. Then, in a press conference meant to trumpet the new jobs and homes his boss has provided for those residents displaced by the latest round of MTR, Walter welcomes a new group to the American middle-class, which he notes is a "mainstay of economies all around the globe" (513). Now that they have jobs at LBI's body-armor plant, he tells them, they're "going to be able to participate in those economies" (513). Walter elaborates upon what middle-class membership entails:

> I want to mention those big new eight-miles-per-gallon vehicles you're going to be able to buy and drive as much as you want, now that you've joined me as a member of the middle class. The reason this country needs so much body armor is that certain people in certain parts of the world don't want us stealing all their oil to run your vehicles. And so the more you drive your vehicles, the more secure your jobs at this body-armor plant are going to be! I want to welcome you all to working for one of the most corrupt and savage corporations in the world! Do you hear me? LBI doesn't give a *shit* about your sons and daughters bleeding in Iraq, as long as they get their thousand-percent profit! . . . Now that you are working for LBI, you can finally make enough money to keep your kids from joining the Army and dying in LBI's broken-down trucks and shoddy body armor! (514–515; emphasis original).

In short order Walter loses his own job and the home he had purchased at a sweet price from his boss. Yet as much as Walter's break from work and marriage ostensibly unfetters him from the bonds of middle-class existence, leaving him free to travel the country with Lalitha to bird-watch, enjoy rollicking sex, and plan the rallies against population growth that have attracted the attention of youth, anarchists, and all manner of fringe elements for whom he has become a YouTube sensation, Walter's behavior should be familiar to anyone who has ever read a white male midlife crisis novel, ranging from Sinclair Lewis's *Babbitt* to John Updike's *Rabbit Redux* and beyond.

If these novels are any indication, Walter's countercultural vacation isn't indicative of a deep need to overturn the social order but a fierce desire to recover his own waning manhood. More than anything previous in the novel, Walter's time off the grid fully exposes the depth of his hypocrisy. After haranguing his audience about the carbon footprint of the trucks they will be able to buy, Walter treats himself to a "gas thirsty" Econoline van for his and Lalitha's cross-country adventure, confirming Hal Rothman's accusation that middle-class Americans will "embrace environmentalism when it is convenient and inexpensive, but when it challenges the comforts to which they are accustomed, they ignore or avoid it" (340). And despite his foaming declaration that "WE ARE ADDING THIRTEEN

MILLION HUMAN BEINGS TO THE POPULATION EVERY MONTH! . . . WE ARE A CANCER ON THE PLANET," (515), lurking in the back of Walter's mind is "a wish that everybody else in the world would reproduce a little less so that he might reproduce a little more, *once* more, with Lalitha. . . . It was the root of all their fucking" (522; emphasis original). Not only does Walter reveal that he is indeed a romantic imperialist, determined to colonize Lalitha's racialized, sexualized body, he betrays the degree to which he is still committed to the suburban fetishization of the Child.

But I'd like to paradoxically suggest that while Walter may reiterate the consumption and reproductive patterns of the middle-class life that he has ostensibly abandoned, with his vitriolic break from the social order he also assumes something akin to what Edelman calls the "structural position of queerness"—a position that revels in its place "outside and beyond political symptoms" (3). Similar to the "mantle of victimhood" that Yudice describes, self-exile from mainstream culture represents yet another choice that is the white male's privilege to make (271). It is a position that represents the best of all worlds, in other words—casting the white male as a heroic martyr who bears no responsibility for the culture he has repudiated. This is the essence of the critique that queer theorist Tim Dean levels against Edelman, whom he accuses of fashioning certain "sufficiently privileged" subjects into "heroic agents" with the power to "deploy the death drive, instead of being simply subjected to it" (127). What links these various sensibilities is the degree to which they all share in the illusion of autonomy that accounts for neoliberalism's broad appeal.

In a similar vein, Heise has noted that the novel that predicts "a dystopian image of the future" is only suitable "for a readership that is privileged enough not to have to cope with such conditions in the present" (75). Walter's dire prophecies throughout the novel partake in the delusion of control that Heise and Dean consider an idiosyncrasy of the "sufficiently privileged." As I stated earlier, however, the novel turns on the shattering event of Lalitha's death, which may have been an accident or, Walter imagines afterwards, the result of someone purposely running her off the road. Either way, Walter is thrust headlong into a world marked by randomness and catastrophe, so that the question "how to live?" is no longer a matter of exercising one's free choice but is an expression of despair in the face of devastating loss and damning failure. The novel's final section, however, steeped in regret and grief, offers a provisional answer to this question that reformulates the ethos that has informed the male-authored suburban novel since its postwar inception.

Failing Man and Other Losers

On the one hand, it might be argued that Walter charts the familiar course of the white male in a midlife crisis novel, which is to say he may suffer a catastrophe, but he emerges relatively unscathed. Earlier iterations posit the midlife crisis as a crucible meant to undercut the protagonist's embarrassing entitlement and prosperity. In Updike's 1971 *Rabbit Redux*, for instance, its eponymous antihero's house burns down, but while the young runaway he's been harboring dies in the flames, he returns to his wife's bed. He emerges in the next installment, *Rabbit Is Rich*, bigger if not better as the new owner of his father-in-law's car dealership, which has gone from a used-car lot to a thriving Toyota franchise, suggesting the adaptability and durability of the hegemonic chain of inheritance. As I've shown in the introduction, writers working on the eve of 9/11 give their protagonists no such quarter: Rick Moody's *The Ice Storm*, Jeffrey Eugenides's *The Virgin Suicides*, T. C. Boyle's *The Tortilla Curtain*, and A. M. Homes's *Music for Torching*, for instance, all feature violent deaths of children ostensibly to issue their own version of Edelman's battle cry to "fuck the social order and the Child in whose name we're collectively terrorized," by violently breaking the line of succession meant to guarantee white middle-class identity in perpetuity (29). But even these apparently self-destructive stories work strategically to reestablish the existing order into the next generation: each may martyr one child, but they also leave behind an as-yet fully formed male child waiting in the wings to reestablish white male authority. After 9/11, writers working in the suburban literary tradition reimagine the mature white middle-class everyman as a figure who emerges from disaster sufficiently chastened to become a relevant but not central member of a changed and changing community. In the case of Lee's *Aloft*, its protagonist is also called upon to assume partial responsibility for a baby who represents the future—albeit an uncertain one.

This is not the case with Walter: he is spared but not redeemed. After Lalitha's death, he retreats to the family cottage on Nameless Lake, abandoning the grand antigrowth agenda for which he was an unlikely hero. Here, among the McMansions that have sprung up all around this once idyllic spot and rendered it yet another victim to suburban sprawl, he has become the neighborhood crank whose efforts on behalf of his beloved songbirds have been reduced to chasing and trapping his neighbor's cat. For a full six years Walter retreats into what queer theorist Judith Halberstam calls "queer time and space," marked by "inertia or time outside of capitalist propulsion" (*Queer Time* 7). Much like Franzen's earlier novels, then, *Freedom* ends not with a bang but a whimper: diminished, disillusioned, and broken, Walter has requested and taken a low-level caretaker's job at the Nature Conservancy he once directed because its "coziness with corporations and millionaires now made him queasy" (584–585). As Walter assesses his work, "He wasn't doing dazzling good on the lands he oversaw, but he wasn't doing any harm either" (585). Colin Hutchinson has argued that the "subversive intent" of Franzen's earlier work "falls victim to a content that emphasizes capitulation and quietism" (194). The same argument might be made against *Freedom*. If, as Franzen asserts, his novel has the capacity to "engage productively with an otherwise scary and unmanageable world," it ultimately does so by advancing a poetics of *un*productiveness (Grossman 48).

This is exactly the aesthetic that Franzen means to advance. In the aftermath of Lalitha's death, in place of the heroically angry opposition advocated by Edelman that has characterized Walter's modus operandi, the novel now locates in failure, abjection, loss, and death a radically new conception of middle-class identity, no longer predicated upon the chimerical allure of self-mastery but in the stark confrontation with what Beck calls "endemic uncertainty" in which "all too swiftly, the 'elective,' 'reflexive' or 'do-it-yourself' biography can become the breakdown biography" (12). In this way the novel participates in what Halberstam calls the "queer art of failure," which she argues "may in fact offer more creative, more cooperative, more surprising ways of being in the world" (*The Queer Art of Failure* 2–3).

Make no mistake: Halberstam's aesthetic, like Edelman's, resides in "the murky waters of a counterintuitive, often impossibly dark and negative realm of critique and refusal" (2). But unlike Edelman, who insists upon a poetics distanced from "crude and pedestrian" political concerns (107), Halberstam celebrates "the negative potential of the queer and the possibility of rethinking the meaning of the political through queerness precisely by embracing the incoherent, the lonely, the defeated, and the melancholic formulations of selfhood that it sets in motion" (*Failure* 148). There might be no better description of Walter's character after Lalitha's death. His new neighbors indeed find Walter "potentially deviant" (*Freedom* 578) and learn to steer clear of him, since "his hermitlike existence now strongly smacked of grief; . . . the enduring sort of grief that, like all forms of madness, feels threatening, possibly even contagious" (579).

But if his neighbors are inclined to avoid him, Walter's own encounter with enduring grief ultimately teaches him a painful lesson about the importance of connection and offers the reader insight into the manner in which the novel works to realize its "subversive intent." The suburban literary tradition has historically participated in the humanist project that Schryer describes, deigning to instruct and refine a rising middle-class readership. Walter's savage welcome to new members of the middle class in West Virginia brutally admits the failure of that enterprise. But in the novel's coda, and in his diminished capacity, Walter speaks to and for a *declining* middle class smarting not only from the events of 9/11 and their aftermath but from a crushing economic downturn: how to live in a world characterized by disappointment, loss, and randomness. Walter's dubious success in West Virginia and his present misery admonish the reader first and foremost to avoid "doing any harm" (585).

Second, however, the novel's conclusion refashions the "putatively universal ideals" that Fitzpatrick argues have provided the scaffolding for the "structures of traditional humanism" that have in turn supported the postwar suburban literary genre: the valorization of the individual who stands alone and in opposition to the world at large (202). In self-imposed exile, Walter is initially the embodiment of this entrenched ethos: "He could feel the outside world closing in on him, demanding his consideration, but as long as he stayed by himself in the woods he was able to remain true to his refusal. He came from a long line of refusers, he had the constitution for it" (590). But if Walter's staunch rejection of his culture's values arguably once bespoke the quiet everyday heroism of the white male suburban protagonist, his behavior is now depicted as myopic and even pathological. Though he contends that he wants nothing more than "to go out every morning and see birds who have nothing do with any of it," his maniacal campaign to protect them is tone deaf to his neighbors' suffering during the deep economic recession, so that "they felt they understood his worry about birds a lot better than he understood what a hyper-refined privilege it was to worry about them" (576). When he kidnaps one neighbor's cat because he determines that the pet must "pay personally for his sociopathy," he betrays his own sociopathy, which is all for naught: his neighbor retaliates by replacing the lost cat with three more (584).

Eventually, however, the "outside world" does demand Walter's attention in a manner he cannot ignore: his ex-wife Patty shows up at his doorstep. If Walter is determined to remain isolated in his pain and suffering, she is equally determined to locate in loss and failure the grounds for renewed connection, even if it means freezing to death in the process. That Patty is ultimately victorious—Walter brings her inside and uses his own body's heat to thaw hers—should not be understood as a move that restores the existing social order. Instead, Patty's return signals a radical reformulation of the bourgeois novel's humanist project. In the final pages the novel fully gives itself over to Patty's "warming influence" (596). It may be through Patty's eyes that Walter sees "out into the cold space of the future in which they would both soon be dead," but it is also this perspective that spurs Walter to "return their look before it was too late, before this connection between life and whatever came after life was lost" (594). In this manner, the novel advances a neohumanist aesthetic that no longer privileges the alienated individual but instead places a premium on the bonds of sympathy, without which, Franzen has recently asserted, "a work of fiction has a very hard time mattering" ("Rooting Interest" 60).

In a recent essay in the *New York Times Book Review*, Garth Risk Hallberg discusses this recent turn by Franzen and his fellow writers—among them, Jeffrey Eugenides, David Foster Wallace, Jonathan Lethem, and Zadie Smith—who now collectively determine the novel's value in relation to its ability to "sustain a sense of connectedness, to resist existential loneliness" (n.p.). Hallberg is suspicious of this mission statement: is the novel meant to confirm for the reader that he or she is not alone? Or does it aspire to the loftier cause of awakening readers to the fact that "there are other people besides ourselves in the world, whole mysterious inner universes" who are "equally real"? The latter best illustrates *Freedom*'s ambitious aim, expressed through Patty's newfound and hard-won compassion for others. Formerly fiercely competitive, Patty has been sufficiently humbled to become adept at submerging her "individual wants, needs and desires" to negotiate an economically just distribution of her grandfather's inheritance among her difficult, variously needy siblings (Harvey 41). In a similar spirit, when asked if she, too, is a bird lover, Patty responds, "No, but I'm a Walter-lover, so I sort of get it" (*Freedom* 595).

Patty's attuned sense of other people's needs and desires provides a helpful model for Walter, who learns to use environmental psychology to advance his conservation agenda: instead of bombarding his beleaguered neighbors with leaflets and lectures, he leads them on nature walks to introduce them to "their local heritage and to see, up close, some of the marvelous life the woods were full of" (596). In place of the commodified view of nature maintained by postwar suburban environmentalists, Walter encourages his neighbors to forge an emotional bond with their environment, thereby extending the humanist project to include nonhuman life.

If the warmheartedness of the novel's conclusion seems more sentimental than subversive, Walter's parting gesture reminds the reader that the novel's reconstituted aesthetic springs from his queer encounter with the "nothingness" of the future (594). Walter rejects the hegemony of hope by breaking the chain of inheritance whereby one generation passes the existing social order on to the next: he guts the structure that has been in his family for three generations—the cottage on Nameless Lake—"leaving only the shell standing, as a haven for owls and swallows" and dedicating the monument of decay to his dead lover, Lalitha (597).

Such a move runs the risk of redeeming Walter and casting him, belatedly, as the heroic antihero of his own story. That argument might possibly be made where Walter's literary counterparts are concerned—Richard Ford's Frank Bascombe at the end of *The Lay of the Land*, for instance, whose fate hangs precariously in the balance at the novel's conclusion. But Franzen forecloses such a reading by giving the last word not to his protagonist but to Lalitha, the "pretty young dark-skinned girl" (596) who so fervently and foolishly believed in Walter and "whose commitment to fighting overpopulation was as practical and humanitarian as Walter's was abstract and misanthropic" (522). It is he who may have failed, but she who lost. And it is she who speaks for the weak, the poor, and the dispossessed human and nonhuman subjects who have been sacrificed in the name of American prosperity and freedom.

4

Dead Man Walking

Philip Roth's Engagement with the Everyman Tradition and the Reimagination of Middle-Class Identity

The Imperative to Rise and Fight Again

For the 2012 Super Bowl, the Chrysler Corporation reprised the risky but successful advertising campaign it had launched the year before—a two-minute, $10 million spot featuring the controversial rap artist Eminem—with another $14 million halftime gambit, this time featuring the iconic actor and director Clint Eastwood. As with the previous year's ad, the spot sought to emphasize the putatively peculiarly American ability to rise and fight again.[1] The ad begins as Eastwood, in silhouette, strides toward the camera to pronounce that "it's halftime in America, too." Then, against a montage of sepia-toned images of rural, urban, and suburban scenes and "average" Americans rising to face the day, the seasoned actor allows, "I've seen a lot of tough eras, a lot of downturns in my life." The soundtrack swells and the montage flips through several black-and-white images of what must be meant to represent a multicultural cross-section of the general population before pausing on an image of firefighters, clearly meant to evoke the "ordinary heroes" who have become part of 9/11's lore. Eastwood then declares, "But after those trials, we all rallied around what was right, and acted as one. Because that's what we do. We find a way through tough times, and if we can't find a way, then we'll make one. All that matters now is what's ahead. How do we come from behind? How do we come together? And, how do we win?" (Chrysler, "It's Halftime in America" [hereafter "Halftime"] n.p.). The camera zeros in on Eastwood's rugged visage as he virtually snarls, "This country can't be knocked out with one punch. We get right back up again, and when we do the world is going to hear the roar of our engines. Yeah, it's halftime, America. And our second half is about to begin" (n.p.).

By all counts, the advertisement was a resounding success. Media pundits and viewers alike declared it the victor of what has become the Super Bowl for television commercials. Arguably, however, nothing signals an advertising campaign's success more than a *Saturday Night Live* parody, and Chrysler's "Half-Time in America" ad earned not one but three segments aired throughout the evening's program, with comedian Bill Hader in the role of Eastwood. The three-part skit takes aim at precisely what the ad means to sell: the enduring notion that American exceptionalism is rooted in the *un*exceptional American's extraordinary resilience. The original advertisement savvily and sentimentally rearticulates the defining characteristics of a beloved American archetype: the everyday hero. Hard-working, scrappy, and physically fit, he has an infinite capacity for rising from the ashes of his past into a bigger, better, and stronger future. As Hamilton Carroll has demonstrated, this rhetorical figure was deployed immediately after 9/11 and has been called up once again to combat the ongoing economic crisis.

SNL's parody skewers this national myth of perpetual regeneration. Emerging from the shadows, Bill Hader, doing a gravelly imitation of Eastwood, intones, "The clock's winding down, America. It's the fourth quarter, and there's [*sic*] no time-outs left. How do I know?" he asks, as the camera pulls back to reveal a full-length view of the performer, dressed as Eastwood in the original, except with his pants now hiked above his waist in a style said to be popular among old men. "Because my pants get higher every quarter," he answers. The skit proceeds to declare that China dominates the world stage because its billion people "work hard," while we have only grown fatter and older.

The parody not only deftly punctures a hole in Americans' inflated sense of themselves as winners, it also calls attention to the fact that the perpetually resilient everyman at the center of the national myth has grown old.[2] For indeed, the high pants, irascible tone, and spotty memory ("what's this ad for, again?" he asks) are meant to poke gentle fun at Eastwood himself, who, at eighty-one when the spot was filmed, is not only past his own halftime, but, according to the actuarial table, well into overtime("Clint Eastwood Chrysler Ad" n.p.).[3]

I have lingered on this advertisement and its parody because, together, they get to the crux of my examination of the male midlife crisis novel since 9/11. In truth, none of the protagonists I examine are at "halftime."

Richard Ford's Frank Bascombe and Jonathan Franzen's Walter Berglund are both in their mid-fifties. Jerry Battle of Chang-rae Lee's *Aloft* is sixty. Under the best of circumstances, these protagonists are well into their third quarter, in other words. These characters' somewhat more advanced age is appropriate to an aesthetic that is less concerned with crisis than with its aftermath. The male-authored suburban novels I discuss contribute to the growing body of post-9/11 literature not by replicating the conditions of large-scale catastrophe but by imagining an anxious, uncertain everyday; they are valuable precisely because they do not chart the critical path to safety and self-mastery. The new suburban novel may thus address a middle-class readership shaken by the effects of crisis, but it does not comfort these readers by leading them back to an imagined "before"; as Frank Bascombe puts it at the end of *The Lay of the Land*, "Before is everlastingly gone" (458).

Thus, these older protagonists suffer loss, disappointment, and illness from which they do *not* rebound, befitting a poetics based on contingency and diminished expectations. These novels distinguish themselves from earlier iterations of the suburban male midlife crisis novel since such "personal illness" narratives (as Ohmann calls them [217]) are also what Margaret Morganroth Gullette labels "cure stories" in her book *Safe at Last in the Middle Years: The Invention of the Midlife Progress Novel* (1989). In these earlier stories the "questing protagonist" moves from "randomness to meaningfulness, or from conflict to resolution, from pain to serenity, from stasis to activity, from defect to fulfillment, from drive to freedom, from loss to recovery" (xiv). Even Updike's quintessential Rabbit, whose restorative run-return-repeat pattern seemingly comes to an end when he succumbs to a fatal heart attack in *Rabbit at Rest* (1990), returns once more to haunt the novella "Rabbit Remembered" (2001). "Not even the grave . . . could exhaust Rabbit's life force," *New York Times* critic A. O. Scott observes. "Rabbit Remembered" also appropriately ends with the prospect of marriage, thereby renewing the genre's vow to sanctify the nuclear family.

In the preceding chapters I've argued that the post-9/11 male-authored suburban novel has renounced its commitment to uphold the established order of production and reproduction that such earlier recovery narratives have so faithfully maintained. The post-9/11 protagonists I've discussed are not rejuvenated (as say, Frank Bascombe breathing deep Florida's salt air in the conclusion of Ford's 1986 *The Sportswriter*) nor restored to their former lives (see him again in the final scene of *Independence Day* [1995]). Instead, Bascombe's prognosis for his prostate cancer remains uncertain at the end of *The Lay of the Land* so that when he thinks of "health," he envisions "something not good or else something that was good but will soon be no more" (481–482). Jerry Battle is last seen in *Aloft* standing in a "scary and unnervingly quiet" gravelike hole, sifting through the everyday artifacts of an irrecoverable past (342). And *Freedom*'s Walter Berglund's confrontation with his own inevitable demise leads him to deliberately gut the home that has been in his family for three generations and leave the shell as a monument to the "nothingness" of the future (597).

But the fact remains that while Frank, Jerry, and Walter may not be fully restored, they are nevertheless granted a reprieve (even Jerry's father, Hank, manages to escape the nursing home in which he'd originally been left to die). By giving their protagonists a second chance—if not necessarily a second half—these novels run the risk of perpetuating the narrative of American exceptionalism that Clint Eastwood so effectively pitches by way of everymen who may be down but are not completely out of the game.

Philip Roth solves the conundrum posed by the replenished everyman by beginning his novel, *Everyman* (2006), just past the point where Lee's *Aloft* ends: Jerry Battle is standing in his grave contemplating it, but Roth's unnamed protagonist is lying in his: the seventy-one-year-old everyman is emphatically dead and underground in a forlorn cemetery somewhere in New Jersey, surrounded by his family above. If the conclusion of *Aloft* suggests this possibility, the opening scene of *Everyman*, in which a smattering of mourners toss handfuls of dirt over the unnamed protagonist's casket, indicates that the story has ended even before it has begun. The novel concludes at the same point, with its protagonist dead on an operating table from cardiac arrest. It might thus appear that Roth is sounding the literal death knell for the suburban literary tradition. As I will elaborate, though, this is paradoxically far from the case. Instead of burying the suburban protagonist, Roth rewrites his story along the design suggested by Ford, Lee, and Franzen.

Roth starts by offering a truly unexceptional everyman who not only fails to be cured but is actually dead before his story even starts. On the one hand, it might be argued that the novel's circular logic—beginning and ending with death—amounts to a lethal form of closure that contradicts my central claim that the twenty-first-century suburban novel is distinguished by an aesthetic of radical indeterminacy. But the novel's subversive potential resides in its determination to fully deny its protagonist the opportunity to begin again. Therefore, let me bring myself full circle as Roth does. As I outline in my introduction, the events of 9/11 immediately instilled in Americans the fear that we had entered a new era of uncertainty and danger, which just as quickly inflamed an overwhelming urge to "return to normal." *Everyman* effectively forecloses that possibility by insisting that there is nothing to which we can return.

Everyman thus appears to make the case that the suburban novel centering on the experience of the white middle-class male has indeed exhausted itself. Pre-2001 novels such as A. M. Homes's *Music for Torching*, Rick Moody's *The Ice Storm*, and David Gates's *Jernigan* rely on all manner of mayhem to violently punish the weak-willed suburban everyman at the center of the male midlife crisis narrative, even if they also offer in his stead a younger, more resilient version with the capacity to rise from the ashes of his father's experience. As I elaborate below, though he offers a decidedly more sympathetic protagonist in his ambitious *American Pastoral* (1997), Roth similarly subjects his everyman to an explosive crisis (and leaves behind not one but three sons who might carry the torch into the future). In contrast, the depleted male body introduced at the beginning of *Everyman* expires neither with a bang nor a whimper. But the ashes-to-ashes trajectory that Roth's post-9/11 *Everyman* maps amounts to a poetics of exhaustion that succeeds in resuscitating the suburban literary tradition. I trace the evolution of Roth's engagement with the white middle-class everyman tradition to counterintuitively argue that the post-9/11 suburban novel, especially as articulated by Roth in *Everyman*, revivifies the suburban subgenre by burying once and for all the resilient everyman who perpetuates what Ford's Bascombe calls the "life-forever lie of the suburbs" to allow for a truly new man: one whose frailty offers him a new path to follow in a world he only temporarily inhabits (*SW* 319).

New Man, Everyman, Last Man, Old Man, and the American Body Politic

In the intervening pages of a novel that begins and ends with a dead body, the narrative loops back to tell us something of *Everyman*'s unnamed protagonist's history, which has followed the established patterns of the male midlife crisis genre: he has suffered the typical marital woes and has worked at a job that has made him financially secure but existentially unsatisfied. The bulk of the text, however, focuses on the last seven years of the everyman's life and chronicles in unrelenting detail his myriad medical issues: a bad heart has led to one procedure after another so that "not a year went by when he wasn't hospitalized . . . and his body seemed threatened all the time" (*Everyman* 70). The everyman thus morbidly muses that were he ever to write an autobiography, he'd entitle it *The Life and Death of the Male Body* (52). It's a title that perhaps befits Roth's own oeuvre and its preoccupation with the corporeal in all of its glory, decay, pleasure, and abjection.[4] But the title's insistence on the generic quality of the male body also hints at the symbolic weight this body has been charged with carrying. Therefore, in order to fully consider the implications of the corpse that frames *Everyman*, I'd like to take a protracted look back at a novel Roth wrote almost a decade before—*American Pastoral* (1997)—in order to examine the impossibly youthful suburban everyman at its center, Seymour (the Swede) Levov. Taken together, the robust Seymour and the depleted everyman narrate a history not only of the life and death of the male body per se but of the American Dream that that body has served and protected.

The Swede is a marked departure from Roth's large stock of dark-complected, prominent-featured, intellectually predisposed, anxiety-ridden characters, and a revealing complement to *Everyman*'s frail, elderly protagonist. A high school athletic star in his World War II–era Jewish working class neighborhood, he is nicknamed "the Swede" and beloved by his community because of his striking blond-haired, blue-eyed "unabashed" "perfection"(*American Pastoral* [hereafter *AP*] 4). If Roth has ventured onto new terrain with his characterization of the Swede, he bears a striking resemblance to John Updike's iconic everyman, Rabbit Angstrom, whom

Updike describes in his introduction to the Everyman's Library edition of *Rabbit Angstrom: The Tetralogy*. Rabbit is, he asserts, "the New World's New Man"—a specimen who is "a natural athlete, a blue-eyed Swede, sexually magnetic, taller than six feet" (xix). Both Rabbit and the Swede, in turn, flesh out the sociologist Erving Goffman's sketch of the quintessential "unblushing" American male, whom he identifies as "a young, married, white, urban, northern heterosexual Protestant father of college education, fully employed, of good complexion, weight, and height, and a recent record in sports" (128). As Goffman notes, every American male "tends to look out upon the world from this perspective, this constituting one sense in which one can speak of a common value system in America" (128).

So entrenched is this "common value system" that we may assume that Goffman's outline pertains, more or less, to the everymen I have examined up to this point—to Ford's Frank Bascombe and Franzen's Walter Berglund, certainly, and probably to Lee's assimilated, anglicized everyman, Jerry Battle. Tellingly, however, although little escapes these protagonists' attention in their observations concerning the physical attributes of the people who cross their paths, we learn precious little about their own bodily configurations. As I discuss in the introduction, thanks to the groundbreaking work of scholars such as Donna Haraway and George Lipsitz among others, it has become something of a truism that white masculinity's power resides in its invisibility.[5] As this line of reasoning goes, Sally Robinson explains, "To be unmarked means to be invisible—not in the sense of 'hidden from history' but rather, as the self-evident standard against which all differences are measured: hidden *by* history" (2; emphasis original). In *American Pastoral*, in contrast, Roth engages the everyman tradition in order to call attention to that which has been elided in these other narratives centering on so-called everymen: the power and privilege that inhere in the unmarked, supposedly unremarkable white male body.

In fact, Roth inverts the genre's conventions by making his everyman the object of our gaze rather than the novel's unseen seer: the Swede is the particular obsession of Roth's alter ego, Nathan Zuckerman, who is also the novel's narrator. Zuckerman grew up with the Swede and worshiped him as a child, he explains, because the Swede vicariously satisfied his own deep-seated desire to "be an all-American kid during the patriotic war years" (*AP* 19). Certainly, the Swede possesses "all the values of youth, virility, activity and physical beauty" that constitute what anthropologist Robert Murphy has identified as the American Ideal in his groundbreaking account of his own disabled body, *The Body Silent* (100). Some fifty years later, Zuckerman avers that the allure of the American Ideal still fascinates him. He marvels that the Swede is

> at home here the way the Wasps were at home here, an American not by sheer striving, not by being a Jew who invents a famous vaccine or a Jew on the Supreme Court, not by being the most brilliant or the most eminent or the best. Instead—by virtue of his isomorphism to the Wasp world—he does it the ordinary way, the natural way, the regular American-guy way (89).

Disability scholar Rosemarie Garland-Thomson calls this "ordinary" American guy the "normate": "the constructed identity of those who, by way of the bodily configurations and cultural capital they assume, can step into a position of authority and wield the power it grants them" (42). Like Goffman's "unblushing male" and Murphy's American Ideal, the normate is the "unmarked, prototypical subject," impossibly and eternally able-bodied, possessed of a set of characteristics "that describes only a minority of actual people" (8). Nevertheless, Garland-Thomson maintains, this composite has come to represent the norm because it "parallels the national ideal in an individualist egalitarian democracy that each citizen is a microcosm of the nation as a whole. A well-regulated self thus contributes to a well-regulated nation" (43). Garland-Thomson underscores "the body's crucial role" in dramatizing the inherent contradictions in the national ideal, given that "the principle of equality implies sameness of condition, while the promise of freedom suggests the potential of uniqueness" (43). Garland-Thomson notes that this paradox essentially issues "a mandate for distinctiveness—the kind that Emerson and Thoreau so vehemently extol in their efforts to formulate an individual self free from all restraint" (43). In her study Garland-Thomson focuses on the "extraordinary body" of the disabled figure, whose "distinctiveness" amounts to "nonconformity incarnate," its "indisputably random and unpredictable character" indicating an "appalling disorder and persistent menace in a social order predicated on self-government" (44, 43). In contrast, I concentrate on the "ordinary body" of conformity incarnate, the white middle-class everyman who has historically attempted to distinguish himself not by transgressing norms but by epitomizing those norms through a physically fit body built to uphold the social order.

Zuckerman confirms that the Swede's "well-regulated" body does indeed help write the national narrative by resolving "the contradiction in Jews who want to fit in and want to stand out, who insist they are different and insist they are no different" (*AP* 19).[6] Of course, the Swede's prominence in his community clearly indicates that he does not so much resolve the contradiction as he is himself a contradiction: an anomaly who lays claim to the universal. But as Zuckerman clarifies, it is the community itself who is invested in eliding the inherent paradox of the exceptional everyman, deifying the Swede as their "household Apollo" because through him it could enter "into a fantasy about itself and about the world, the fantasy of sports fans everywhere: almost like Gentiles (as they imagined Gentiles), our families could forget the way things actually work and make an athletic performance the repository of all their hopes" (3). In other words, the Swede is the guarantor of the American Dream itself, an everyday hero who embodies at once the "principle of equality" and "the potential of uniqueness" (Garland-Thomson 43) that assure his immigrant community that America is a land of opportunity that steers all of its citizens "relentlessly in the direction of success," as Zuckerman puts it (*AP* 41). Zuckerman acknowledges that the "hope" that the Swede embodies amounts to a "bizarre, delusionary kind of sustenance" (4), but its grip remains so powerful over his imagination that he obsessively "thinks about the Swede for six, eight, sometimes ten hours at a stretch" (74) and determines to fashion out of the scant knowledge he has a "realistic chronicle" of both the dream that the Swede embodies and the "tragedy" that ostensibly ruptured it (89, 86).

Indeed, as far as Zuckerman is concerned, far from being "hidden by history" (Robinson 2), the Swede is not only "fettered to history," he is "an *instrument* of history," deployed strategically to remind the nation of our inborn strength and mettle (*AP* 5; emphasis original). Zuckerman goes so far as to liken his everyman to John F. Kennedy, "another man of glamour exuding American meaning" (83). It is a comparison that is provocative for a number of reasons, as I will explore more fully in the latter portion of this chapter, but not least because the Swede is a poster boy for the physical fitness campaign that was Kennedy's pet project. Consider that at the height of the Cold War, for instance, President John F. Kennedy determined it a matter of vital national interest to take to the pages of *Sports Illustrated* in order to argue that a strong nation depends upon able-bodied male citizens:

> It was men who possessed vigor and strength as well as courage and vision who first settled these shores and, over more than three centuries, subdued a continent and wrested a civilization from the wilderness. It was physical hardihood that helped Americans in two great world wars to defeat strong and tenacious foes and make this country history's mightiest defender of freedom. ("The Vigor We Need" [hereafter "Vigor"] n.p.)

This triumphal historical narrative was part and parcel of Kennedy's rhetorical strategy to rally an increasingly flabby populace onto the physical fitness bandwagon. Studies conducted in the late 1950s had revealed that victory in the war notwithstanding, there was great disparity between the nation's hardy self-image and its actual physical shape. While the draft rolls for World War I revealed that one in three draftees was unfit for combat, by World War II the armed forces had to reject almost half of its draftees or give them noncombat positions (Dallek and Kravitz n.p.). In the wake of World War II, the nation's physical fitness had only worsened. As I discuss in the previous two chapters, living memorials—parks, playgrounds, ball fields—fostered a suburban life built around recreation—an initiative largely spearheaded by the Federal Security Agency, whose mission it was to promote "the health of all of the citizens of the Nation" by building "self-disciplined individuals who reject soft living" (Shanken 133). Nevertheless, by the early 1950s, 57.9 percent of American children failed at least one of three basic fitness tests, compared to less than 9 percent of European children (Kennedy, "Soft American" n.p.). These findings originally induced President Eisenhower to form the President's Council on Youth Fitness, but it was President Kennedy who would enthusiastically embrace and promote the cause during his presidency, asserting that

> the stamina and strength which the defense of liberty requires are not the product of a few weeks of basic training or a month's conditioning. These only come from bodies which have been conditioned by a lifetime of participation in sports and interest in physical activity. Our struggles against aggressors throughout our history have been won on the playgrounds and corner lots and fields of America. (n.p.)

Kennedy lent considerable sex appeal to the campaign to equate private life with public service. In one sense Kennedy's crusade was successful: his emphasis on the strong, energetic body gave rise to the modern fitness movement and a multibillion-dollar industry that continues to grow with the promise that, with a modicum of self-discipline, a better, stronger body awaits us all.[7] On the other hand, at almost 31 percent, America continues to have the most obese population in the world by no small margin. In terms of life expectancy, the United States ranks an unimpressive thirty-eighth on the global list.[8] I point these facts out, not to demean the government's efforts on behalf of physical fitness, but instead to suggest that our investment in the illusively resilient body is exactly that: an investment with far more at stake than the success of the fitness and diet industries. After all, it is our supposed health and vigor that marks us as American, so that Clint Eastwood can say with certainty that what makes us special is that "we can't be knocked out with one punch" (Chrysler, "Halftime" n.p.) and conservative pundits can declare vehemently that "universal healthcare may not be unconstitutional, but it is un-American" since we are a nation of able-bodied, self-reliant citizens (Weinger n.p.). In his bodily strength and independence, the image of the eternally fit white American male is possessive individualism's beloved mascot: he is patriotic not only because he can defend his country but, more important, because he requires nothing from it.

Throughout his brief presidency, Kennedy demonstrated his commitment to the nation's poor, disenfranchised, disabled, and senior citizens with numerous measures that provided emergency economic assistance, pressed for fair housing and equal employment opportunities for blacks, and expanded Social Security benefits. But he also fostered the mythos of the ageless, self-reliant body with both his fitness campaign and his own self-presentation. Kennedy literally went to great pains to project an image of uncontested vigor and virility. It would be decades after his assassination before the extent of his myriad ailments would become clear: in addition to Addison's disease, colitis, asthma, and allergies, the president suffered so from a degenerative bone disease and rheumatoid arthritis that he could barely climb a flight of stairs or even put on his own socks. Kennedy spent his entire political career hiding this disabled body from public view and carefully crafting an image of invulnerability.[9]

For instance, in the same issue of *Sports Illustrated* in which President-elect Kennedy chides his fellow Americans for "getting soft," a puff piece proclaims that "Jack" Kennedy is a "savage contestant," "whether sailing, swimming, skin-diving, golfing or playing touch football" ("Jack Kennedy" n.p.). The article goes on to describe Kennedy's well-publicized experience during World War II, when his PT boat was sunk by a Japanese destroyer and he managed to swim for five hours while towing a crewmate before finally arriving on shore. The author asserts that were it not "for a hardiness of body and toughness of spirit developed through rough-and-tumble games," Kennedy probably would "not be alive today," thus linking his heroic service to country with a physical resilience that is the product of avid participation in recreational athletics (n.p.).[10]

Never mind that Kennedy's preferred sports—sailing, skin-diving, golf, and touch football on the family compound—bespoke a background of leisure, privilege, and inherited wealth. "Jack's" "rough-and-tumble" play, his "savage" competitiveness, and his remarkable ability to rise and fight again cast him as the ultimate exemplar of the ordinary hero—an everyman whose inborn hardiness makes him exceptional. It was in this capacity that he was to be emulated by the *Sports Illustrated* demographic: middle-class men and their sons, whose own proving grounds were the "playgrounds and corner lots and fields" of suburban America (Kennedy, "Vigor" n.p.).

On the one hand, Kennedy advanced bodily youth, health, and endurance as the qualities "average Americans" would need to meet the public demands and personal sacrifices that his so-called New Frontier would require: we could not afford to be a "tired nation" in the face of such challenges as the "unsolved problems of peace and war, unconquered problems of ignorance and prejudice, unanswered questions of poverty and surplus"(Kennedy, "New Frontier" n.p.).[11] On the other hand, the premium placed on strength and stamina did not summon the "average American" to a future in which athletic teamwork would teach citizens to find collective solutions to social problems, but to an imagined past where individual winners "were greeted as heroes and received rich rewards" ("Soft American" n.p.). For as Kennedy well understood, the lifestyle encouraged by mass suburbanization had not developed a citizenry committed to vigorous competition but just its opposite: "New forms of transportation have made it unnecessary to walk to school or to the office or the corner store. New forms of entertainment have consumed much of the time which was once used for sports and games," Kennedy conceded ("Vigor" n.p.). His fitness campaign sought to reinvigorate the men who had settled the postwar suburban frontier by stirring up nostalgia for an older, mythic frontier and the figure of the rugged individual who "won the West" thanks to his sheer physical determination and hardiness.

This is precisely the role that the Swede imagines for himself when he moves to the idyllic WASP enclave of Old Rimrock, New Jersey, and fancies that "he was settling Revolutionary New Jersey as if for the first time" (*AP* 310). Unlike *Aloft*'s Italian American everyman Jerry Battle, who joins the rank and file of the white middle class by taking up residence in one of the new, suburban ranch-style incubators for assimilation, the Jewish American Swede, like Ford's Frank Bascombe, locates himself among the established landed gentry. Paradoxically, this does not instill in the Swede a sense that he has become part of a long-standing community but, on the contrary, that he has won his spot in suburban paradise by dint of his own hard work and competitive edge. Comparing himself to Johnny Appleseed, a beloved figure of American folklore who tamed the wilderness of western New York and Pennsylvania in order to plant his apple trees, the Swede revels in "pull[ing] on his boots and walk[ing] the five hilly miles into the village and the five hilly miles back" just to get the Saturday paper (316).

In this manner, the Weequahic-born, third-generation Jewish immigrant claims for himself a role in the foundational national fairy tale of the self-reliant subject who charts his own journey across the limitless frontier. The Swede sees himself in vigorous opposition to his neighbor, Bill Orcutt, whose lineage stretches back to Jefferson and so represents the tired notion of inherited wealth and privilege associated with the old guard of WASP elites. The Swede is a new man for a new world order—one who can and has successfully pulled himself up by his own bootstraps.[12] Indeed, as Zuckerman notes, the Swede belongs, like the Irish American Kennedy, to a generation credited with resetting the "clock of history" so that a "whole people's aims" were "no longer limited by the past" and its prejudices and exclusions (40). But the story that the Swede narrates to himself not only hearkens back to a particular version of the nation's imagined history, it ignores the fact that the glove manufacturing business that has made him wealthy is a family business he himself inherited, and its success depends on the hard labor of others, first in Newark, then in Puerto Rico, and finally to "wherever in the Far East the labor force was abundant and cheap" (26). Nor does the Swede's frontier fantasy take into account what will only later become clear: the "new" American order that the Swede represents has not supplanted the established order but has unwittingly served its needs: Bill Orcutt, after all, has been sleeping with the Swede's wife.

Of course, this drama is secondary to the novel's chief irony, which is that the Swede turns out not to be Johnny Appleseed, issuing forth the blessed fruits of freedom and democracy. Instead, his seed begets the Rimrock Bomber, his morbidly obese, stuttering daughter, Merry—hardly a prime example of the physically fit suburban youngster that President Kennedy deemed necessary to secure "the future of freedom in the years to come" ("Soft American" n.p.). Too much time in front of the television has alerted Merry to the horrors that exist beyond the borders of Rimrock. From the comfort of her living room, she witnesses a Buddhist monk on the other side of the world self-immolate in protest to the Vietnam War, causing her to wonder, "Do you have to m-m-melt yourself down in fire to bring p-p-people to their s-senses? Does anybody care? Does anybody have a conscience?"(*AP* 154). Merry attempts to awaken the citizens of her sleepy suburban community to the terrible price of their privileges and freedoms by blowing up the local post office, which inadvertently kills a local doctor and sends the Swede's well-ordered life into chaos.[13]

Merry's emphatically unflattering characterization led critics initially to read *American Pastoral* as a reactionary text that holds the radical movements of the 1960s accountable for quashing the "contagious" "upsurge of energy" that Zuckerman fondly remembers coursing through the generation that came of age in the hope-filled years immediately following World War II (40). But as Sam Cohen rightly points out, the novel is neither an "anti-1960s screed" nor a nostalgic reminiscence of "the more innocent America that preceded that allegedly ruinous decade" (63). Instead, Cohen reads this novel-within-a-novel as an extended meditation about the ways we have chosen to remember that history and the stakes involved in "how stories of the past get told" (64)—whether about the fabled Greatest Generation or the equally mythologized countercultural revolution that followed it. Legend holds that both the Greatest Generation and the protesting youth movement it spawned made a radical break with the past, if what we mean by the past is the established order long presided over by "the Holy Protestant Empire," as the inimitable Alexander Portnoy dubs it in Roth's groundbreaking 1969 novel, *Portnoy's Complaint* (*Portnoy's Complaint* 39). I'd argue, however, that *American Pastoral* demonstrates the degree to which the Swede and his daughter, Merry, are both "fettered to history," are, indeed, "*instrument*[s]" of an old story that has proven remarkably resilient (*AP* 5).

As we've seen, the Swede's "superordinary" body faithfully serves that old story by telling the tale of disciplined self-reliance upon which a liberal democracy depends (86). In contrast, we might read the stuttering Merry's outsize figure in the same manner that Garland-Thomson advances the extraordinary body, as one whose "appalling disorder" threatens "a social order predicated on self-government" (44, 43). To better understand the nature and efficacy of that threat, I'd like to consider Merry alongside her fictional contemporary, the sexually voracious Portnoy, who similarly comes of age in the 1960s. Cohen also reads these two characters in conversation to argue that in *American Pastoral* Roth returns to the themes of his earlier work in order to "reconsider the historical time that produced the writer and the work" (66). I similarly read Merry as a response to the character who made Roth a literary superstar, but I do so to arrive at a somewhat different conclusion.

To be sure, the ranting analysand Portnoy, like the "angry, rebarbative" Merry (85), is in possession of an "ungovernable, recalcitrant" body that appears to threaten the existing social order (Garland-Thomson 41). But if Roth's depiction of Portnoy's insatiable body was widely credited with productively initiating his uptight middle-class readers into the new freedoms of the sexual revolution, Roth characterizes Merry as a purely destructive force whose bomb accomplishes no social good whatsoever but instead transports her family and by extension the nation "out of the longed-for American pastoral and into everything that is its antithesis and its enemy" (*AP* 85).

Perhaps the fruitless fury that emanates from Merry's body is evidence of the author's determination to reevaluate the relative merits of the social movements that rocked the 1960s. But Merry's characterization does not indicate a conservative turn on the author's part. Instead, from the vantage point of the late 1990s, when the end of the Cold War and the longest economic boom in history collaborated to announce the clear victory of capitalism, Roth took the occasion to reassess the degree to which the upheavals of the 1960s had actually succeeded in disrupting the "anticipated American future that was simply to have unrolled out of the solid American past" (85). After all, Democratic President Clinton's "Third Way" capitalism was not so very different at all from the kinder, gentler conservatism that his Republican predecessor, George Bush, had advocated before him, nor from the trickle-down economic policies of that president's predecessor, the neoliberal *par excellence* Ronald Reagan.

Looking back from this position, we might see that while Portnoy's desire to shake free from the inhibitions of family, community, and religion and his impulse toward self-gratification may have been initially shocking, they were wholly consonant with a social order predicated upon the "liberation of the individual to pursue his own ends, subject only to the loose restraints of a free society," as President Kennedy himself put it in his 1962 *Sports Illustrated* article, not long before Portnoy arrived on the scene to pursue and pursue again his own ends ("Vigor" n.p.). So much for Kennedy's so-called New Frontier of social responsibility. Like the President's ostensibly resilient body, Portnoy's compulsively masturbating self retells in particularly salacious fashion the foundational legend of the self-reliant, virile individual who spreads the seeds of freedom and democracy far and wide.

In this context, we can better grasp the implications of Merry's revolting body, which despite its capacity to shock and even devastate, ultimately fails to destroy "the dependable father whose center is the source of all order" (*AP* 230). Unquestionably, Merry's explosions do real damage: lives are lost, property is destroyed, a family is devastated. To the Swede's "particular form of Utopian thinking," Merry's turn to violence, like her stuttering, is incomprehensible. But what truly horrifies the Swede is the version of his daughter that he encounters five years after the bombing, when he locates her in a rank tenement right in Newark. She is all but unrecognizable, having denied her body to the point of emaciation by taking to extremes the principles of her adopted religion, Jainism, which advocates nonviolence and self-sacrifice. She has also "mastered miraculously the agitated stuttering," causing the Swede to muse that "her being able successfully to explain and to talk was now the worst thing of all" (250). Her impeccable speech and the foul odor wafting from her wasted body articulate all too clearly the true threat that Merry poses to her father's cherished belief system: what he recognizes as the "inhuman horror" of her "selflessness" and "monstrous altruism," which has no place in a narrative that celebrates the "self-seeking," self-reliant individual and his "desire to go the limit in America with [his] rights, forming [himself] as an ideal person" (250, 85).

Indeed, Merry's putrid body has the same devastating effect on her father that Robert Murphy attributes to that of the disabled figure in general: it serves as a "visible reminder[ ] to the able-bodied that the society they live in is shot through with iniquity and suffering, that they live in a counterfeit paradise, that they too are vulnerable" (Murphy 117). In Franzen's *Freedom*, the poor, the weak, the wounded, and the dispossessed gnaw at the edges of his middle-class characters' consciousness, similarly identifying for readers what has been excised from the triumphal narrative of prosperity and individual liberty that the suburban way of life was written to tell. Merry, on the other hand, occupies the very center of *American Pastoral*—a position that speaks both to her body's terrifying power and its paradoxically limited capacity to truly unsettle the façade of her father's attractively built frame.

It's true that the sight and smell of his daughter—the "chiseled-out eye sockets" that he recognizes as his own and "the smell of everything organic breaking down"—so unmake the Swede that he uncontrollably vomits into her face (265). But this intimate encounter with decay and mortality so traumatizes him that the Swede just as quickly works to restore a sense of order: he not only flees from Merry but begins the process of remaking himself and revising his story. Ruminating on all of the horror his daughter has done, seen, and experienced, he concludes, "You protect her and protect her—and she is unprotectable. If you don't protect her it's unendurable, if you do protect her it's unendurable. It's all unendurable. . . . If only that beautifully chiseled body had never been born" (272). As might be expected, in his self-pity and self-justification, the Swede reverts to the everyman's default setting by conflating Merry's misery with his own while also absolving himself of all responsibility for the ills that befall him and those around him (19). But the Swede does not simply deny his role in the current catastrophe. He disavows his own daughter, whose monstrous body cannot be assimilated into the success story his own "beautifully chiseled body" has been built to demonstrate.

As Cohen argues, *American Pastoral* is a story about the stories we tell ourselves. More particularly, the novel is about the tenaciousness with which we cling to those stories, and how we edit and refashion them in order to make them cohere. The countercultural revolution of the 1960s, as much as any other chapter in our nation's history, has been revised into a compelling drama that attests to our unique national character. Cohen argues that the fall of the Berlin Wall in 1989 prompted writers working in the 1990s to bring triumphant closure, and the 1960s have been treated to just this sort of revisionist refashioning. Yes, the period was marked by upheaval and violence that put our nation to a severe test, but everything "turned out all right in the end" (Cohen 161). People of different backgrounds came together to agitate for equal rights, resources, and freedoms for disenfranchised people of color, women, and homosexuals, proving, as the Swede did a generation before, that that the "clock of history" has once again been "reset" so that the unencumbered individual could "go the limit in America" (*AP* 40, 85). It is an old yarn that reveals again our infinite capacity for making it new.

Portnoy's body, unruly but virile, told well this seductive tale of possibility and rebirth to a readership eager to test their own limits and craft their own identities. In contrast, Merry's stinking, starving body stands out as what Garland-Thomson calls "an icon of all human vulnerability" with the disturbing potential to narrate a far darker tale (41). Merry's is a body, in other words, that makes no sense within the framework of the feel-good national narrative that informs the novel's present tense—a Clintonian America whose catchy theme song, "Don't Stop Thinking About Tomorrow," cheerfully directs the body politic into the "anticipated American future" (*AP* 85). Nor does her disruptive potential jibe with Zuckerman's own sanguine mood, which is decidedly and uncharacteristically nostalgic for the "solid American past" from which he, like the Swede, sprang (85).

But Garland-Thomson also notes the paradoxical role that an "icon" such as Merry plays in the "cultural project of American self-making" (41, 5). On the one hand, Merry's body, reeking of decay, reminds us that without invitation or warning, disability descends on everyone. On the other hand, an extraordinary figure such as Merry also serves as a receptacle for society's anxieties, absorbing and isolating the "disavowed elements" of the American Ideal so that it can continue to "appear as master of both destiny and self" (41). This is the role that Zuckerman assigns to Merry. He may place her at the center of his story, but he is interested in her character only inasmuch as she shapes his protagonist's character into a more commanding—and ultimately comforting—version of the American Ideal: the everyday hero. Merry is merely the catalyst who transforms the Swede in Zuckerman's eyes from a mere "god or a demigod" into someone deserving of a writer's attention: "another assailable man" whose "tragic fall" is "worth thinking about" (*AP* 89, 88).

As I've already noted, Zuckerman goes so far as to compare his childhood hero to none other than President John F. Kennedy. As Zuckerman reasons, not only were both men "privileged sons of fortune," but the president was "assassinated while still in his mid-forties just five years before the Swede's daughter violently protested the Kennedy-Johnson war and blew up her father's life" (83). It is a humorously inflated comparison, of course. It is also riddled with contradictions. The Swede certainly was not struck down while in his prime. Nor is there solid evidence that Merry's bomb did, in fact, "blow up" her father's life: by Zuckerman's own account, whatever may have befallen his childhood hero in the intervening years, by the time he sees him again in 1985, the Swede is as resplendent as ever in a "suit that fit him so exquisitely he seemed even taller and leaner than I remembered him in the uniform of one sport or another" (16). Further, he has not only replicated his perfect suburban life, he has expanded upon it: he has remarried and is the father of three handsome, athletic boys. The sloppy logic of Zuckerman's bizarre comparison thus reminds the reader that he is as much a character in this novel as is the Swede, with motivations of his own that his creator, Roth, offers up for our scrutiny.

In the introduction, I argue that authors writing in the pre-9/11 suburban literary tradition depict crises that work conservatively to reestablish social cohesion by instilling in readers a nostalgic desire to return to an earlier era when white patrician masculinity still had authority. *American Pastoral* similarly narrates a crisis in the form of "the monster Merry" who "detonates" her father's "perfect life" (67). But whereas the catastrophes that mark contemporaneous novels such as A. M. Homes's *Music for Torching* and Rick Moody's *The Ice Storm* work to summon in readers a desire to return to a strong, paternalistic status quo, the crisis at the center of *American Pastoral* serves to *distract* us from the fragility of that status quo—to wit, the banal, everyday terror that stalks the ordinary, "assailable" male body. By comparing his boyhood hero to the eternally boyish

John F. Kennedy, Zuckerman strives to cement in our imagination and his own a version of the Swede who is forever young and forever virile—one who could only be annihilated by a devastating act of pure violence. Zuckerman, after all, remembers "those scrimmage pileups from which the Swede would extricate himself, always still clutching the ball," and he reminisces:

> How seriously I'd fallen in love with him on that late-autumn afternoon long ago when he'd transformed my ten-year-old existence by selecting me to enter the fantasy of Swede Levov's life—when for a moment it seemed that I, too, had been called to great things and that nothing could ever obstruct my way now that our god's benign countenance had shed its light on me alone. (72)

It is this enduring fantasy that underwrites the "realistic chronicle" that Zuckerman goes on to concoct: a compelling drama that attributes the Swede's "tragic fall" to the "fury, and the violence" of "little Merry's darling bomb" (68). So gripping is the story that Zuckerman invents, we lose track of what we learn at the novel's outset: that the Swede has died unremarkably from prostate cancer. The same disease that has left Zuckerman himself impotent and incontinent "had managed the most astounding thing of all by carrying off the indestructible hero of the wartime Weequahic section, our neighborhood talisman, the legendary Swede" (64). It is Zuckerman himself, not the Swede, who is the novel's "questing protagonist" and who seeks in his depiction of the iconic unmarked everyman to write a comforting "cure story" that moves "from defect to fulfillment, from drive to freedom, from loss to recovery," as Gullette puts it (xiv). Or, as Zuckerman himself puts it, "in the wake of all the other isolating losses, in the wake of everything gone and everyone gone," the disease has robbed him of all but his abilities as a writer, so that "his aging powers had now but a single and unswerving aim, a man who would be seeking his solace, like it or not, nowhere but in sentences" (*AP* 64). Read in this way, the novel represents Zuckerman's own heartbreaking gambit to stage a violent crisis that preserves the feel-good fiction that it takes a catastrophic event to fell the resilient everyman who, after all, "can't be knocked down with one punch" (Chrysler, "Halftime" n.p.). Some fifty years later Zuckerman's own declining body illustrates well why we persist in clinging to the myth of the self-reliant, eternally youthful everyman; he may provide only the most "bizarre, delusionary kind of sustenance" (4), but the alternative to his story is just too grim to contemplate.

Yet oddly, in the aftermath of the 9/11 terrorist attacks, when our sense of collective vulnerability would seem to call for exactly this kind of solace, it is this grim tale that Roth narrates in his depiction of the decidedly ordinary and inescapably dead body of an unnamed white middle-class protagonist in his 2006 novel, *Everyman*. Unlike so many of his previous indelibly drawn protagonists—whether the neurotic Portnoy or the beautiful Swede—Roth's everyman is not marked by difference: he is "not flamboyant or deformed or extreme in any way" (30). In fact, the text asserts that where its dead everyman is concerned, "it's the commonness that's most wrenching, the registering once more of the fact of death that overwhelms everything" (14–15). Thus, Roth's prototypically unmarked everyman embodies both the normate and its inevitable failure—a wrenchingly familiar reminder to those who identify with this position that at best we are all only "temporarily able-bodied" (Garland-Thomson 14). It is to this novel that I now turn to argue that the post-9/11 suburban novel, as exemplified by Roth's contribution, advances a poetics of prostration that not only admits but embraces what Zuckerman would not: "the assailability, the frailty, the enfeeblement of supposedly robust things" that radically reimagines middle-class male identity (*AP* 426).

Dead Reckoning

At a trim 182 pages, Roth's *Everyman* differs markedly from the other books I've engaged in this study. As their titles and their heft suggest, *The Lay of the Land* (496 pages), *Aloft* (384 pages), and *Freedom* (608 pages) all participate in the sweeping tradition of the Great American Novel, which is to say that these expansive works, like Roth's own pre-9/11 contribution to the genre, *American Pastoral* (432 pages), depict questing individuals whose various personal crises mirror the state of the nation. Whether we determine that these novels engage this tradition in order to undermine the mythos of American exceptionalism, as I argue they ultimately do, they unquestionably teem with the sights, sounds, and strains of American history and culture in order to comment on the shaping of national character. *Everyman*, on the other hand, is stripped all but clean of the effluvia of current events that typically make up the suburban everyman's stream of consciousness. Whole decades, for instance, are dismissed thus: "Twenty-two years passed" (41). *Everyman's* austere prose perhaps aligns it less with the voluble male-authored suburban novel than with the "elegy, the lament, and the dirge," as Ross Posnock asserts (51).

Perhaps, but the novel does not particularly grieve the passing of the everyman at its center. It may begin at his graveside funeral in a decrepit cemetery somewhere along the New Jersey Turnpike, but the opening does not work to establish its protagonist as the epitome of sympathetically drawn white male victimization. Instead, the scene insists upon the quotidian nature of his fate: "That was the end. No special point had been made. . . . Up and down the state that day, there'd been five hundred funerals like his, routine, ordinary . . . no more or less interesting than any of the others" (13–14). The novel's conclusion is just as brusque in its description of its everyman's death: "he never woke up. Cardiac arrest. He was no more, freed from being, entering into nowhere without even knowing it" (182). For a novel that quite literally revolves around its protagonist's dead body, it is paradoxically intent on minimizing its import.

Mark McGurl argues that *Everyman*—along with Roth's three other recent brief, death-obsessed novels, *Indignation* (2008), *The Humbling* (2009), and *Nemesis* (2010)—participates in an aesthetic he identifies as "post-heroic individualism." In contrast to earlier novels such as those by, say, Updike, Ford, and Roth himself, which imagine their questing protagonists in heroic opposition to the institutions that threaten to constrain them, *Everyman* is not predicated along this predictable individual vs. institution axis. To be sure, the everyman struggles mightily, but the battle is waged against his own betraying body. A successful advertising executive who has been thrice divorced, Roth's everyman may once have fully participated in the restorative run-return-repeat behavior that maps the familiar trajectory of the male-authored suburban novel and which bespeaks the individualistic pursuits of its questing protagonist, but now, "eluding death seemed to have become the central business of his life and bodily decay his entire story" (71). Hardly a triumphant portrait of American virility and self-reliance, Roth's everyman, on Medicare and collecting Social Security, is certainly not characterized as heroically pitted against the institutions that now sustain him. Further, we already know how the protagonist's quest will end: this may be an illness story, but it is by no means what Gullette calls a "cure story": the everyman is inarguably unsuccessful in his determination to fend off death (xiv).

The novel may thus fully engage the genre's familiar tropes, but only to invert their meaning. Consider, for instance, the difference between Ford's thirty-six-year-old Frank Bascombe in the iconic conclusion of *The Sportswriter* and Roth's seventy-one-year-old everyman in a similar setting in the months before his death. Having fled his home, his job at the glossy sports magazine, and his family in a moment of personal crisis, Frank seeks and finds rejuvenation on a "lithesome" beach in Florida, where he feels like "a kid" again and marvels at the sensation "of being let loose, of being the light-floater" (*SW* 375). We find out in the next installment, *Independence Day*, that Frank goes on to celebrate his renewed sense of manhood by cavorting throughout Europe with a much younger woman. In this manner, Frank Bascombe is arguably the embodiment of the American Ideal—a youthful, virile, and independent everyman who attests to our national self-reliance and resilience.

Roth similarly relocates his ailing everyman to the beach in the wake of a crisis. In this case, though, it is not an ultimately self-actualizing personal crisis that has brought him here but the anxiety-inducing September 11 terrorist attacks that "had subverted everyone's sense of security and introduced an ineradicable precariousness into their daily lives" (*Everyman* 65–66). The twin desires for safety and self-mastery impel Roth's everyman to likewise leave behind his family, his work, and his former home to resettle in a suburban retirement community on the Jersey shore—a move that does not reinvigorate him but instead "mark[s] the beginning of his vulnerability and the origin of his exile" (135). The everyman's quest for safety in a suburban setting calls to mind Bernice Murphy's observation that in suburbia the enemy resides within. In the films and popular texts that Murphy analyzes, that threat is often supernatural—poltergeists, zombies, vampires—and yet potentially surmountable. In Roth's novel, it turns out that the danger within—illness, infirmity, death—is both natural and overpowering.

From his park bench on the ocean's boardwalk, he takes to ogling the "robustly healthy young women" who jog by, but although "following their speedy progress with his gaze was a pleasure, . . . at bottom the mental caress was a source of biting sadness that only intensified an unbearable loneliness" (101). When he summons the nerve to make a sexual overture to one of these nubile joggers, however, she momentarily indulges the flirtation, causing him to get an erection that makes him feel, similar to Frank Bascombe, "as though he were fifteen," which invites him to participate in the national myth of perpetual regeneration and to experience "that sharp sense of individualization, of sublime singularity that marks a fresh sexual encounter or love affair" (134).

The sexual pursuit of the much younger woman is, of course, typical behavior for the male middle-class everyman. If we are to believe Francis Fukuyama, more than simply assuaging ennui, sating a libidinal craving, or even recovering lost youth, the sexual encounter is also the means by which the everyman satisfies the "universal desire for recognition," or what Fukuyama calls "thymos," borrowing Plato's term. In his controversial treatise, *The End of History and the Last Man* (1992), Fukuyama asserts that "sexual conquest is not usually just a matter of physical gratification—one does not always need a partner for that—but reflects in addition the need to have one's desirability 'recognized' by the other" (176). According to Fukuyama's terms, it is the quest for recognition that not only distinguishes us as human but has inevitably pulled us in the direction of liberal democracy—the "end point of mankind's ideological evolution" that marks the so-called end of history because it promises its citizens universal recognition (xi). Yet paradoxically, Fukuyama also asserts that the very survival of the liberal democratic state depends upon "the degree to which [its] citizens seek to be recognized not just as equal, but as superior to others" (xxiii). In the absence of war and conflict, men wage the battle for prestige with demonstrations of bodily mastery in the private sphere—in activities such as "sports, mountain climbing, auto racing" and "sexual conquest," which have "no 'point' other than to make certain people winners and others losers" (319). In this context, the prototypical everyman's sexual exploits are not only illustrative of national virility but can be read as thymotic bids for glory prized by a system that feeds on competition and conquest.

In contrast and following Nietzche, Fukuyama might disdainfully dismiss Roth's aging everyman as a so-called "*last man* . . . the creature who reportedly emerges at the end of history" (xi; emphasis original). In such a setting, the last man is reduced to "desire and reason, clever at finding new ways to satisfy a host of petty wants" and "unable to feel any sense of shame in himself for being unable to rise above those wants" (301). Unquestionably, despite his fleeting sensation of "sublime singularity," the aging everyman's unseemly public erection does not rise to the thymotic ideals of self-regulation and individual dignity that prop up a liberal democracy. The incident also reveals that the notion of universal, reciprocal recognition is nothing more than a false, placating promise. Though the young female jogger seductively assures the everyman that she finds him both fit and distinctive and alluringly tucks his phone number into her sports bra, she disappears immediately after, never to jog his way again, leaving him bereft, humiliated, and alone.

The scene thus elaborates the political stakes of what McGurl identifies as the novel's ethos of "post-heroic individualism" by calling attention to all those individuals who go unrecognized—the old, the infirm, and, by extension, the poor, the marginalized, and the exploited. Such an argument may sound like a stretch in relation to an upper-middle-class everyman who may be existentially lonely but is clearly materially privileged and hardly has a history of disenfranchisement. But the very credentials that allow the everyman to lay claim to the universal—he is straight, white, middle class, and male—reconfigure our understanding of what constitutes universal experience. Unlike *American Pastoral*'s unassimilable Merry, there is nothing extreme about the everyman: he is variously described as "moderate," "square," "conventional and unadventurous," and so "average" that the descriptor bears repeating four times in a single page (*Everyman* 30–31). And yet, very much like Merry, he, too, winds up decaying, anonymous, and desperately alone. In this manner Roth's universal everyman paints a distressing portrait of what individualism looks like when divested of its heroic ability to rise and fight again. At the very least, then, Roth's ordinary, aging protagonist counteracts the figure of the robust and resilient white suburban everyman at the same time that he issues a sturdy critique of the state's failure to distribute recognition, rights, and resources fairly among its variously needy citizens.

Of course, it might be argued that the chronically ill everyman is just one more member of the walking-wounded white men's club that Sally Robinson discusses. Hamilton Carroll, for instance, contends that the strategy that maintains white male privilege is best understood according to the concept of lability, since the term incorporates both mutability and mobility but also means "liable or prone to lapse" (10). Carroll asserts that such perceived frailty represents the "sleight of hand" by which white masculinity gathers for itself "rights and recognition by citing itself as the most needy and the most worthy recipient of what it denies it already has" (10). Leaving aside for the moment the fact that the everyman's body is not "prone to lapse" but has *already* lapsed, thereby rendering any claims to injury moot, the frail everyman may be needy, but in the novel's formulation that neediness does not entitle him to more than his fair share of self-pity. Instead, his own vulnerability instills in him compassion for similarly needy bodies. *Everyman* thus moves beyond critique to offer an alternative to thymos as a source of dignity: the capacity to fully recognize others' humanity.

Note, for example, that immediately after his demoralizing encounter with the young woman on the boardwalk, the everyman learns that his second ex-wife, Phoebe, has had a debilitating stroke. The two divorced bitterly over two decades earlier because of his affair, not incidentally, with a much younger woman. Now, however, when he hears of her stroke, he immediately goes to the hospital. In one of the novel's most affecting scenes, the everyman does what his kind rarely does: he listens intently as Phoebe haltingly admits her terror at being paralyzed, all the while gently stroking her hair and remembering everything he can "about this candid, unaffected woman" (140). In another similar scene, during an art class the everyman conducts for his fellow retirees in his condominium, one of his elderly students is so overwhelmed by her chronic back pain that he offers her his bedroom so she can lie down. Again, the everyman soothes her and listens as she expresses her anguish, her suffering, and her shame. He muses that the woman is "embarrassed, humiliated, humbled almost beyond her own recognition. But which one of them wasn't? They were all embarrassed by what they'd become. Wasn't he? By the physical changes. By the diminishment of virility. By the errors that had contorted him and the blows—both those self-inflicted and those from without—that deformed him" (91).

It is a crucial moment when the everyman not only acknowledges the humanity of the shattered woman beside him but admits to himself what Zuckerman refused to see in the Swede: his own depleted body, which he tellingly likens to deformity, able-bodiedness having uneventfully become a thing of the past. Far from devolving into an occasion for self-pity, however, the experience instills in the everyman a sense of intimate connection to and responsibility for his fellow sufferer. In this manner the everyman helps to convert the amenity-rich but spiritually depleted "lifestyle enclave" that Robert Bellah describes into what Bellah would call a "community of memory" of sorts (73). As Bellah elaborates, an authentic community of memory tells "painful stories of shared suffering . . . and if the community is completely honest, it will remember stories not only of suffering received but of suffering inflicted" (153). The everyman's encounter with others who once felt "in the middle of everything" but now feel "in the middle of nothing" prompts him to acknowledge accountability for the "errors" that have left him so alone at this point in his life (*Everyman* 88). If the typical Rothian protagonist rants à la Portnoy against the various wrongs that have been done unto him, in this novel the everyman takes stock of the pain he has caused others in his individualistic pursuit of pleasure: the two sons from his first marriage who have never forgiven his abandonment; his second ex-wife, Phoebe, and their beloved daughter, Nancy, who remains devoted to him; the mother who died while he was enjoying an extramarital tryst in Paris; the older brother he has shut out because he begrudges him his good health. Not that his stark recognition of the circumstances that have left him so painfully alone changes anything. His sons remain estranged. Phoebe's stroke dashes his plan to move in with his daughter and grandchildren. His mother is still dead. His brother has gone to Tibet. And two weeks later his pain-riddled art student quietly kills herself with an overdose of pills. The aging everyman's acceptance of responsibility does not translate into heroism, nor does the narrative offer any promise of fixing that which is ineradicably broken: the everyman's maxim, repeated by his daughter at his funeral, is "there's no remaking reality. . . . Just take it as it comes" (5).

We have, of course, seen something like this moment in each of the novels I've discussed thus far. The experience of loss and the proximity of death cause these flawed everymen—Frank Bascombe, Jerry Battle, Walter Berglund—to become "more wise and generous and self-sacrificing" than they have heretofore been (*Aloft* 319). All of these post-9/11 suburban novels, in other words, engage the ethos of post-heroic individualism that McGurl argues informs *Everyman* by offering protagonists who learn to see themselves in relation to the larger world rather than in opposition to it. These novels also respond to the events of 9/11 by advancing an aesthetic of contingency that counteracts the typical official response to national catastrophe, which is to spin a triumphalist fairy tale that fashions victims into heroes and reimagines the event itself—whether a world war, a terrorist attack, or financial meltdown—as a test of character that demonstrates its citizens' true grit. In contrast, the unexceptional everymen of these novels are neither victims nor heroes, and they certainly do not emerge from disaster bigger, better, or stronger.

Everyman, however, rethinks the very notion of crisis by offering us a protagonist who is dead at the novel's outset. The catastrophe, utterly commonplace and completely terrifying, has already happened, and as the novel loops back to arrive at the same conclusion, it reminds readers of the obvious: it is, always was, and always will be unavoidable. This does not mean that loss is not devastating. As the everyman's brother puts it, standing over his grave, "We can say of him what has doubtless been said by their loved ones about nearly everyone who is buried here: he should have lived longer. He should have indeed" (5). Far from minimizing death, the novel insists only that all of life is precious and deserves to be mourned.

This is the insight that informs Eric Cazdyn's book *The Already Dead: The New Time of Politics, Culture, and Illness* (2012), in which he notes, "Though we fall at different speeds and with varying degrees of recognition, we are freefalling together in the global abyss and living together as the already dead" (10). And yet, Cazdyn argues, new medical technologies have encouraged us to think in terms of what he calls "the new chronic mode" (6). He might well be describing the everyman's quest for security in a suburban retirement community when he defines this mode as a limbo state "that cares little for terminality or acuteness, but more for an undying present that remains forever sick, without the danger of sudden death. The maintenance of the status quo becomes, if not quite the ultimate goal, what we will settle for, even fight for" (5). Extending his analysis beyond the medical to include the political, economic, and cultural realms, Cazdyn asserts that we have given up the "utopian desire to cure" and instead determine only to manage the disease, stabilize the economy, secure the homeland (6). Cazdyn insists instead that we embrace our right to die. It is assuredly not Cazdyn's aim to advocate for euthanasia or legalized suicide. Nor does he ignore the billions who necessarily live outside the confines of the new chronic—the urban, rural, and global poor and those living and fighting in war zones for whom loss of life is all too familiar. Rather, he invites his privileged readers to consider the degree to which the existing power structure benefits by severing death from everyday life and figuring it instead as "the great terrorist from beyond"—a vicious, extreme enemy that must be vanquished at all costs (6). This strategy was certainly effective in the immediate aftermath of 9/11, when the horrific losses of that day left an entire nation jittery in anticipation of another attack. The national response—which included but was not limited to two wars and untold Afghani and Iraqi civilian deaths in addition to thousands of military casualties—reveals just how lethal the practice of keeping death at a safe distance can be.[14] It is in this context that Cazdyn asserts that to claim our right to die is also to claim "our right to dream—and live in—a radically different present than the one we now inhabit" (7).

The post-9/11 male-authored suburban novels I have engaged modestly strive to achieve precisely this aim in their reconception of middle-class identity, the basis of which is no longer the false promise of self-mastery and security, but is instead frailty and instability. These novels further suggest that in our vulnerability and inevitable decline, we are all intimately connected to and responsible for one another. *Everyman* operates somewhat differently to arrive at the same conclusion: in this novel, it is the absolute certainty of our death that rewrites the suburban narrative. I began this book by wondering how the story would end for *Mad Men*'s remarkably glamorous advertising executive, Don Draper. If Roth's retired ad man's trajectory is any indication, this is where it ends: in obscurity and an unremarkable death.

Even more definitively than Franzen does in *Freedom*, Roth's novel, beginning and ending with a corpse, breaks from the "anticipated American future that was simply to have unrolled out of the solid American past" (*AP* 85). The novel may lay to rest the figure of the perpetually resilient everyman, but in the process it introduces a truly new specimen: an everyman whose foregrounded dead body starkly reinterprets Clint Eastwood's dictum that "all that matters is what lies ahead." Certainly his follow-up question, "How do we win?" seems beside the point (Chrysler, "Halftime" n.p.). The novel makes clear that we are all losers, after all. But its final paragraph—the everyman's last reverie before he slips under the anesthesia and "into nowhere"—also makes lyrically clear what is to be gained from the losing: a precious present, which is over in an instant. Recalling his "unscathed" boyhood body riding the waves of the Atlantic ocean, the everyman marvels,

> Oh, the abandon of it, and the smell of the salt water and the scorching sun! Daylight, . . . penetrating everywhere, day after summer day of that daylight blazing off a living sea, an optical treasure so vast and valuable that he could have been peering through the loupe with his father's initials at the perfect priceless planet itself—at his home, the billion-, the trillion-, the quadrillion-carat planet Earth! (*Everyman* 183).

It is a gorgeous passage that eloquently rewrites the human equation: it is not a matter of having our individual worth recognized but of taking full measure of the invaluable, fragile world that surrounds us. The thymotic urge to demonstrate mastery beyond his grasp now, the everyman instead revels in being "penetrated" by the sun and the sensation of being one with the "living sea." *Everyman* thus fully realizes what all of the other male-authored suburban novels I consider suggest in a shared aesthetic that is bound up in loss, failure, and death: the freedom that inheres when we abandon the notion of our preternatural resilience, give up striving, and just let go.

5

That's What She Said

The Everyman in Recent Suburban Fiction by Anne Tyler, Gish Gen, and A. M. Homes

The White Middle-Class Male and Women's Struggle for Recognition

The so-called war on terror may drag on along with its insidious "us versus them" rhetoric, but the famous feud between Jonathan Franzen and Oprah Winfrey that likewise began in the fall of 2001 officially came to an end on September 17, 2010, after Franzen apparently sent Winfrey the galleys of *Freedom* along with a personal note. Winfrey rewarded Franzen's peacemaking gesture by choosing his novel, which she described as an "epic family saga that has everything—sex and love and even rock and roll," for her televised book club. Two months later Franzen, once ostensibly determined to keep his work on the "shelf reserved for high literary art," appeared on Winfrey's show to offer apologies, accept forgiveness, and schmooze with the audience about the inner workings of his emotionally challenged characters (Fitzpatrick 2). Ironically, however, just as Franzen, like *Freedom*'s protagonist Walter, was giving himself over to the "warming influence" of a tough but tender woman in the spirit of conciliation and connectedness, female authors banded together to identify Franzen as the enemy's leader in the ongoing battle of the sexes (*Freedom* 526).

It began when the bestselling author Jodi Picoult tweeted, "Would love to see the NYT rave about authors who aren't white male literary darlings" and gathered steam when fellow author Jennifer Weiner, under the hashtag "Franzenfreude," tweeted, "Call for non-Franzen novels about love, identity, families, The Way We Live Now. I pick Anne Tyler's DIGGING TO AMERICA." Soon every major media outlet in the country was compelled to weigh in on the literary establishment's gender bias—a worthy enough activity, perhaps, that revealed what anyone paying attention over the last several decades already knew: that the literary powers that be always have and still do pay more attention to male writers than to female writers, so that the struggle for equal rights and recognition continues.[1] As Weiner's tweet suggests, and as she herself acknowledges elsewhere, the commercial women's fiction she writes has different aims than the literary fiction Franzen writes.[2] But what of a novel by a similarly established literary novelist such as Anne Tyler's *Digging to America* (2006)? First of all, it bears mentioning that Tyler's novel, like Franzen's, earned not just one but two *New York Times* book reviews and that her work over the years has garnered considerable critical and scholarly attention. My aim here, however, is not to dispute the disproportionate amount of hosannas heaped on "white male literary darlings" as opposed to their worthy female colleagues but to determine instead how these female authors themselves have opted to depict the figure of the white middle-class male in their recent fiction. Whatever the realities are on the ground, established authors such as Tyler, Gish Jen, and A. M. Homes do not portray him as the enemy in their respective post-9/11 novels, *Digging to America*, *World and Town* (2010), and *May We Be Forgiven* (2012). Instead, these novelists reimagine the white middle-class male in much the same way that their male peers do, which is to say that they offer this figure a decentered but meaningful role in a changed and changing environment.

Over the last four chapters, I have argued that the events of 9/11 and their lingering aftermath have impelled writers such as Franzen, Richard Ford, Chang-rae Lee, and Philip Roth to return to the suburban literary tradition in order to refashion the white middle-class male protagonist at its center. This character, influenced by the women in his midst, learns to see himself in *relation* to the larger world rather than in opposition to it. By valuing affiliation over alienation, these novels purposefully subvert the neoliberal values of self-mastery, privacy, and property ownership that have shaped middle-class experience in order to imagine new, flexible, and responsible modes of being and belonging in an uncertain everyday. These novels thus also appear to bridge the longstanding divide that has segregated men's from women's domestic fiction, which has ostensibly always privileged interconnection over independence.

In this chapter I focus on the depiction of the white middle-class male in Tyler's, Jen's, and Homes's post-9/11 suburban novels to argue, not only that their characterizations of this figure closely resemble the evolved white middle-class male I identify in Ford's, Lee's, Franzen's, and Roth's post-9/11 suburban novels, but that this shift is indicative of these novelists' similar determination to overturn the ethos of individualism that has arguably likewise informed female-authored middle-class fiction in the decade preceding 9/11. Weiner synopsizes female-authored fiction about middle-class experience as revolving around "love, identity, families," but as I will discuss further below, in the 1990s these entanglements were mediated by the values of individualism, security, and property ownership that had become so entrenched as to appear commonsensical, as David Harvey asserts (3). As Jen's, Tyler's, and Homes's pre-9/11 suburban novels illustrate, under the guise of equal opportunity the neoliberal agenda works to consolidate white male authority.

In the fragile post-9/11 landscape that Tyler, Jen, and Homes depict in their recent novels, however, the balance of power has apparently shifted. *Digging to America*, *World and Town*, and *May We Be Forgiven* depict deeply flawed, seriously lacking white middle-class male characters who have variously lost their wives, their jobs, their homes, and their health. As we shall see, the suffering that these white male characters endure is, to some extent, punishment for their past deeds. However, as is the case in the male-authored fiction I discuss in the previous chapters, these men learn not only from their mistakes but from their newly forged relationships with strong female characters to come to terms with their diminished circumstances and take responsibility for themselves and others in a shifting community of sufferers. Importantly, these are not one-sided affairs but reciprocal relationships. As the women in these novels collide and collude with these defeated and marginalized white males, they, too, learn to reevaluate their own entrenched and perhaps narrow assumptions about the nature of power and privilege within an expanded frame.

In a 2006 essay entitled "Feminism Meets the Free Market," for instance, author Jane Smiley chronicles her own experience and that of a small group of peers who came of age in the heady 1970s when "the world seemed to lie before us" (202). Nevertheless, Smiley expresses real misgivings about what the feminist movement came to mean:

> It turned out that if we feminists were going to succeed (gain power, gain influence, change the world, get famous, achieve economic security . . .), it had to be according to the individualistic American model. Success

> became defined by surviving change and adversity, being adaptable and tough, and understanding and possibly making use of the perquisites of power. (208)

Smiley concedes that her and her peers' choices "seemed to be purely personal ones" (202). "Our lives," she reflects, "played themselves out in free-market terms, not in common-good terms. We 'made it' one at a time rather than as a group" (208). As I will elaborate, these novels also seek to correct feminism's course for a new and uncertain era. In *Digging to America*, *World and Town*, and *May We Be Forgiven*, Tyler, Jen, and Homes rise to the occasion of 9/11's ongoing aftermath and attendant sense of precariousness with widely scoped stories that share a moral vision committed to the common good. These novels thus pointedly dispense with the binary divisions—men versus women, youth versus age, freedom versus constraint, us versus them—that have underwritten earlier works that center on middle-class female characters' struggle for self-actualization in a landscape shaped by white male privilege. Instead, they imagine their middle-class male and female characters on an equal footing; it is the ground that has become so distressingly shaky that they must navigate it together.

In my introduction I argue that male writers who have returned to the suburbs in the wake of 9/11 do not offer this space as a retreat from the larger world but suggest instead that the world has come to the suburbs. Tyler, Jen, and Homes are every bit as insistent on this score: the communities they conjure are ethnically, racially, and economically diverse environments in which identity and belonging are not abstract concerns to be mulled over at one's leisure but are concrete problems with real and dire consequences. Against this backdrop, the upper-middle-class women and men in these stories put their own problems in perspective as they learn to engage in group projects that seek to build new alliances with those who have been forgotten, ignored, or exploited by the existing social order.

Of course, this sort of coalition building is a delicate endeavor that runs the risk of equating rather than illuminating the range of suffering and uncertainty that differently situated populations experience. The novels I engage here are sensitive to these distinctions. As we shall see, in their earlier work Tyler, Jen, and Homes offered middle-class female protagonists who strain against the confines of stifling homes and the demands of entitled men in search of individual fulfillment. In contrast, their post-9/11 novels advance protagonists who recognize the relative privileges they enjoy and so pursue collective solutions on behalf of characters who are truly vulnerable. These female-authored narratives may thus unseat the white middle-class male from his position at the head of the table, but they do not claim moral authority, nor do they seek to wrest control of the story. Instead, they include the figure of the white middle-class male in an ongoing, open-ended conversation that allows for a multiplicity of perspectives at a table whose shape is still being determined.

The Neoliberal White Protestant Male in 1990s Female-Authored Suburban Fiction

Elaine Showalter concludes *A Jury of Her Peers* (2009), her comprehensive history of American literature written by women, on a triumphant note, proclaiming that by the 1990s "American women writers had traversed the three stages of feminine, feminist, and female writing, and had moved into the fourth stage: free" (494). Showalter elaborates what that freedom entails: "No longer constrained by their femininity, women were free to think of themselves primarily as writers, and subject to the same market forces and social changes . . . as men" (494). Showalter champions the work of Jen, Tyler, and Homes as examples of a new, unencumbered era in women's writing, which she identifies under the catchall label "Anything She Wants." But as I will elaborate, these authors' pre-9/11 contributions to middle-class suburban literature underscore the inherent contradictions of being "free," bound up as this term has become with the free-market values of self-determination and privacy that serve and preserve white male privilege.

Gish Jen's 1996 novel, *Mona in the Promised Land*, for instance, centers on Mona Chang, an adolescent who comes of age in the heady late 1960s and '70s that concern Smiley in the fictionalized suburb of Scarshill, New York. Indeed, the novel may be set in the vicinity of the stifling suburbs that Friedan calls "comfortable concentration camps"(282), but Jen describes Mona's little corner of the world as a hotbed of playful experimentation where her winning protagonist and her peers are determined to make the most of the various opportunities for self-actualization that the new era affords them. After all, as far as Mona is concerned, being "American means being whatever you want" (8). Mona, for instance, the second daughter of upwardly mobile Chinese immigrants (chronicled in Jen's first novel, *Typical American* [1991]), decides to convert to Judaism after tagging along with her friend Barbara Gugelstein to her temple's youth group. Mona's love interest and eventual husband, Seth Mandel, is a part-time Marxist radical who dabbles in all manner of -isms and lives in a teepee in his parents' sprawling backyard. Barbara, in the meantime, the daughter of a wealthy financier, decides to dabble in social action and redress centuries of racial injustice by inviting the devastatingly handsome Alfred, the black line cook from Mona's parents' restaurant, to stay at her parents' mansion after he is evicted from his apartment and while her parents are away—a grand social experiment that turns into a raucous house party-cum-consciousness-raising session that they dub Camp Gugelstein—a utopian effort to find collective solutions to poverty and racial injustice. Showalter reads the novel as a celebration of a radically altered landscape in which girls and by extension all underrepresented groups are free "to change their names, their religion, and their nationalities" (502). I would argue, however, that the novel dramatizes the degree to which the liberating "market forces" that Showalter identifies continue to be controlled by a patriarchy that may invite select minority members to feast at its table, but only one at a time, as Smiley points out, and only according to its established rules.

This is evident in the novel's depiction of a minor character who exerts major control over the narrative: Mr. Ingle, the wealthy white Protestant father of one of Mona's school friends, Eloise. Mona encounters Mr. Ingle when she goes to visit her older sister, Callie, a Harvard student who, along with her black roommate, Naomi, is spending the summer waitressing at an exclusive resort in Rhode Island. Naomi explains that she and Callie are taking field notes for a paper they plan to write on the ways of the resort's privileged white Anglo-Saxon Protestant patrons. They enlist Mona in their project, which involves observing this subculture's speech patterns, conversation topics, and leisure habits in their native habitat and among their own kind, and Mona agrees to infiltrate the Ingle family inner circle and report her findings.

Initially the girls are convinced that they are in control of the anthropological diversion they've devised. At first glance Mr. Ingle, with his

"Nantucket red pants" and tennis hat perched ridiculously atop his head, seems merely to be a particularly entertaining exemplar of the WASP tribe (172). It becomes apparent, however, that it is he who is in charge of the game and its rules, and he who will determine its outcome. This is suggested at the outset of his family's arrival, when his four hypercompetitive sons and daughter take to the tennis courts, which they monopolize over the course of their stay at the expense of the other guests at the hotel. As they explain to Mona, they have learned well their father's "great lesson in life," which is that "*You've got to know how the game is played*" in order to win (177; emphasis original).

Mona learns for herself how the game is played when she is invited to go to dinner with the Ingles. As it happens, the normally commanding Naomi is their waitress for the evening, and Mona is appalled to see that she bows her head submissively to Mr. Ingle. For the Ingles' part, they likewise do not engage Naomi, even when they find out that she is attending Harvard with Mona's sister. Only invited guests can feast at their table; the model minority Mona may be provisionally accepted, but the African American Naomi is not yet welcome.

At first glance the scene, played out in a stuffy bastion of exclusive white privilege that the hotel's threadbare guest towels suggest has worn thin, reads as an offensive but fairly typical and toothless example of casual racism that says more about the Ingles' outmoded parochialism than it does about Mona's and Naomi's prospects in the larger world. But the scene ends on a menacingly foreboding note when Mr. Ingle is called from the table for a business phone call. Upon his return, he has an inscrutable look on his face and refuses to respond to his wife's cryptic comment that "that poor man has a family too" (183). Only later will Mona piece together that, at that moment, Ingle had made the decision to fire Barbara Gugelstein's father as part of a "ritual purification" after his investment firm was caught in shady dealings—despite the fact that Gugelstein had nothing to do with the questionable transactions (230). As a result, Barbara's family is forced to vacate the mansion. The family will be fine—they are able to move back into their smaller home—but their eviction as a result of Ingle's ruthlessness also forestalls any future efforts Mona, Barbara, and Seth might make to recreate and improve upon the equitable, open society they had attempted to forge with Camp Gugelstein.

The novel's epilogue, then, in which we find out that all of the adolescents in the novel have grown into successful adults with satisfying lives and careers, does not signal that women and minorities have been victorious in redrawing the landscape. Of all the disadvantaged campers of Camp Gugelstein, only Alfred is mentioned, having been brought into the fold by marrying Barbara's cousin, who paid for his college education. Berlant recalls George H. W. Bush's invocation of the "thousand points of light." This was his signature plan to enlist private citizens to take over the government's role in addressing social problems: "This brightly lit portrait of a civic army of sanctified philanthropists was meant to replace an image of the United States as a Great Society with a state-funded social safety net" (*Queen of America . . .* 7). In the conclusion to *Mona*, we learn that all of the characters' social activist instincts have indeed been safely confined to the private sector: Mr. Ingle's daughter does "foundation work," Alfred and Barbara's cousin are "Mr. and Mrs. Community Organization." Naomi, a successful producer, is ready to "rest on her laurels" and "bake bread and make applesauce" and "volunteer[ ] in a youth program" (297). Mona and her friends have thus grown up to be model citizens who narrate the myth of American exceptionalism to a new audience and, in so doing, testify to the enduring power of what Smiley calls the "individualistic American model" that has long served the white Protestant male establishment.

Showalter's obvious delight in Mona's ability to write her own success story is understandable in the context of women's struggle to put an end to "second-class status, critical denigration, and self-censorship" (442). Oddly, though, Showalter inadvertently participates in the very rhetoric that has worked to exclude women from the literary canon in her valorization of the individual who triumphs over a constraining society. Over thirty years ago, in her seminal essay, "Melodramas of Beset Manhood: How Theories of American Fiction Exclude Women Authors," Nina Baym argued persuasively that the American literary canon is organized around the work of a narrow range of white Anglo-Saxon middle-class males who write about the putatively universal "struggle of the individual against society" (132). Baym notes that this is the narrative arc that describes the fiction of Melville, Hawthorne, and Twain, but we can see the tenaciousness of this model in the "pre-canonical" texts that Richard

Ohmann identifies and that were written between 1960 and 1979—decidedly domestic-centered, middle-class fiction by Updike, Roth, and Salinger that nevertheless imagines society as a "hostile force" that threatens to "annihilate" the individual who strives to be "invulnerable" to its demands (212). And we find it again in Franzen's description in his 1996 *Harper's* essay of the group of writers with whom he identifies: "angry, confused, lonely white males [who] write *at* and against the culture" (51; emphasis original).

But as Showalter's celebratory reading of *Mona* as a novel of "self-creation" indicates, it isn't just that we overvalue male-authored fiction but that we have been led to prefer narratives that revolve around the triumph of the individual over stories that grapple with the challenges and rewards of connection, cooperation, and compassion (all of which are the values that inform the spirit of Camp Gugelstein but which are marginalized by a patriarchy-driven market). That this is the case is evident in the outrage that greeted an earlier essay by Jane Smiley, "Say It Ain't So, Huck: Second Thoughts on Mark Twain's 'Masterpiece,'" published in *Harper's* just a few months before Franzen's "Perchance to Dream" essay in 1996. Smiley heretically decries not only the canonization of Twain's *The Adventures of Huckleberry Finn* (as opposed to Harriet Beecher Stowe's *Uncle Tom's Cabin*) but also the privileging of an entire body of literature that advocates "the ultimate distraction, lighting out for the territory." "The real loss," Smiley insists, "is not to our literature but to our culture and ourselves, because we have lost the subject of how the various social groups who may not escape to the wilderness are to get along in society" (66). Smiley goes on to assert that "if literature is to have any purpose, it is to help us face up to our responsibilities" (67).[3] For Smiley, those responsibilities include a willingness to engage the world beyond the realm of the private and the emotional in order to publicly tackle structural inequity.

According to Smiley's terms, one might dismiss Anne Tyler's fiction, which centers fairly exclusively on the vicissitudes of middle-class family life, out of hand. Feminists in particular have taken umbrage with her body of work, which they charge advances an aesthetic of quietism and capitulation rather than resistance and change.[4] Feminist scholar Alice Petry, for instance, bemoans the fact that Tyler's novel *Breathing Lessons* (1988), about a "ditzy housewife" who by novel's end recommits herself to her reserved husband, won that year's Pulitzer Prize. "After two decades of ardent feminism," Petry frets, "was this award at some level intended to be a public endorsement of the seemingly antifeminist ideas increasingly evident in Tyler's fiction?" ("Tyler and Feminism," 41). For her part, Tyler has hardly ingratiated herself with feminist critics; during the heyday of the women's liberation movement, in a series of negative reviews of various feminist works in the early 1970s, she denigrated what she felt were these stories' "really strident, bitter, look-what-men-have-done-to-us" approach (cited in Jones 272). In an interview with Petry, Tyler clarifies her position: "Certainly I don't hate liberated women as such; I assume I am one myself, if you can call someone liberated who was never imprisoned" (*Understanding Anne Tyler*, 18–19). Tyler, an intensely private woman, has been outspoken about her decision to organize her writing life around the needs of her children and husband. In a 1992 interview, for instance, she asserted that she was vigilant about only working from 8:05 to 3:30, when her children were in school, so that she could devote the rest of her time to being "wife, mother, cook, housekeeper, laundress" (Michaels 40). Tyler's fervent commitment to her private life does not so much make her a throwback to an earlier era as an exemplar of the so-called family values that had so thoroughly saturated the culture after the Reagan presidency that Hillary Clinton would find herself at the center of controversy in the months before her husband's 1992 election for daring to say that she was happy to work outside the home.[5]

In her 1995 novel *Ladder of Years*, however, Tyler imagines just such a woman who feels imprisoned by her life in her suburban home and opts to liberate herself: feeling unappreciated by her husband and children, forty-year-old Delia Grinstead impulsively wanders off during a family beach vacation to start a fresh life unencumbered from her past. But as much as Delia's adventure recalls similar flight narratives by, say, Updike and Ford, *Ladder of Years* is not properly a female midlife crisis novel but a coming-of-age narrative, since Delia, with her babydoll dresses and her tendency to translate her experience through the gauze of fairy tales and the romance novels she devours, is a study in arrested development. In this sense, her narrative invites comparison to Mona, perhaps, who similarly tries to invent herself from scratch, but more particularly to another famous literary figure, Huck Finn, who, like Delia, runs away from home. Huck sought to break free from the constraints of a feminizing society; Delia shakes off the golden handcuffs of a benevolent paternalism that has kept her in childlike thrall. The beloved daughter of a kindly doctor, she married his equally decent if distracted junior partner when she was just seventeen and has lived with him in her childhood bedroom ever since, serving as his receptionist and raising her own children in a house in which she herself never actually grew up.

Far from eschewing responsibility, then, Delia's decision to "light out for the territories" is the path she takes to maturity and a life more fully attuned to the larger world. In a new town where she knows no one and no one knows her, Delia, like Mona, is free to craft her own identity, a self-fashioning process that empowers her. For the first time in her life, for instance, she lives on her own and works outside the home. Quickly, however, it becomes clear that *Ladder of Years* is not a celebration of independence but of interdependence. Delia may originally seek self-fulfillment in her escape, but she ultimately forges meaningful bonds in an ad hoc community she helps to build. Her newfound sense of mutual responsibility persuades her that she cannot untangle herself from the web of connections—a realization that leads her to return to her husband and her family and resume her role as wife and mother.

Delia's decision to recommit herself to her marriage provides yet more fodder for feminist scholars who find that Tyler's work "serves a static, politically conservative line on life," as Susan Gilbert asserts (139). Perhaps, but Delia's husband, Sam, likewise undergoes a transformation. Sam is of a piece with Tyler's stock of male protagonists, who are "instantly recognizable as a distinct species," as Michiko Kakutani describes them, "basically well meaning but detached and more than a little passive" ("Late Midlife Crisis . . ." n.p.). Sam, in other words, is an everyman we might easily find in male-authored suburban fiction. While Delia is gone, Sam becomes more engaged with the emotional and practical demands of the family life that had formerly been her exclusive domain, an experience that Delia notes approvingly has had the effect of melting the "ice water" in his "veins" (*Ladder of Years* 283). In this manner *Ladder of Years* anticipates the everyman's trajectory in the male-authored post-9/11 novels I have discussed. In this case, however, while the female character may still be the agent who thaws the white everyman, it is the absence of her "warming influence" that challenges Sam to reconsider his role in the household.

The changes that Delia inspires lead Paul Christian Jones to read *Ladder of Years* as a postfeminist text that offers the home as just one of many places that might "benefit from the independence, self-awareness, strength, and confidence of women" (281). Further, he asserts that Delia participates in the "remaking of one's world" that feminist fiction demands (281–282). I would suggest that the novel does not remake a world built around the prerogatives of white male privilege but only updates it. To be sure, the novel's transformative possibilities are undercut by its sentimental insistence that one can indeed go home again. Delia's reoccupation of her home participates in the same nostalgic project that informs Richard Ford's *Independence Day*, likewise published in 1995, which also centers on a protagonist who moves away only to come back with "the feeling of renewal" that impels him to transform his cold and impersonal community into one that encourages a sense of "homey connectedness" (91). In their suggestion that the lost home of our dreams can be recovered, both *Independence Day* and *Ladder of Years* participate in a form of nostalgia that shores up the existing power structure by blotting out bad or inconvenient memories that might tell a different story of struggle and exploitation. As opposed to the self-interested patriarch Mr. Ingle, who manipulates outcomes from behind the scenes in *Mona in the Promised Land*, authority in *Ladder of Years* takes the benign shape of a father figure who nurtures all those who seek his care. Sam, after all, is no ruthless financier but an old-fashioned physician who still makes house calls to anyone who asks, thus hearkening back to the notion of a kinder, gentler capitalism when the man with the biggest house on the street still selflessly served the common good.

In her book *Neodomestic Fiction*, Kristin Jacobson likewise reads recent male- and female-authored domestic fiction side by side in order to identify a subgenre that she sees emerging in the 1980s in response to feminist backlash and the imperatives of "family values" as codified and enforced by Reaganite conservatives (35). Jacobson argues that this "neodomestic fiction" productively reimagines domestic space as unstable in order to call attention to the exclusions built into the single family house and to challenge the status quo, which she sees these novels accomplishing through the recurring motif of home renovation and remodeling that carves out what Homi Bhaba has called a "third space" designed to "set up new structures of authority" and "a new area of negotiation" (cited in Jacobson 18–19). The 1990s domestic fiction I examine here, however, responds to a recently renovated White House presided over by a benevolent white male new democrat, Bill Clinton. The epilogue to *Mona in the Promised Land*, for instance, which concerns Mona's marriage to Seth Mandel, suggests that she and her cohort occupy just such a "third space." Their personal success and their continued interest in public service invokes Clinton's Third Way agenda and the wedding of free market imperatives and progressive social initiatives. But as the novel demonstrates, the alterations to this space are purely cosmetic: Mona, who playfully invented and reinvented herself throughout the novel, has deferred her ambitions in order to be a stay-at-home mother, not because this is her choice but because she and her husband, Seth, now fully immersed in mainstream society as a professor "married to his tenure prospects," can't sort out how to "divvy up child care duties" (298).

In *Ladder of Years* Delia does not merely destabilize the traditional family home, she temporarily abandons it—a move I've suggested has the effect of transforming it from within. But it is her husband, Sam, who undertakes the renovations while she is away. Their home may feel more comfortable and capacious thanks to his decision to install air conditioning and remove much of the old, heavy furniture, but the basic structure remains unchanged. The penultimate scene that takes place at the family's dining room table may testify to the era's spirit of inclusiveness: all of the table's leaves have been inserted to accommodate the hodgepodge cast of characters who have been invited to share in the "infinitely expandable" meal that Delia prepares (314). It is Sam, however, who sits at the head of the table. And the final scene depicts Sam and Delia intimately reunited in their marriage bed in her father's home, a scene that sanctifies the restoration of the established order and the primacy of privacy.

On the surface, two writers could not be more different than Anne Tyler and A. M. Homes. Indeed, Showalter heralds A. M. Homes as one of a group of writers whose work participates in what she identifies as "the extreme female gothic," since it partakes of the same gory sensationalism that is "the initiation rite into the contemporary boys club of contemporary fiction and art" (497). Critics and readers alike were outraged by her novel *The End of Alice* (1996), about a pedophiliac murderer who reminisces while serving a life sentence in prison, responding with the same fury they had heaped upon Bret Easton Ellis's controversial novel, *American Psycho*. Homes's subsequent novel, *Music for Torching* (1999), is arguably more mainstream and perhaps even more disturbing. It fits neatly into what Bernice Murphy identifies as the suburban gothic tradition, since it unearths the deviance and brutality lurking in the hearts of seemingly normal, upstanding citizens, so that the danger comes not from some predatory outsider but from within the community itself.

In my discussion of *Music for Torching* in the introduction, I outline Homes's portrayal of the novel's despicable and dangerously irresponsible white male protagonist, Paul Weiss. He is, in fact, part of a team: his wife, Elaine, is equally immature. In this sense she bears an odd resemblance to *Ladder of Year*'s Delia—another ahistorically drawn character who seems to have missed the women's movement. Elaine is a numbingly bored stay-at-home housewife who has no other particular aspirations of her own. Her attempts at self-fashioning range from experimenting with smoking crack, dabbling in a same-sex love affair with her neighbor, and engaging in random sex with a cop who is casing her house. But neither she nor her equally odious husband can muster the energy to cook a meal for their children, so in the opening chapter, they kick over the backyard barbecue and maniacally douse their house in lighter fluid in a bid to burn it down. Later, holed up in a motel, Paul suggests they should "build a fortress" to protect themselves from the outside world. "To protect us from each other," Elaine corrects. "From ourselves," Paul further emends. True to the suburban gothic tradition, Paul and Elaine discover that they are their own worst enemies. Yet their initial desire for radical change quickly fades. Instead, they determine to renovate their smoke-damaged house—a project that neither destabilizes the existing home nor offers a new footprint but instead merely buttresses a fatally flawed model. By the time the novel reaches its devastating conclusion, when Paul and Elaine's youngest son is held hostage at school and shot by a classmate due to their own self-indulgent myopia, it seems plain enough that A. M. Homes's intent in *Music for Torching* is to destroy, once and for all, a hollow American dream built around property ownership and the nuclear family.

Yet as I discuss in my introduction, by creating a cast of characters so self-absorbed that they are viscerally repugnant and setting them in motion in a world where the consequences are unthinkably real, *Music for Torching* elicits in readers a natural desire for a strong authority figure who will set things right again. Further, the novel reinforces the Thatcherian principles of privacy and personal responsibility that provide the framework for the suburban ethos that the novel ostensibly sought to overturn in the first place. According to the novel's schema, the devastating school shooting in the final scene is not a random event, nor does the novel nod toward a larger cause, such as inadequate gun control laws, or larger cultural and social issues ranging from Americans' love affair with violence to inadequate mental health care. Instead, *Music for Torching* holds the parents alone wholly accountable for their son's presumed death, so that it is a failure of the individual and the family, not society, that is to blame. Like their male colleagues, then, in their pre-9/11 suburban novels, Jen, Tyler, and Homes may offer stories that dabble in challenging the status quo, but they ultimately work conservatively to reaffirm a neoliberal agenda organized around the unit of the individual and her family. Baym notes that in canonical male-authored fiction the "society" that the male individual struggles against is overrun by busybody females. In the female-authored fiction I examine in this section, female protagonists struggle against a society dominated by white men in a battle that appears rigged from the start. Such fatalism excuses their middle-class female protagonists for their powerlessness to change anything more than their own circumstances. In the wake of 9/11 and its anxious aftermath, however, these same novelists do indeed offer stories that stage a "new area of negotiation" that allow for alternative, flexible community formations in which all are exhorted to mutually participate. As is the case in the novels I've discussed by Ford, Lee, Franzen, and Roth, the spaces that Jen, Tyler, and Homes imagine are hardly utopian, but are marked by contingency and anxiety that render the boundaries of middle-class experience as porous and open to change.

The Female-Authored Post-9/11 Suburban Novel, Broadly Defined

Even casual readers of Anne Tyler's fiction are familiar with the territory that she has carved out for herself: the suburbs of Baltimore, which she depicts as an environment that is suffocating, self-enclosed, and impervious to the forces of either history or current world affairs. But while Tyler's post-9/11 novels are still set in Baltimore's outskirts, this space is now affected by the vicissitudes of time and events beyond its borders. Nor do her more recent novels conclude on the note of optimism that reaffirms the enduring bonds of marriage and blood kinship. Her 2004 novel,

The Amateur Marriage, for instance, opens immediately after the attack on Pearl Harbor in 1941 and concludes on its sixtieth anniversary, just three months after the 9/11 attacks. The novel centers on a married couple who are old standbys in Tyler's repertoire—the high-spirited, impulsive wife and the reserved, overly sensible husband. But in this novel opposites do not learn to compromise and recommit to their marriage. Instead they divorce, their differences irreconcilable.

In *Digging to America* Tyler strays even further afield from her standard formula with characters whom we have never encountered before in her fiction: a middle-aged man and woman who are coequals in every way and who come together, go apart, and come together again in open-ended fashion as they navigate a world characterized by loss and radical change. Further, the setting differs considerably from Tyler's standard terrain. Susan Gilbert has complained that Tyler's fiction advances a "nostalgic vision of an America of private houses and private lawns" (139). But is clear from the outset of *Digging to America* that this novel, though likewise set in Baltimore and its environs, is different territory indeed, subject to the winds of change and outside forces. The novel, anchored uncharacteristically in time, opens on Friday, August 15, 1997, not in one of Tyler's typically fusty family homes but in a public setting the very definition of which is flux: the Baltimore/Washington International Airport, where two families await the arrival of their adopted Korean babies. One is an outsize, boisterous, all-American clan, the Donaldsons, who have made a party out of the event, complete with balloons, banners, video cameras, and buttons that proudly identify the players by their impending roles: MOM, DAD, GRANDMA, GRANDPA, COUSIN, etc. The other couple who have come to meet their baby for the first time are Sami and Ziba Yazdan, who bring with them Sami's elegant and reserved Iranian-born mother, Maryam. Thus begins the unlikely friendship that unfolds over the ensuing years and the course of the novel. But if the initial setup promises to deliver a Tyleresque meeting of opposites—stasis versus change, gregariousness versus reticence, Americanness versus foreignness—the novel does not intersect neatly along binary lines in its engagement with such disparate topics as transnational adoption; assimilation and cultural identification; the debates over public versus private schools; the vicissitudes of child care and working motherhood; the issue of racial profiling; and the realities of illness, aging, and dying. Instead, it takes up its diverse subject matter in order to more fully consider belonging, identity, privacy, and connectedness from multiple perspectives that do not resolve, reconcile, or in any way answer the questions the novel raises.

While the narrative perspective shifts from chapter to chapter, the bulk of the novel's action is translated through the alternating perspectives of the novel's two grandparents, Maryam Yazdan and Dave Donaldson. Maryam, having left her family behind in Iran before the age of twenty and become widowed before the age of forty, is a fiercely independent woman who lives a carefully arranged life in her own fastidiously tidy house. For his part, Dave Donaldson has been recently widowed and is "rackingly, achingly lonely" as he "rattle[s] around the house with far too much time on his hands" (125). Dave's profound sense of isolation and lack of purpose is exacerbated by his recent retirement as a junior high science teacher at a private girl's school where he was revered by his students, leaving him feeling listless, rudderless, and irrelevant: "It was like walking down a red carpet and then turning to find the attendants rolling it up behind you. He was gone. It shook his whole view of himself to discover how much he minded" (143). These circumstances might seem to place him among the pantheon of displaced, beleaguered white middle-class males at the center of male-authored suburban novels who are specialists in the art of self-pity and the sense of spiritual isolation that deflects attention from their privileged status while providing the means for recouping their authority in a shifting cultural landscape. Except in Dave's case, what has been lost can never be recovered. His deceased wife, Connie, is never coming back, and his position at the head of the class was over "not only for the year but forever" (125).

Kristin Jacobson asserts that the neodomestic novel unsettles domestic space in productive ways that allow for its renovation. In the anguished months after his wife's death, however, Dave, "a competent repairman, woodworker, seat-of the-pants inventor," determines to clear the house of forty years worth of clutter and undertake small repairs in a burst of energy and industry, only to look around at the end of his second day of labor and find that the house looked "much, much worse than when he'd begun" (145). Anticipating Walter Berglund, the protagonist of Franzen's *Freedom*, who throughout the novel sounds the refrain "how to live?," in his frustration, anguish, and grief Dave cries to himself, "Oh, what was the *point*, what was the *point*, what was the *point*?" (152; emphasis original). Thus,

Digging to America and, indeed, all of the male- and female-authored post-9/11 novels I examine do not just destabilize the traditional home but suggest that it is irrecoverably lost, in part because the idealized sense of home we hold in our memories never existed in the first place. It is this sense of longing for a lost home they know exists only in their imagination that provides the basis for Maryam and Dave's budding romance. Maryam, for instance, admits to Dave, "You think everything would be different if only you belonged. 'If only I were back home,' you say, and you forget that you wouldn't belong there either, after all these years. It wouldn't be home at all anymore." Dave tries to reassure her that "you belong just as much as I do . . . We *all* think the others belong more" (216; emphasis original). Far from equating Dave's recent loss with Maryam's protracted loneliness, however, the novel carefully parses out these characters' and others' differently situated experiences in order to explore what it means to belong. According to the novel's logic, belonging itself is problematic.

Indeed, Maryam's and Dave's shared sense of homelessness does not pave the way for them to create a new home for themselves. Theirs is a delicate dance that is often characterized by missteps and misunderstanding that may carve out a "new space for negotiation," but those negotiations are fraught and not necessarily resolvable. When Dave exuberantly proposes to Maryam in front of both of their extended families, Maryam is so abashed that she accepts just to avoid further embarrassment. The following day, awash in regret, she exclaims to her daughter-in-law, "He is so American. . . . He takes up so much space. He seems to be unable to let a room stay as it is; always he has to alter it, to turn on the fan or raise the thermostat or play a record or open the curtains" (252). She breaks off their twelve-hour engagement and the two don't speak for over a year, both festering in anger, resentment, and wounded feelings.

The two ultimately reunite, but only in the most provisional sense, and in service to the larger needs of the family: Dave's daughter has breast cancer, so they both pitch in to help with babysitting and providing meals. In the final scene, Dave and his entire extended family appear at Maryam's door to coax her to come to a party hosted by her son and daughter-in-law—the raucous annual two-family gathering that includes all of their mutual aunts, uncles, cousins, and friends. It is not his party, in other words; he is just one member of an eclectic crowd whose size and shape varies, depending on the year. Maryam ultimately relents and chases the crowd out into the street, calling out "Wait for me!" (330). The novel thus ends on a note of hopeful possibility, but it does not provide closure, nor does it provide a restored or renovated home. After all, unlike *Ladder of Years*, which left its husband and wife in the intimacy of their marriage bed, this novel concludes where it began, in a public space: this time on the street, where a kaleidoscopic crowd meets, clashes, and gathers together to celebrate, to protest, and occasionally to achieve something for the common good.

Gish Jen's novel *World and Town* likewise revolves around the relationship of a woman of color and a white Protestant male, both in late middle age and both independent. The novel is also strikingly similar to *Digging to America* in its engagement with issues of belonging and identity, which it also narrates from a variety of perspectives—in this case, from the points of view of characters who are not only racially and ethnically diverse but who also represent various class positions. We can detect echoes of *Digging to America* in *World and Town*'s time frame, as well: Tyler's novel begins approximately three years before September 11 and ends about three years after, while *World and Town* opens in the months before that day and concludes several months later. The day itself thus falls like a pebble in the middle of both novels, its causes and effects rippling in either direction across national borders and other sites of historical trauma.

The novel's central character is Hattie Kong. At sixty-eight she has returned to Riverlake, a quaint town in Vermont, to salve a "loneliness beyond words" and to "reconstitute herself" after losing both her husband and best friend to cancer in quick succession and retiring from her job as a high school science teacher (25). There, she reencounters her childhood friend, Carter Hatch, who has also returned to Riverlake to lick his wounds and assuage his feelings of bitter loss, regret, and guilt. Like Dave Donaldson, Carter is a widower: in Carter's case, however, his wife had divorced him first, he explains to Hattie, "then died without asking for me once. As if I were this Terrible Mistake" (98). He is also estranged from his daughter and has recently lost his younger brother, who was killed in a drunk-driving accident for which Carter feels vaguely accountable, since the two had never outgrown their sibling rivalry. And, like Dave and Hattie both, Carter has also recently retired from his teaching post—in his case, though, as the head of his own lab at a nearby prestigious university—a tradition passed down from Carter's father to all of the sons with the expectation that one of them would win the Nobel Prize. Empty-handed of the big prize, he has to acknowledge "that a moment comes when you are past your prime—when your challenge is to accept it with grace" (100).

Carter's characterization engages and complicates Jen's earlier portrayal of Mr. Ingle, another figure of the white Protestant male establishment. Carter, after all, is not a ruthless financier but a teacher and scientist who may have capitalized on what sociologist R. W. Connell calls the "patriarchal dividend," but has also contributed to the greater good. Further, he is not the puppet master, but one who has let himself be mastered by his father's lofty expectations. Jen does not render Carter either a victim or a saint. He and Hattie, for instance, have a fraught history. Hattie, whose father was Chinese and whose mother was an American missionary, was sent by her parents to America amidst the chaos of the Cultural Revolution and came to live with Carter's privileged family in Riverlake, where she served as the brothers' Chinese tutor. She and Carter were especially close and occasionally sexually involved, and she followed him into the sciences and even worked as a graduate student in his lab. But when she applied for a tenure-track position, he refused to make the case for her appointment, fearing unfounded rumors of impropriety. Decades later Hattie still smarts from resentment and her complex feelings for Carter. As in *Digging to America*, *World and Town* narrates an ongoing, often tense conversation between the white Protestant male and the foreign-born female of color, not so much to settle differences but to air them.

Further, Carter's and Hattie's heartaches may be challenging for them, but they do not compare to the suffering and loss of the Chhungs, the Cambodian family who has settled precariously in the abandoned trailer at the edge of Hattie's property. As Hattie takes in the porta-potty perched just beyond their rusted homestead; watches them digging in inhospitable soil to create a patch they can garden; and comes to learn something of the untold atrocities they suffered in Cambodia under Pol Pot, she concludes, "*The sorrows of the rich are not real sorrow; the comforts of the poor are not real comforts*" (24–25; emphasis original). The disparity between Hattie's and Carter's privilege and the hardships the Chhungs have endured is drawn on a broader canvas when she tries to explain to Chhung, the family patriarch, what she has just witnessed on television: the World Trade Center attacks, people leaping from windows, the devastation played over and over again, giving her the sense that "no one was ever going to move past this." She tells Chhung that "many people died. Many, many people" (267). She realizes that she must surmount not only a language gap but an experiential one as well, since "she knows, of course, that it will not seem like so many people to the Chhungs; that like her parents, they counted hardship by the millions. The millions wounded, the millions dead" (267). Without minimizing the devastation wrought by the 9/11 attacks, Hattie understands them in the context of "the vista of global suffering," as Michael Rothberg puts it ("'There Is No Poetry In This'" 148), and recognizes that Chhung's affectlessness is the symptom of a man who has been saturated in trauma. Nevertheless, he is not an easy man to help.

It is thus to Hattie's credit that she not only persists in reaching across this cultural divide but that she forms an uneasy alliance with Carter on the Chhungs' behalf, enlisting his help in order to ease their burdens and help them integrate into the community, which is itself rife with tension and a sense of anxiety in this "age of flux," as Hattie calls it (13). This is not to say that the two are figured as heroes, however. Though the novel's dynamics are similar to those outlined in Clint Eastwood's 2008 film, *Gran Torino,* in which Eastwood plays a rugged white savior who sacrifices himself in order to protect his upstanding Hmong neighbors from menacing outside forces, in *World and Town* the Chhungs' problems are far more complex than Hattie and Carter are capable of solving. Chhung is an alcoholic who abuses his adopted son, Sarun. Sarun, in the meantime, has become embroiled with a gang and its nefarious dealings. The family's mother, Mum, speaks no English and is all but helpless in these strange surroundings. Their troubled but bright daughter, Sophy, has been in and out of foster homes and has been gathered in by the fundamentalist church in town, which sets her on a course to save herself and renounce her family if they won't find their way to Jesus. Their problems are way beyond the scope of any individual's capacity to help, in other words. What is called for, in the first place, is everyone's mutual desire for and willingness to change. It is up to Chhung to decide to give up drinking. It has to be Sarun's decision to break his ties with the gang, and Sophy must recognize for herself that the fundamentalist church has divided her against her family.[6] But they can accomplish none of these things without enlisting the help of public services.

Indeed, what begins as a fairly shallow paternalistic/maternalistic initiative on Carter's and Hattie's part—Carter teaches Sophy guitar, Hattie teaches her Chinese—grows more meaningful over the novel as the Chhungs' situation reaches a crisis point and they need help navigating the health care system as they seek medical treatment for Sarun and for Chhung, who needs rehabilitation and counseling. They also need to find a source of income for Mum and get the teenagers enrolled in public school. Mutual participation guarantees all of this, but Jen does not suggest that these solutions are permanent. The Chhungs' trailer is only a temporary shelter, after all, and there are rumblings that they may move, since they miss being among other "black hairs" and are not sure they "could ever get used to the cold" (455). The novel assiduously avoids participating in the conservative project of restoring a sense of order, security, and authority.

Part of the way the novel avoids the trap of advancing a utopian vision that merely burnishes the status quo is by offering Carter a tenuous position at best in the narrative. Jurca argues that the fictional white male house owner garners the reader's sympathy by portraying himself as spiritually homeless even as he enjoys the privileges of material homeownership (4). As it happens, though, Carter only rents in town, the family's imposing patriarchal home having been sold and torn down to the ground. Thus Carter, while plenty privileged, is in fact homeless, so that his place in the community is provisional. Further, his sense of being displaced does not provide the grounds for isolation, but leads him to expand his sense of himself in relation to others and hold himself accountable for the sins of his past: "Can you forgive me?" he asks Hattie. "I know I'm years late with this, but I ask your forgiveness" (460). Hattie's intimate grasp of the cold reality that we are all only temporary residents in the world fills her with a sense of "defining grace, bittersweet and hard-won" that allows her also to put the past in perspective in order to more adequately respond to the demands of the present (461).

In *Mona in the Promised Land* an oppressive white male authority figure provided a screen for its male and female characters' limited contributions to the common good and their adherence to the ethos of personal upward mobility. *World and Town* offers its characters no such air cover. The world has indeed come to the town, so both Hattie and Carter must learn to see beyond their own limited problems in order to join the collective effort to address the issues of adequate housing, employment, education, transportation, and health care to meet the needs of the underserved members of their community. The narrative thus overturns an existing order predicated on self-determination and weaves instead a public safety net for a fragile population.

As its title suggests, A. M. Homes's novel *May We Be Forgiven* is also centrally concerned with issues of forgiveness and atonement. In this novel Homes returns to the same upscale suburban terrain of New York's Westchester County that provided the setting for *Music for Torching* and where one might spot the "ghost of John Cheever, going for a ride" (471). Perhaps unsurprisingly, then, she once again focuses on the experiences of a passive, habitually self-absorbed white middle-class male (471). But though Homes still indulges her inclination to shock and revolt, the trajectory of this novel could not be more different from her earlier work.

Music for Torching ends in catastrophe; *May We Be Forgiven* begins with a crisis and then spends the next several hundred pages exploring the ethical imperatives of its aftermath. The novel opens on Thanksgiving Day. The protagonist and narrator, Harry Silver, is a guest at his brother George's sprawling, ostentatiously appointed house for a lavish dinner, and the scene he sets suggests we are in for another tale full of hateful characters who will slash, burn, and maim their way through the story. George's children, Nathaniel, twelve, and Ashley, eleven, are glued to their handheld devices, "the only thing in motion their thumbs" as they text furiously and "kill digitized terrorists" (2). When Harry clears a few plates into the kitchen in an effort to help George's wife, Jane, she kisses him passionately, suggesting we are in for yet another novel revolving around the bored and tawdry assignations of self-absorbed suburbanites. Not long after this night, Jane summons Harry to help her: George has driven through an intersection, slamming into a minivan, killing a mother and father and leaving the son in the backseat an orphan. It is unclear whether it was an accident or George acted on a violent impulse. He voluntarily hospitalizes himself, and Harry stays with Jane initially as a source of comfort, but they quickly launch into a full-blown, torrid affair. Things take a drastic turn from the expected course, however, when George finds out, escapes from the hospital, and bludgeons Jane to death with a lamp while Harry is in bed beside her, effectively leaving Nathaniel and Ashley orphans. All of the above transpires in the first 45 pages of the novel. The remaining 440 pages follow Harry's path to making amends for his part in destroying his brother's family.

It perhaps goes without saying that, stylistically, Homes's violent, sexually explicit, and surreal novel has nothing in common with either *Digging to America* or *World and Town*. Yet Harry is lacking in all of the ways that Tyler's and Jen's white male protagonists are; his abasement is just more complete. Like Dave and Carter, he is a teacher—in his case, a professor of history or, more specifically, Nixon studies.[7] Harry doesn't retire from teaching; he is fired, having spent years toiling on a Nixon biography he is incapable of finishing and failing to attract more than a handful of students to his classes. Harry is also homeless—not out of choice, but because his wife unceremoniously evicts him from their Manhattan apartment when she finds out about his affair with George's wife. With nowhere to go, he takes up residence in his brother's vacated house—George is locked up in a psychiatric facility and his children are in boarding school—and initially behaves in the manner we might expect of Homes's particular variation of the prototypical sad-sack everyman—with equal portions desultory debauchery and staggering self-pity. He uses his brother's computer to meet suburban housewives and enjoys a round of anonymous lunchtime trysts until the children of one of those women take him hostage and he swears off the habit.

Utterly alone with the exception of his brother George's dog, he curls up on a park bench and wails, "*Look at me*, homeless in a public park. I curl into a ball, a fucking human ball in the corner of the park . . . I'm nothing, just a guy, a truly average Joe—which is probably the worst part of it all, knowing that I am not in any way exceptional or distinguished" (103; emphasis original). In the depth of his abjection, Harry might represent the Cheeveresque everyman taken to his logical extreme, whose function, Timothy Aubry argues, is to instruct his male middle-class readers "how to be properly miserable" ("Cheever and the Management . . ."). Harry's bid for attention can also be read, however, as part and parcel of the "universal desire for recognition," or what Francis Fukuyama calls "thymos," borrowing Plato's term in his unapologetic apologia for the neoliberal state, *The End of History and the Last Man* (1991). According to Fukuyama, it is the struggle for recognition that not only distinguishes us as human, but has inevitably pulled us in the direction of liberal democracy, since the desire for recognition impels us to compete—whether on the battlefield, the athletic field, or in the field of commerce (xi).

As was clear from the opening scene, Harry has always been engaged in a thymotic battle for prestige with his brother George, the final prize being George's wife, Jane. In what I'd suggest is the novel's turning point, Harry comes to terms with what his bloody competition has wrought. Talking to himself, he says, "*Look at me*—even though no one's come out and said it, you know as well as I do, I'm as much a murderer as my brother, no more, no less. I say it to myself—and I am undone" (103; emphasis original). It is a pivotal moment in which Harry not only holds himself accountable but reinterprets the universal desire for recognition for a new generation of middle-class readers by calling on them to recognize the tired, the poor, the wretched, and the homeless among them, because they are one and the same.

Thus begins Harry's transformation. He establishes ties with George's troubled children, currently shunted off to boarding school, and the orphaned child, Ricardo, who survived George's car crash, for whom he applies to become a foster parent. He strikes up a friendship with an elusive young woman in the grocery store, and in short order he finds himself attached instead to her elderly parents, who move in to George's house along with Ricardo and Ashley, who has moved back home after being sexually abused by a female teacher. There is also a trip to an African village that Nathaniel has been engaged with helping over the years, a sustaining friendship with one of his lunchtime trysts, and ties he develops with the people who own his favorite Chinese takeout place, so that by the following Thanksgiving Harry hosts a feast for all of these people and more and marvels at his sense of "benevolence and free-floating goodwill" (478). The novel thus comes full circle in shamelessly sentimental fashion to apparently offer a corrected version of the white male seated securely at the head of an infinitely expandable table to which all are welcome—a vision that merely dresses up the existing social order.

Perhaps, but then again this is not Harry's house, and the money he has used to fund this feast is not his own but his brother George's, which Harry has seen fit in his absence to redistribute judiciously for the common good rather than for personal pleasure or to display status. The conclusion is insistently hopeful, to be sure, but it neither restores nor renovates the lost home of our imagination. George's luxurious house may be commodious, but it is still nothing more than a temporary shelter: his prison term is only seven years. As has been the case with all of the post-9/11 male- and female-authored suburban novels I have discussed throughout, it is up to a female character to instruct the men in her midst how to "live with lack," as Kaja Silverman puts it (65). Fittingly, it is George's abused daughter, Ashley, who says grace at the table: "I do not think of all the misery, but of the glory that remains. Go outside into the fields, nature and the sun, go out and seek happiness in yourself and in God. Think of the beauty that again and again discharges itself within and without you and be happy" (481). Cy, the old white man at the table who is on "his last legs," guesses that Ashley is quoting Walt Whitman, the poet laureate of individualistic self-actualization and the distinctly American talent for renewal and regeneration (478). But Ashley corrects him: it turns out that it is from Anne Frank's diary. The passage thus elicits a complex range of associations, from the vast capacity for human evil, suffering, and grace, to the incredible beauty of fragile, finite life. It is on this note that Harry "rises to the occasion" to ask, "May we be forgiven," which he notes is an "incantation," since both atonement and forgiveness must be constantly won and rewon in the struggle for truly universal recognition (479).

If, as Weiner suggests, the female-authored middle-class novel's special province is its ability to show us "the way we live now," Tyler's, Jen's, and Homes's novels make clear that we now live in a world that has grown increasingly more harrowing, uncertain, and dangerous. Tales devoted exclusively to individual woes—the travails of marriage, the trials of dealing with ungrateful men and children, the quest for personal fulfillment—no longer suffice. Instead, Tyler, Jen, and Homes take seriously Smiley's assertion that it is literature's job to "help us face up to our responsibilities" by offering stories that challenge readers to think beyond the lines of gender, class, race, ethnicity, sexuality, nationality, and all of the other categories that divide us in order to imagine new alliances ("Huck" 67). These novels thus reconceive the familiar subject matter of middle-class suburban fiction—what Weiner identifies as "love, identity, families"—in broader, more flexible terms that carry with them an ethical charge to set aside petty grievances so that we, too, can rise to the occasion of a fragile, needy world that demands all of our attention.

NOTES

INTRODUCTION

1 Junod, who gave Drew's photograph its name "The Falling Man" in a 2003 *Esquire* article of the same name, is not the first to identify *Mad Men's* opening credits with what has become 9/11's quintessential image. In fact, Junod is responding to controversy in the blogosphere surrounding the advertisement for *Mad Men's* fifth season in 2012. The ad features the same silhouette of a businessman in free fall, but because it is a still image and because the skyscrapers have been stripped of their corporate content, the advertisement more strikingly evokes "The Falling Man." Scholars noted the connection before the controversy erupted, however. See Anker and Edgerton, respectively.

2 In 2006 the Brookings Institution issued a report that revealed that as of the year 2000 more immigrants and people in poverty lived in metropolitan areas outside the city (see Fuentes and Warren). The most recent Brookings Institution report, issued in May 2010, finds that the immigrant population in suburbs has only increased since then: "Suburban Asians and Hispanics already had topped 50 percent in 2000, and blacks joined them by 2008, rising from 43 percent in those eight years." The report notes a new phenomenon it calls "bright flight," which refers to the number of young white professionals now opting to live in cities closer to work and amenities, so that the suburban population is not only more ethnically diverse, it is increasingly older and poorer. There are several indications that this trend will continue: in another first, in the nation's one hundred largest metropolitan areas, black, Hispanic, and Asian residents now constitute a majority of residents younger than eighteen—presaging a benchmark that the nation as a whole is projected to reach in just over a decade. In the meantime, suburbs are home to the vast majority of baby boomers, the first of which turned sixty-five in 2011, increasing the burden on already strained social services. Add to this steadily increasing poverty in the wake of the 2008 financial crisis, and the support structures in these formerly robust communities are at their breaking point. See Roberts and Luhby, respectively.

3 This is not to say that there haven't also been novels depicting the suburban experiences of immigrants, people of color, and homosexuals since 9/11, such as

Alicia Erian's *Towelhead* (2005), Jhumpa Lahiri's *The Namesake* (2005), Laila Halaby's *Once in a Promised Land* (2007), Junot Diaz's *The Brief, Wondrous Life of Oscar Wao* (2007), and Colson Whitehead's *Sag Harbor* (2009), among others. In addition, Karen Tongson offers a queer-of-color suburban archive of novels, performance art, and hip hop that she argues reclaims and reinvents abandoned suburban space.

4 The proponents of neoliberalism insist that an unimpeded market—"the invisible hand of Adam Smith"—is a benign force that invites all to feast at its table. Postwar suburbanization, which made home ownership a reality for so many Americans for whom this had not previously been possible, has therefore been a shining beacon for the neoliberal celebration of individual property ownership. Needless to say, however, evidence abounds that since the suburbs' inception, property value has been manipulated by exclusionary practices. Douglas S. Massey and Nancy A. Denton first outlined the argument in *American Apartheid: Segregation and the Making of the Underclass* (1993), tracing the degree to which federal lending practices were, by design, racist. Taking its cue from the earlier Home Owner's Loan Corporation (HOLC), the FHA maintained on a grand scale the practice of "redlining," a color-coded ratings system that evaluated the risks associated with loans made to specific urban neighborhoods. Those central-city neighborhoods that were racially and ethnically mixed were color-coded red and virtually never received loans (51–54). In addition to the policy of redlining, The FHA also published a technical bulletin entitled "Planning Profitable Neighborhoods," which advised developers on how to concentrate on homogenous markets for housing (cited in Mary Beth Haralovich, 75–76). When the Supreme Court ruling in 1948 outlawed racially restrictive covenants, homeowner associations quickly learned to rely on restrictive covenants that targeted specific behaviors in order to exclude people of color to protect their all-important property values. Ironically, this approach may have grown out of a proposal from Robert Weaver, noted for being the first African American to hold a cabinet position, who suggested replacing restrictive racial covenants with those that targeted instead certain objectionable practices in order to preserve property values. See Evan McKenzie's *Privatopia* (1994). Exclusion from the feast of capital created by suburbanization was not only a matter of race: Rosalyn Baxandall and Elizabeth Ewen chronicle the McCarthy Housing Hearings in 1947, which bear witness to the degree to which the federal government colluded with big business interests to exclude labor unions from participating in the impending housing boom in order to keep building costs down (see pp. 87–105).

5 The following is a breakdown of casualties of the Twin Tower attacks from surrounding suburbs: 694 from New Jersey; 500 from Long Island; 112 from Westchester County; and 65 from Connecticut. See the following websites for numbers:http://www.statemaster.com/graph/cri_ter_vic_of_911-crime-terrorism-victims-9-11; http://longisland.newsday.com/911-anniversary/

victims; http://ww.nytimes.com/2002/09/15/nyregion/lost-to-9-11-112-names-from-westchester-and-putnam.html.

6 See note 1.

7 Keith Wilhite has recently written on the way that recent fiction moves beyond this reified vision of suburbia to reflect, critique, and negotiate a changing suburban landscape.

8 In a discussion of "the new suburban poverty" in the *New York Times*, Lisa McGirr observes that "the climbing rates of suburban poverty mark a definitive end to the Fordist model of mass production and consumption, and its most internationally recognized poster child: homogeneous middle-class families cradled safely in ever expanding suburban developments" (n.p.).

9 A *Time* magazine article declares, "The American suburb as we know it is dying," but goes on to argue that this space should be "recycled" to create economically and environmentally sustainable environments: "Otherwise, we're just eating up more land and resources" (Walsh n.p.). Further, as Karen Tongson reminds readers about the California suburbs that are the object of her study, they have largely been "reconstituted as service economies and repopulated as residential apartment communities for low-wage immigrant workers reliant on service sectors for sustenance." Thus, when creative urbanites and academics celebrate the suburb's decline and the city's ascendance, "whose demise are we celebrating?" Tongson wonders (13).

10 Approximately three quarters of the victims were white, male, middle class and between thirty and fifty years old. Approximately 8 percent were black, 9 percent Hispanic, and about 6 percent Asian. New York and New Jersey combined accounted for about 87 percent of the victims. See Beveridge.

11 The following excerpt from Rudolph Giuliani's address to the United Nations on October 1, 2001, sums up the story of American exceptionalism quickly espoused by pundits of all stripes: "This massive attack was intended to break our spirit. It has not done that. It's made us stronger, more determined, and more resolved" (n.p.).

12 Consider, for instance, a New York firefighter, Mike Moran, whose brother was killed in the Twin Towers attack and who appeared on what has become a de rigueur spectacle in the wake of a catastrophic event: the televised fundraiser. Introduced by the actor Michael J. Fox and speaking to a jam-packed Madison Square Garden audience of uniformed first responders as well as to the nation, he raged, "Osama Bin Laden! You can kiss my royal Irish ass!" to thunderous applause before adding, "And I live in Rockaway! And this is my face, bitch!" This moment, and indeed the entire event, felt more like a rowdy pep rally than a collective display of grief and sorrow. http://www.youtube.com/watch?v=a1EoZ_nwYIk.

13 In a discussion of several popular and acclaimed films about suburbia—among them, *Pleasantville* (1998), *The Truman Show* (1998) , and Todd Solondz's edgier

Welcome to the Dollhouse (1996) and *Happiness* (1998)—Samuel Freedman notes that by the 1990s the suburbs had already outgrown its image as a dystopia of white upper-middle-class privilege, having grown "ever more varied by race, class, and ethnicity and eluding the grasp of all but a handful of perceptive artists and entertainers" (n.p.). He credits Junot Diaz's story collection *Drown* (1996) and Tamara Jenkins's film *The Slums of Beverly Hills* (1998) with presenting a more "complex portrait of suburbia circa 2000" (n.p.).

14 These scholars and others can be credited with initiating so-called whiteness studies; invisibility, of course, is understood to mean the claim to universality and its attendant power and privilege, not underrepresentation. See, for instance, Donna Haraway, *Simians, Cyborgs, and Women* (1991); Toni Morrison, *Playing in the Dark* (1992); Ruth Frankenberg, *White Women, Race Matters* (1994); George Lipsitz, *The Possessive Investment in Whiteness* (1998); Robyn Wiegman, *American Anatomies* (1995); and Dana Nelson, *National Manhood* (1998).

15 Graydon Carter is credited/mocked for being the first to assert that "there's going to be a seismic change. I think it's the end of the age of irony." Just as quickly as critics such as Rich, Rosenblatt, and others jumped on board to embrace this sentiment, others lambasted him for this pronouncement, not only claiming that it was too soon to make such a prediction (it was), but also questioning both the definition and the productive uses of irony. See, for instance, David Beers. Michiko Kakutani offered a historical overview of cultural production in response to large-scale crisis, citing the rise of film noir, for instance, in the aftermath of World War II in her essay, "The Age of Irony Isn't Over After All; Assertions of Cynicism's Demise Belie History." At the end of the first tumultuous decade of the twenty-first century, Carter's precipitous prediction came in at #6 on *Newsweek*'s list of "Top Ten Worst Predictions of the Decade." See Peyser. To commemorate the tenth anniversary of the attacks in 2011, *The Atlantic Wire* undertook an investigation to see who, in fact, was the first to wrongly predict irony's demise and traces it back to Andrew Coyne, who apparently pronounced irony dead in Canada's *National Post* on September 12, 2001. See Randall.

16 While there have been no scientific studies, white knight syndrome has been associated with firemen, security guards, and to a lesser extent police officers who set fires and stage crises in order to act as hero at the scene. See Cave. More recently, and in the swirl of controversy surrounding the Kony 2012 initiative sponsored by the dubious charity organization Invisible Children, whose viral Youtube video brought worldwide attention to the child atrocities committed by Ugandan warlord Joseph Kony, author Teju Cole excoriated what he called the "White Savior Industrial Complex": on his Twitter account he posted a seven-part response that began, "From Sachs to Kristof to Invisible Children to TED, the fastest growth industry in the US is the White Savior Industrial Complex. The white savior supports brutal policies in the morning, founds charities in the afternoon, and receives awards in the evening." He concluded, "The White Sav-

ior Industrial Complex is not about justice. It is about having a big emotional experience that validates privilege." See his extended discussion of the subject in *The Atlantic.*

17 Even before the Great Recession that began in 2008, a third of the middle class was identified as having slid down the economic ladder. See Acs.

18 In fact, *The Company Men* is not so much interested in forging cross-class alliances as it is in creating sympathy for its newly precarious upper-middle-class characters who must face all sorts of fresh indignities, such as no longer being able to afford country club memberships, expensive sports cars, or Xboxes for their children. Nystrom notes that what this film is really mourning, however, is the demise of an "old boy network" under the pressure of neoliberal capitalism. In what amounts to a deus ex machina, the film offers a Hollywood ending that restores the efficacy of this old boy network when the wealthiest of the three protagonists uses his still vast fortune to start his own shipbuilding company and rehires all of his recently displaced friends and coworkers. As Nystrom points out, the lone ship on the horizon in the film's final scene may rescue the narrative's upper-middle-class workers, but it leaves no room for the film's unseen but "thoroughly fetishized" laborers.

CHAPTER ONE

1 In response to this assault, Whitehead remarked afterward, "I would like to warn the many other people who panned the book that they might want to get a rain poncho, in case of inclement Ford" (Schuessler n.p.).

2 A number of critics focus on Frank Bascombe's Southern heritage and Ford's debt—especially in *The Sportswriter*—to Walker Percy. See, for instance, Fred Hobson, "The Sportswriter: Post-Faulkner, Post-Southern?" and Martyn Bone, "The Postsouthern Sense of Place in Walker Percy's *The Moviegoer* and Richard Ford's *The Sportswriter.*" Along these lines, Matthew Guinn reads the suburban setting merely as an antithesis to an outdated agrarian, guilt-laden version of the South; Guinn argues that "the *Sportswriter* novels are Ford's protest against such a South" (197). Martyn Bone similarly reads the late capitalist New Jersey landscape as an indication of Ford's insistence on separating himself from a Southern tradition that is obsolete. I follow Bone in highlighting the sense of community that Bascombe advances in the late capitalist setting in *Independence Day.* However, while Bone reads the novel *against* the "southern literary shibboleth[s]" of "sense of place" and "community" ("New Jersey Real Estate . . ." 107), I read the trilogy *within* a suburban literary tradition that has never allowed for the possibility of either. Similarly, though I follow Jeffrey Folks's argument that Frank moves from "solitude back to society" (87), Folks claims that the process requires Frank to "divest" himself of the "security and contentment within a deadening suburban environment" (86), while I argue that it is Frank's aim to reclaim these

things for himself in *Independence Day* by way of imagined traditions; it is not until *The Lay of the Land* that he imagines just such divestment in order to reimagine a suburban environment that cannot be escaped but only reshaped. Folks's essay is ontologically focused on Frank's privileging of "immanence" over Percyean transcendence. See also Corner and Duffy, respectively.

3 Virtually every mainstream review identifies Frank Bascombe as an "everyman," though the author himself demurs, claiming that "the truth is that Frank Bascombe as everyman was never my intention." See "Nobody's Everyman" (n.p.). Nevertheless, Frank identifies the various phases of his life of white upper-middle-class male privilege according to what he thinks of as a universal life stage. The three novels cover, respectively, the Dreaminess of young middle age; the Existence Period, which encompasses late middle age; and the Permanent Period, which constitutes whatever time follows.

4 If nothing else, postwar suburbs provided plenty of fodder for a new bumper crop of social critics such as Betty Friedan (*The Feminine Mystique*), C. Wright Mills (*White Collar: The American Middle Classes*); David Riesman (*The Lonely Crowd*); William Whyte (*The Organization Man*), and many others. Though Herbert Gans ostensibly moved to Levittown, New Jersey, to dispel many of the assumptions of his mentor, Whyte, Gans's study did little to challenge the already congealed "suburban myth" he had identified. More recent contributions from M. P. Baumgartner (*The Moral Order of the Suburb*) and Robert Putnam (*Bowling Alone*) may have updated this damning sociological perspective but offer little to change the widespread perception that suburbia is "intellectually debilitating, culturally oppressive, and politically dangerous, breeding bland mass men without respect for the arts of democracy" (Gans xxviii).

5 See note 1, Introduction.

6 Cohen outlines the forces that combined to make postwar suburbs socioeconomically homogenous, among them house prices, which fairly quickly began sorting residents along class lines. By 1961, for instance, only 50 percent of Levittown's residents were white-collar workers, down from 62 percent in 1950 (201). This sorting process had the effect of driving up prices so that blue-collar workers such as firemen and policemen, for instance, could not afford to live in—or even near—the towns they worked. Cohen notes further that the same loan practices that kept the suburbs racially segregated also established boundaries along class lines. Both federal and private lenders considered newly built homes in white middle-class communities a more sound investment than a mortgage in a racially diverse, economically mixed community. For this reason, prosperous communities enacted zoning ordinances that established strict codes concerning lot and house size, for instance, that effectively precluded the building of affordable housing for low- and moderate-income individuals and families. Affordable housing continues to be one of the more contentious issues facing the suburbs today. Citizen groups seeking to curtail or limit growth in the

name of pollution, overcrowding, and congestion have been criticized by advocacy groups for making excuses to exclude the poor, the working class, immigrants, and senior citizens in the interest of preserving property values. See Cohen, 200–240; and Kirp et. al.'s *Our Town: Race, Housing, and the Soul of Suburbia*, which chronicles in detail the protracted legal battles in 1975, 1983, and 1986 in Mount Laurel, New Jersey, over the provision of affordable housing for the town's poor that resulted in the Fair Housing Act of 1985; this act may have enacted into law the principles of fair housing, but it also made provisions for municipalities to agree to fund housing in other communities in the region.

7 The term "neoliberalism" refers to nineteenth-century notions of liberalism as defined by the work of Adam Smith, David Ricardo, and John Stuart Mill. As Harvey points out, neoliberal theory is at heart inconsistent: in order to insure a "free market," government can and should use force. Harvey notes that "neoconservativism" has emerged to redress these inconsistencies. Like neoliberalism, neoconservativism is primarily concerned with maintaining market freedoms and protecting a ruling economic elite by way of endorsing corporate power, free enterprise, and market freedom. It likewise shares a fundamental mistrust of democracy. However, it differs from the way neoliberalism has reshaped political practices in two respects: "first, its concern for order as an answer to the chaos of individual interests, and second, in its concern for an overweening morality as the necessary social glue to keep the body politic secure in the face of external and internal dangers" (82).

8 Bellamy also outlines the role Gordon Lish played in making Knopf a "citadel for literary Republicanism" by sponsoring the books of Raymond Carver and others. Carver biographer Carol Sklenicka describes the degree to which Lish intervened in Carver's writing—slicing away huge chunks of prose to Carver's dismay. In this manner, Lish's editorial hand seems to have functioned much like the invisible hand of Adam Smith.

9 Irving Howe fretted in a 1954 essay entitled "This Age of Conformity" that "some intellectuals . . . have 'sold out.' . . . But far more prevalent and far more insidious is that slow attrition which destroys one's ability to stand firm and alone: the temptations of an improved standard of living" (10). As far as Howe and his fellow intellectuals were concerned, the intellectual vocation simply could not be realized "by a commercial civilization" (30), since "every assumption of contemporary American life favors the safe and comforting patterns of middlebrow feeling" (31). Thus, writers such as John Cheever had essentially sold their souls to the middlebrow devil by publishing in such commercial publications as the *New Yorker.* For Howe and his cronies, any engagement with bourgeois culture was debasing, and though the exigencies of life might force a writer to publish in the *New Yorker* and "worse, far worse," "for every writer who has survived the *New Yorker* one could point to a dozen whose work became trivial and frozen after they had begun to write for it" (31).

10 Critics and scholars have similarly charged AMC's hit television show *Mad Men*, which chronicles the bad behavior of 1960s advertising man Don Draper, with allowing readers "to indulge in a most unlovely—because wholly unearned—smugness" (Schwarz n.p.). Jeremy Varon is among several contributors to the collection *Mad Men, Mad World: Sex, Politics, Style, and the 1960s* who counters this charge, asserting that "*Mad Men* screams that we have not found a solution to the happiness problem (at least among an influential slice of American life). If we had, why would our culture continually stage the saga of upper-middle-class discontent, with *Mad Men* itself emerging as the latest, captivating edition?" (270–71).

11 In total, 694 New Jersey residents died in the September 11 terrorist attacks. http://www.statemaster.com/graph/cri_ter_vic_of_911-crime-terrorism-victims-9-11.

12 Harvey supplies the following statistics to support his argument that neoliberalization's central aim is to restore economic and political power to a ruling elite. He notes that in 1996 the net worth of the 358 richest people "was equal to the combined income of the poorest 45 per cent of the world's population—2.3 billion people," and that "the world's 200 richest people more than doubled their net worth in the four years to 1998 to more than $1 trillion. The assets of the top three billionaires [were by then] more than the combined GNP of all least developed countries and their 600 million people" (34–35). A recent article in the *New York Times* suggests that this trend is beginning to change: recent data indicates that over the past two years the very rich have become poorer, and many may not return to their former levels of wealth. As the article articulates, these changes beg the question as to whether tough times for the rich will signal better times for the middle class and poor, "given that the huge recent increase in top incomes coincided with slow income growth for almost every other group" (Leonhardt n.p.).

13 Sociologists such as Robert Bellah in *Habits of the Heart* distinguish between group participation among a homogenous group that merely advances members' self-interest with a broader sense of responsibility to a diverse community. Bellah notes, for instance, that "when thinking of the imperative to 'love thy neighbor' many . . . Americans . . . consider that responsibility fulfilled when they love those compatible neighbors . . . of their own lifestyle enclave, while letting the rest of the world go its chaotic, mysterious way" (179). Stephen Grant Meyer traces the history of institutional and individual racism that has fostered "NIMBYism" in his book *As Long As They Don't Move Next Door* (2000). See also David L. Kirp, John P. Dwyer, and Larry A. Rosenthal's *Our Town: Race, Housing, and the Soul of Suburbia* (1996), which chronicles the fierce legal battle in Mount Laurel, New Jersey, in the 1970s over the provision of affordable housing for the town's poor and its legacy. The suburbs' burgeoning immigrant population has

only made these battles more intense. While the spotlight has recently been on Arizona and its recent passage of anti-immigration legislation, the suburbs of New Jersey have likewise been riven by the issue. In 2006, for instance, Riverside became the first municipality to pass an ordinance making it illegal to hire undocumented workers. By the following year, the town's economy had collapsed and the law has since been rescinded. See Belson and Capuzzo.

14 Four mail centers—including that of Princeton, after which Haddam was modeled—were closed in central and southern New Jersey after mail tainted with anthrax was discovered in October 2001. In all, six postal workers apparently contracted anthrax, as did one woman from the Trenton area, unconnected to the postal system or the news media (Chen and Greenhouse).

15 Frank Bascombe's description of a Sponsor's work parallels the mission of FAVOR, or "Friends Assisting Victims of Terror," a volunteer group organized by residents of Middletown, New Jersey, which lost fifty residents in the 9/11 attacks, to assist the town's widows in myriad ways. In *Middletown, America: One Town's Passage from Trauma to Hope* (2003), Gail Sheehy describes the work of FAVOR in her depiction of the way that the disaster has transformed this New Jersey suburb, once an unfortunate example of the alienating effect of geographic sprawl, into a community in which people have come together to comfort one another, forging out of grief and sorrow lasting bonds. "Proof of the pudding," Sheehy asserts, is that thirty-one of the thirty-three widows, all of whom initially worried that they might be considered "socially undesirable" in a traditional "bedroom community," have elected to stay among neighbors who have embraced them with "warmth and support" (343).

16 Ford expressed precisely this sort of visceral empathy in an op-ed after Hurricane Katrina, a catastrophe that especially pained him and his wife, since the peripatetic couple consider New Orleans their home (see Brinkley): "we want to project our sympathies straight into the life of a woman standing waist-deep in a glistening toxic current with . . . no particular reason for hope . . . We would all give her hope. Comfort. A part of ourselves. Perform an act of renewal" ("A City Beyond" n.p.).

17 Harvey's book outlines the many neoliberal initiatives undertaken globally and in the name of freedom, from the installation of Pinochet in Chile in 1973 to the latest Iraq war. Harvey quotes Bush, who justified the preemptive war in the name of freedom: "Freedom is the Almighty's gift to every man and woman in this world. . . . As the greatest power on earth we have an obligation to help the spread of freedom" (6).

CHAPTER TWO

1 Keith Wilhite's essay, "Contested Terrain: The Suburb as Region," reads *Aloft* and Jonathan Franzen's novel *The Corrections* (2001) from a regionalist perspective and determines that in Lee's novel "the single-family home emerges as the site for a reimagined and recalibrated scale of living" (632).

2 Critics have indeed been somewhat dismissive of *Aloft*. In addition to James Wood's dismissal of the novel as the "feebler . . . thematic poor cousin" to Lee's first two books, *Native Speaker* (1996) and *A Gesture Life* (71), John Homans similarly finds that there is "an airy lightness and inconsequentiality about *Aloft* (think: Zoloft) that's both charming and cloying" (n.p.).

3 See Rosalyn Baxandall and Elizabeth Ewen's study, *Picture Windows: How the Suburbs Happened* (2000), which focuses on Long Island's Levittown, where *Aloft* takes place. The authors note that even before 9/11 these Long Island suburbs, once at the forefront of the postwar housing boom that promised a better life, had once again "become a bellwether for the nation's older suburbs" now struggling "to adapt to an uncertain and threatening future" (231). In 1997, for instance, Long Island had the highest rate of AIDS of any suburban area in the nation; in 1992, 40,000 people were homeless in an area that values homeownership as a primary social value. The area's infrastructure—bridges, roads, water, and buildings—is decaying, while the rising cost of taxes, housing, and utilities has caused more foreclosures on Long Island since the 1930s (230–31), a crisis that has only deepened since the subprime mortgage bubble burst. See Henry and J. Roberts.

4 Writing in *The Guardian*, for instance, Maya Jaggi describes Jerry Battle as "a suburban American Everyman who appears to have more in common with the protagonists of John Updike or Richard Ford" than with his previous protagonists. For his part, Lee, who was teaching at Princeton (the basis for Ford's depiction of the fictional suburb Haddam) at the time *Aloft* was published, asserts in an interview that Ford's *Independence Day* is "definitely one of my favorite books." He adds that he has taught Ford's work to students, although their reaction to *The Sportswriter* depends on whether the reader loves or hates the narrator, since "being inside someone's head for such a long time . . . can be unbearable if it's not someone you like." See Marshall. Both Bascombe and Battle share the habit of regarding their lives in terms of universally experienced life stages. Bascombe describes midlife as the Existence Period, which stretches into the Permanent Period. Battle is similarly adept at containing the messiness of his life with pithy, reductive labels such as "Turbulent Early Years" and "Waning Passions: A Late-Middle Passage" (17).

5 Anker considers, for instance, Frederic Beigbeder's *Windows on the World* (2004); Don DeLillo's *Falling Man* (2007); Jonathan Safran Foer's *Extremely Loud and Incredibly Close* (2005); Colum McCann's *Let the Great World Spin* (2009); Ian Mc-

Ewan's *Saturday* (2005); Joseph O'Neill's *Netherland* (2008); and Jess Walter's *The Zero* (2006), among others.

6 David Roediger cites Louis Adamic's 1942 study, *What's Your Name*, which discussed the motivation that prompted immigrants to "promiscuously" change their "foreign-sounding" names "for the sake of a job" (Roediger 218–219).

7 Such is the conclusion Lauren Berlant similarly draws in her treatise, *Cruel Optimism* (2011), which is "about what happens to fantasies of the good life when the ordinary becomes a landfill for overwhelming and impending crises of life-building and expectation whose sheer volume so threatens what it means to 'have a life' that adjustment seems like an accomplishment" (3).

8 As World War II scholar Christina Jarvis argues in "'If He Comes Home Nervous'" (2009), the rapid rehabilitation and reassimilation of returning veterans "was vital to the continuous operation of America's economic and war machines" (99). Of particular concern were veterans returning with so-called battle fatigue. Jarvis notes that between January 1942 and June 1945 there were approximately 1,000,000 hospital admissions, 1,750,000 Selective Service rejections, and 457,000 discharges for "neuropsychiatric disorders" (99). Jarvis has chronicled the vast body of military pamphlets and advice literature that was meant to help struggling soldiers adapt to civilian life as quickly as possible. The advice ranged from working outdoors to "dumping" one's haunting war memories on a psychiatrist (103), but was univocal in its directive that the returning soldier put the past firmly behind him and get on with his life. In his influential treatise *Veteran Comes Back* (1944), for instance, sociologist Willard Waller allowed that "every veteran is at least mildly shell-shocked" (115), but argued that recovery was a matter of "bringing one's self to accept a little dull job and to marry a woman who is a good ordinary woman and to buy a suit of clothes with two pairs of pants" (129).

9 Waller (234–45) chronicles the government's virtual abandonment of WWI veterans—who were provided the pittance of sixty dollars upon their return—and the scandalous graft and mismanagement associated with the building of veterans' hospitals.

10 As Brodkin argues, while GI benefits were theoretically offered to all returning veterans, "in practice women and black veterans did not get anywhere near their share" (42). Women's Army and Air Force units, for instance, were initially organized as auxiliaries and thus not eligible for military benefits. After that status changed in July 1943, women had to reenlist in order to receive benefits; many women thought they had been demobilized and simply returned home. Those who remained received so little counseling that their access to benefits remained hidden (42). The barriers obstructing black veterans from reaping their rightful GI benefits were even more daunting: though the armed forces were thoroughly segregated throughout World War II, black enlisted men served under white officers and received a disproportionate share of dishonorable dis-

charges, which deprived them of their benefits. Those who did get an honorable discharge were offered low-paid, menial jobs. In terms of taking advantage of the GI Bill's educational benefits, their defacto exclusion from white colleges left only severely overcrowded black colleges as an alternative. See pp. 42–44. George Lipsitz points out that while the FHA and the VA financed more than $120 billion worth of real estate between 1934 and 1962, less than 2 percent of this real estate was available to nonwhite families, and most of this was in segregated areas (6).

11 Never before and never since has the government provided its veterans such benefits. In combination with the Federal Housing Administration's postwar revisions of the 1934 Housing Act, the GI Bill made it possible for white veterans to become the owners of homes with no capital investment and for banks and other investors to underwrite their mortgages with little risk. A powerful private housing lobby, led by William Levitt, was instrumental in convincing Congress that the private industry was capable of providing housing quickly and cheaply. With the aid of Senator McCarthy, Levitt and a powerful lobby comprised of the National Association of Home Builders and the National Association of Real Estate Brokers among others undertook a massive campaign to convince both Congress and the public that public housing was tantamount to socialism, using racism as a fear tactic. One campaign, for instance, asserted that "certain undesirable persons—i.e. Negroes and Mexican-Americans—would be eligible for public housing and would therefore become neighbors of the established residents" (Baxandall and Ewen 94). For its part, the FHA did not merely steer residents to all-white suburbs; it guaranteed racially homogenous communities by way of its lending practices, to wit, the practice of "redlining," a color-coded ratings system that evaluated the risks associated with loans made to specific urban neighborhoods. Those central-city neighborhoods that were racially and ethnically mixed were color-coded red and virtually never received loans (51–54). In addition to the policy of redlining, The FHA also published a technical bulletin entitled "Planning Profitable Neighborhoods," which advised developers on how to concentrate on homogenous markets for housing (Haralovich 75–76). When the Supreme Court ruling in 1948 outlawed racially restrictive covenants, homeowner associations quickly learned to rely on restrictive covenants that targeted specific behaviors in order to exclude people of color and protect their all-important property values. See McKenzie.

12 Lipsitz asserts that whiteness "has a cash value: it accounts for advantages that come to individuals through profits made from housing secured in discriminatory markets; through the unequal educational opportunities available to children of different races; through insider networks that channel employment opportunities to the relatives and friends of those who have profited most from present and past racial discrimination; and especially through intergenerational transfers of inherited wealth that pass on the spoils of discrimination to succeeding generations (vii)."

13 In contrast to Waller's description of a blighted generation of soldiers "haunted by the specter of insecurity" (248), a 1942 advertisement for *Better Homes and Gardens* assured readers that "all the fighting power of the nation" was focused upon securing for soldiers and their families "the one thing they value most: a happy and livable home" which would include "a new and better room for Junior, a den for dad. New furniture for the living room. A glassed in porch" (Baxandall and Ewen 83).

14 *Life's* editors note that there were 15,132 men killed to date, but that the Armed Services lists casualties before it releases names, which could not be published until next of kin were notified (15).

15 Jarvis describes the way that the Office of War Information and the media controlled and manipulated images of the dead to bolster support of the war on the homefront, such as forbidding the publication of photographs of dead soldiers. See Chapter Five of her book, *Male Bodies at War.*

16 See Roediger 208; Matthew Frye Jacobson, who notes that where unions sought to exclude immigrants, big business concerns unsurprisingly lobbied on their behalf (65–66); and Baxandall and Ewen, who outline Levitt's various public relations campaigns against unions, as well as his building practices, which excluded union workers altogether (See especially Chapters Eight and Ten).

17 Paradoxically, if modern appliances were ostensibly designed to make life easier for the woman of the house, the veteran suffering from "combat nerves" was advised to "work outdoors—hard physical work is best" (Jarvis 2009, 110). Therapeutic labor was thus built into the suburban home-owning experience. Levitt, for instance, contractually obligated residents to mow their lawns and enforced it by inspecting properties and billing laggards (Baxandall and Ewen 144). Lawn mowing, bush trimming, and do-it-yourself projects not only functioned as therapy for returning veterans, it limited opportunities for men to gather together in ways that might be politically dangerous (Kelly 6). Levitt reasoned that a homeowner could not be a communist simply because "he has too much to do" (Larabee 84).

18 As Shanken notes, while the traditional memorial had honored sacrifice, the heroics of war, and/or victory, the living memorial "eschewed these associations for a celebration of democracy, community, and 'better living,'" which it promoted by way of recreational facilities (135). Thanks to the Federal Security Agency (FSA), which found in the living memorial a way to advance its agenda, namely, to promote "social and economic security, educational opportunity, and the health of the citizens of the Nation," participation in physical fitness activities became the equivalent of a patriotic act (133).

19 Examples of the comparison between the September 11 attacks and Pearl Harbor are legion. For a sampling of headlines that labeled September 11 "A New Day of Infamy," see *The Archives of Global Change in the 21st Century* (September11news.com).Tom Englehardt asserts that the rush to equate the two events represented an attempt to reclaim what he calls "Victory Culture" (305–307).

20 In his address to Congress immediately after 9/11, President Bush may have reminded Americans that "no one should be singled out for unfair treatment or unkind words because of their ethnic background or religious faith," but his simultaneous assertion that "either you are with us or you are with the terrorists" set the tone for the racism behind the government's practice of indiscriminate racial profiling under the so-called Patriot Act; extraordinary rendition; and the bait-and-switch tactics that justified the Iraqi invasion to the American people. As one U.S. army veteran of the Iraq war describes his experience in the military, "I began to hear new words like 'towel head,' 'camel jockey' and—the most disturbing—'sand nigger.' These words did not initially come from my fellow soldiers, but from my superiors—my platoon sergeant, my company first sergeant, my battalion commander. All the way up the chain of command, viciously racist terms were suddenly acceptable" (Prysner n.p.).

21 At the war's outset, three quarters of Americans supported the invasion of Iraq. See "Public Attitudes Towards the War in Iraq." In contrast, widespread antiwar demonstrations took place across the globe on February 15, 2003, "the largest occurring in Rome, Italy, where a crowd of 3 million gathered to protest against the USA's threat to invade Iraq. Police figures report that millions more demonstrated in nearly 600 cities worldwide: on the same day, 1.3 million rallied in Barcelona, Spain, 1 million participated in a peace march through the streets of London, UK, and 500,00 people in Melbourne and Sydney, Australia, joined the biggest marches since the Vietnam War peace protests" (*Guinness World Records*).

22 Kelly observes that "in Levittown in the Spring of 1991, yellow ribbons and flags were flying in support of the troops in the Persian Gulf and of the president who sent them there. Similarly, throughout the 1960s and 1970s, the postwar suburbs remained apart from the civil unrest taking place in the cities and universities" (6).

23 In addition to his war-like surname and his nickname, The Tank, Hank is also likened to a "fucking Field Marshall Rommel" who gives his workers marching orders (290–291). He is counted as a member of the Greatest Generation (246) and is described as having gone "AWOL" and being "MIA" when he escapes the nursing home (264, 286).

24 Recent critics have followed Ruth Leys in her scathing critique of the moral implications of the theory of transmissible trauma advanced by Cathy Caruth. Amy Hungerford, for instance, extends this critique to suggest the limits of literary and psychoanalytic theories of trauma in general, which, in making trauma "both generic and transmissible," assign to texts themselves "the body of the person and with it the pathos of life and death that belongs to that body" (88). Michael Rothberg has attempted to recuperate the theories advanced by Caruth, Felman, and others by sorting out the conceptual error of conflating "victim" and "traumatized person." He argues that "not all traumatized subjects are vic-

tims, and the fact of being traumatized does not necessarily imply the kind of moral capital that sometimes accrues to it" (232).

25 Daisy's impulsive behavior suggests borderline personality disorder (BPD), which includes symptoms such as excessive spending, risky sexual behavior, substance abuse, insomnia, extreme oscillation between bouts of abject docility and furious rebellion, and suicidal thoughts. See "Borderline Personality Disorder." Herman asserts, however, that BPD is most often a misdiagnosis for posttraumatic stress disorder (PTSD): her own investigation has documented histories of severe childhood trauma in 81 percent of cases of BPD, and she further adds that the relationship between the symptoms associated with BPD and childhood trauma have "now been confirmed in numerous other studies" (125–26).

26 The unbidden recollection of a traumatic event has long been understood to be a staple feature of PTSD. Caruth, for instance, describes Freud's astonishment at the recurring traumatic dreams of World War I veterans suffering "war neuroses," because "it cannot be understood in terms of any wish or unconscious meaning, but is, purely and inexplicably, the literal return of the event against the will of the one it inhabits" ("Trauma and Experience" 5).

27 For behaviors common to domestic abusers, see Herman's discussion of this pattern of behavior, which includes isolating the victim from loved ones and objects of symbolic importance; the use of intermittent rewards; and physical abuse (78–82). The haphazard courses of action in dealing with World War II soldiers suffering from posttraumatic stress disorder might also be said to include instances of shaming, denying compensation, drugging, and bribing. Perhaps the most famous instance of shaming soldiers suffering from "psychoneuroses" is General Patton's infamous slapping and kicking of two hospitalized soldiers. See "Army & Navy—COMMAND: War's Underside." Though Patton was excoriated for his behavior, public opinion still overwhelmingly considered soldiers suffering "psychological breakdown" to be malingerers. Early in the war, "psychoneurotics" were often dishonorably discharged or held in jail until they could be institutionalized (Jarvis 2009, 100), and even the ostensibly enlightened Waller recommended withholding pensions (168–69). After the war, suspicion gave way to grave concern at the perceived threat these returning soldiers posed to economic and domestic order. Military and civilian doctors touted the miraculous properties of sodium pentothal, which allowed patients to "purge" distressing memories and reclaim their manhood (Jarvis 2009, 102–106). Finally, the unprecedented benefits provided by the GI Bill served as an institutional bribe to returning soldiers to leave the past behind them.

28 Cumings's account corroborates the revisionist history uncovered by South Korean historians of these massacres. See Jager.

CHAPTER THREE

1 By all accounts, *The Corrections* was a smashing critical and popular success, winning the National Book Award and selling millions of copies, no doubt only boosted by the public relations debacle that resulted from Franzen's vocal discomfort over the book being selected by Oprah Winfrey for her televised book club, after which she promptly de-selected the book. The controversy also helped launch his reputation for arrogance. Kathleen Fitzpatrick, for instance, reads the Oprah incident as evidence of Franzen's determination to sequester his work from the fiction by women and people of color that Oprah usually features (2).

2 This is the essence of his *Harper's* essay, "Perchance to Dream: In the Age of Images, a Reason to Write Articles," which he later revised under the title "Why Bother?" for his essay collection *How to Be Alone* (2002).

3 Confirming Charles McGrath's declaration that the "suburbs are a state of mind," Franzen asserts that the idea for *Freedom* originated with a voice he heard in his head that belonged to "this discontented suburban mom who had a certain kind of laugh, and a certain kind of sarcasm, and a certain kind of rage" (Grossman 45).

4 For a full discussion of the way that neoliberals infiltrated common-sense thinking, see Harvey, especially Chapter Two, "The Construction of Consent."

5 Lalitha is a representative of what *New York Times* reporter Helene Cooper identified as the "new elite" immediately after President Obama's election. They are "a cohort of the best and the brightest whose advancement was formed, at least in part, by affirmative action policies" that brought minorities to the "institutions that for much of the nation's history have groomed America's leaders." While the election of the nation's first black president is a landmark occasion, as Cooper implies, the mythos of American exceptionalism and the ethos of individualism have been propagated by exceptional individuals. To what extent does this "new elite" merely provide a fresh face for an old guard who has followed E. Digby Baltzell's advice nearly half a century ago to "absorb talented and distinguished members of minority groups into its privileged ranks"? (x).

6 The single-minded focus on one's own children also provided justification for the racism at the heart of so-called White Flight. As Kenneth Jackson explains, the mass migration of blacks from the South that began during World War I, coupled with the 1954 Supreme Court Decision that made school segregation unconstitutional, impelled millions of white families to flee the cities for what they considered the better educational opportunities (as measured by standardized test scores) and a safer social setting to be found in the suburbs (289–290). Jackson caustically asserts that suburban schools "promised relief from the pervasive fear of racial integration and its two presumed fellow travelers—interracial violence and interracial sex" (289–90). See also Massey and Denton; Meyer; and Ellen.

7 In the United States during the 1960s and '70s, the concern over the so-called

population explosion reached a head with the publication of books that Walter likewise read and talks about: Paul Erlich's *The Population Bomb* (1968) and the Club of Rome's *The Limits of Growth* (1972). Ursula Heise discusses the vicissitudes of the debate as well as literary and visual engagements with the issue. See Chapter Two.

8 Kotkin projects these demographics in his study *The Next Hundred Million: America in 2050* (2010).

9 For a discussion of the implications of declining birthrates for developed nations such as France, Italy, and Sweden, see Kramer.

10 The latest projections for population growth, which take into account both birthrates and immigration, are markedly lower than Kotkin originally forecast. In fact, the Census Bureau's new projected population for 2050 is 399.8 million, well below the 439 million that had been projected in 2008. See Cohn.

11 Clearly, Walter taking a punch on Lalitha's behalf would do nothing to change the racist's perspective. Nevertheless, the novel outlines the moral stakes of Walter's behavior in the early description of his wife Patty's rape as a teenager and her subsequent anguish over her parents' determination to remain silent on the matter.

12 Mei Mei Evans articulates the contours of this argument nicely: "Nature is encountered (and subsequently conquered) by a (white) male figure, who then wrests from the confrontation an instatement or reinstatement of his hegemonic identity" (182). See also the Roundtable Discussion in this collection for a discussion of the opposition between environmental justice and mainstream environmentalism (Adamson 15–28).

13 Jeffrey Williams implicitly contradicts the notion that the "new class" of academics ushered in by the postwar expansion of the university were unfazed by petty bourgeois concerns. He argues that over the past sixty years the academic novel has increasingly "grafted with the mid-life crisis novel, the marriage novel, and the professional-work novel to become a prime theater of middle class experience" (562).

CHAPTER FOUR

1 The 2011 ad featuring the gritty rap artist Eminem announced Chrysler's miraculous comeback after being pulled from the brink by the auto bailout of 2008. Against a backdrop of gray-toned images of Detroit, the announcer asks, "What does a town that's been to hell and back know about the finer things in life? It turns out, plenty. You see, it's the hottest fires that make the hardest steel" (Chrysler, "Imported" n.p.).

2 Godfrey Hodgson outlines the myriad arenas in which America lags behind other nations: income inequality, education, health care, our criminal system, etc. See Hodgson's Chapter Five for a summary of these failings.

3 Eastwood himself inadvertently called attention to his advancing age in his odd performance at the Republican convention when he went off script to deliver a rambling, at times incoherent, lecture to an empty chair he pretended was occupied by President Obama.

4 Arguably all of Roth's fiction pertains in its preoccupation with bodily concerns, though certainly *Portnoy's Complaint* (1969) is the most famous of Roth's obsessive explorations of lust. His 1972 novella, *The Breast*, however, might be the oddest: in that work the protagonist David Kepesh, à la Kafka's Gregor Samsa, turns into a female breast. Bodily pain, illness, and death are also preoccupations of Roth's. See *The Anatomy Lesson* (1983) for an extended examination of chronic pain.

5 See note 10, Introduction.

6 Along similar lines, Andrew Hoberek argues that *Goodbye, Columbus* (1959) introduces the figure of the Jewish intellectual as an "organization man with a difference" (90).

7 In the year 2006, for instance, the fitness industry in the United States, as measured by health club memberships and exercise equipment sales, totaled $22.3 billion. This figure, of course, does not include the clothing, diet supplements, exercise videos, etc., that are also part of this industry. See Archer.

8 Combined, 68.8 percent of Americans are either overweight or obese, and that number is rising. See Chou and Kane for an overview of the statistics on weight-related disease such as diabetes, high blood pressure, and heart disease.

9 For a summary of Kennedy's medical problems and a sense of the efforts he and his inner circle went to conceal them from the public, see Robert Dallek's article in the *Atlantic Monthly*. Dallek documents that Kennedy was so hobbled by chronic pain and degenerative bone disease he could barely climb a flight of stairs, and he couldn't put on his own socks. Dallek also writes that "he took steroids for his Addison's disease, pain-killers for his back, antispasmodics for his colitis, antibiotics for urinary-tract infections, antihistamines for allergies and, on at least one occasion, an antipsychotic (though only for two days) for a severe mood change that Jackie Kennedy believed had been brought on by the antihistamines" (n.p.). For a fuller discussion, see Dallek's biography, *An Unfinished Life*.

10 Kennedy was originally 4-F until his father intervened. For a discussion of Kennedy's naval career, the PT-109 disaster, and Joseph Kennedy's efforts to turn the disaster into a public relations opportunity, see Fleming.

11 For a description of the scope of Kennedy's fitness campaign, see "The Federal Government Takes on Physical Fitness" published on the JFK Presidential Library's website, which asserts, "It is not too much to say that the council's fitness programs were a way of encouraging the nation's youth to participate in the 'New Frontier'" (2).

12 For a thorough treatment of the significance of Johnny Appleseed to Roth's engagement with American mythmaking in *American Pastoral*, see Pozorski.

13 The Swede himself is convinced that the "television transmitting the immola-

tion *must* have" been responsible for Merry's radical behavior (153). His conviction dovetails with concerns of critics of the era, who, as Lynn Spigel explains, "also worried about [television's] harmful effects, particularly its dissemination of debased knowledge" and its ability to "reverse good habits of hygiene, nutrition, and decorum, causing physical, mental, and social disorders" (193).

14 As of 2012, a total of 4,804 US and international soldiers have been killed in Iraq and 3,230 U.S. and international soldiers have been killed in Afghanistan. See ICasualities.org. As of June, 2011, an estimated 132,000 civilians have been killed in the wars in Afghanistan and Iraq. See Ackerman.

CHAPTER FIVE

1 A study by Slate.com concluded that of the 545 books reviewed between June 29, 2008, and August 27, 2010, 338 or 62 percent were written by men and 207 or 38 percent were written by women. Of the 101 books that received two reviews in that period, 72 were written by men and 29 were written by women ("Fact-Checking the Franzenfreude").

2 Weiner acknowledges, "I don't write literary fiction—I write books that are entertaining, but are also, I hope, well-constructed and thoughtful and funny and have things to say about men and women and families and children and life in America today. Do I think I should be getting all of the attention that Jonathan "Genius" Franzen gets? Nope. Would I like to be taken at least as seriously as a Jonathan Tropper or a Nick Hornby? Absolutely" (Pinter n.p.).

3 The essay drew more letters than *Harper's* had ever received for one of its articles. One in particular ranted sarcastically that "now that Smiley has ripped the lid off this literature racket, it may be time to scrap the notion of art altogether and replace it with a new paradigm under which the moral standing of each work is evaluated on a daily basis as to how precisely it matches the day's moral fashion" (Fiore 83). This reader and others took Smiley to task for what they saw as her capitulation to political correctness. The aesthetic Smiley advances, however, which advocates for broadly held social responsibility, counteracts an identity politics predicated on the self-interest of individual minorities.

4 John Updike, for instance, perhaps understandably admires the tendency of Tyler's fiction to explore the "fundamental American tension [that] is felt between stasis and movement, between home and escape" in which "the end of traveling is to return," a trajectory that sums up the motion in his Rabbit tetralogy ("Loosened" 121.) But Updike also frets over a "familiar class of Anne Tyler heroines" who are "alarmingly passive in the large curve of their lives—riders on male-generated events" (124).

5 Clinton created a tempest in a teapot when she allowed, "You know, I suppose I could have stayed home and baked cookies and had teas, but what I decided to do was to fulfill my profession, which I entered before my husband was in public

life." Just as infuriating to conservative pundits was her outspokenness on public policy issues and her assertion that she would have a voice in her husband's administration should he win. See "Making Hillary Clinton an Issue."

6 Critics have taken exception to Jen's unfavorable depiction of Evangelical Christians. *Washington Post* critic Ron Charles, for instance, notes:

> Particularly in a novel about tolerating and respecting people's beliefs, it's disappointing to be led down the straight and narrow way toward the holy grail of liberal cliches: the hypocritical Christian, clutching her baby Jesus while spouting a doctrine of hate. Late in the novel Jen inserts a whole chapter—"What Went Wrong"—to explain how someone might fall into such bitter religious fervor, but to the extent it demonizes fundamentalists, it's fundamentally condescending ("Gish Jen's 'World and Town').

I would argue that in the divisive aftermath of 9/11, she is critiquing the notion of any religious rhetoric that foments incendiary "us versus them" thinking—whether Muslim, Christian, or otherwise.

7 Harry's career is, of course, a heavy-handed nod to Don DeLillo's novel *White Noise*, whose protagonist, Jack Gladney, is a professor of Hitler studies. Throughout the novel Harry spots the elusive Don DeLillo in all sorts of odd places—at the hardware store, in the diner, in an elevator, etc.

WORKS CITED

Abraham, Nicolas, and Maria Torok. *The Shell and the Kernel: Renewals of Psychoanalysis*, vol. 1. Nicholas Rand, ed., trans., and intro. Chicago: U of Chicago P, 1994.

Ackerman, Spencer. "Afghanistan, Iraq Wars Killed 132,000, Report Says." *Wired* 29 June 2011. http://www.wired.com/dangerroom/2011/06/afghanistan-iraq-wars-killed-132000-civilians-report-says.

Acs, Gregory. "Downward Mobility from the Middle Class: Waking Up from the American Dream." The Pew Charitable Trust Foundation, September 2011. http://www.pewtrusts.org/uploadedFiles/wwwpewtrustsorg/Reports/Economic_Mobility/Pew_PollProject_Final_SP.pdf.

Adamson, Joni, and Rachel Stein. "Environmental Justice: A Roundtable Discussion with Simon Ortiz, Teresa Leal, Devon Pena, and Terrell Dixon." *Environmental Justice Reader: Politics, Poetics, and Pedagogy*. Tucson: U of Arizona P, 2002.

"The American Purpose." *Life* 5 July 1943: 39. Editorial.

Anderson, Sam. "The Precisionist." *New York Magazine* 12 August 2010. http://nymag.com/arts/books/reviews/67497.

Anker, Elizabeth S. "Allegories of Falling and the 9/11 Novel." *American Literary History* 23:3 (Fall 2011): 463–482.

Archer, Sally. "Fitness and Wellness Intertwine: A Major Industry Rises." *Idea Health and Fitness Association*. July 2007. http://www.ideafit.com/fitness-library/fitness-and-wellness-intertwine-major-industry-rises.

The Archives of Global Change in the 21st Century (September11news.com). http://www.september11news.com/USANewspapers.htm.

"Army & Navy—COMMAND: War's Underside." *Time* 29 November 1943. http://www.time.com/time/magazine/article/0,9171,791151-2,00.html.

Aubry, Timothy. "Cheever and the Management of Middlebrow Misery." *Iowa Journal of Cultural Studies* 3 (Fall 2003). http://www.uiowa.edu/~ijcs/suburbia/aubry.htm.

———. *Reading as Therapy: What Contemporary Fiction Does for Middle Class Americans*. Iowa City: U of Iowa P, 2011.

Bachner, Sally. *The Prestige of Violence: American Fiction 1962–2007*. Athens: U of Georgia P, 2011.

Baltzell, E. Digby. *The Protestant Establishment: Aristocracy and Caste in America*. 1964. New Haven, CT: Yale UP, 1987.

Bangs, Jean Murray. "How American Is Your Way of Living?" *House Beautiful* September 1950: 80+.

Barrett, James R., and Roediger, David. "Inbetween Peoples: Race, Nationality and the 'New Immigrant' Working Class." *Journal of American Ethnic History* 16:3 (Spring 1997): 3–34.

Baumgartner, M. P. *The Moral Order of a Suburb*. New York: Oxford UP, 1988.

Baxandall, Rosalyn, and Elizabeth Ewen. *Picture Windows: How the Suburbs Happened*. New York: Basic Books, 2000.

Baym, Nina. "Melodramas of Beset Manhood: How Theories of American Fiction Exclude Women Authors." *American Quarterly* 33:2 (Summer 1981): 123–139.

Beauregard, Robert A. *When America Became Suburban*. Minneapolis: U of Minnesota P, 2006.

Beck, Ulrich. *World Risk Society*. Cambridge: Polity Press, 1999.

Beers, David. "Irony is Dead! Long Live Irony!" *Salon* 25 September 2001. http://www.salon.com/2001/09/25/irony_lives.

Beigbeder, Frederic. *Windows on the World*. New York: Hyperion, 2004.

Bellah, Robert N., et. al. *Habits of the Heart: Individualism and Commitment in American Life*. 1985. Updated ed. Berkeley: U of California P, 1996.

Bellamy, Joe David. "A Downpour of Literary Republicanism." *Mississippi Review* 14:1/2 (Winter 1985): 31–39.

Belson, Ken, and Jill P. Capuzzo. "Town Rethinks Laws Against Illegal Immigrants." *New York Times* 26 September 2007. http://www.nytimes.com/2007/09/26/nyregion/26riverside.html?scp=3&sq=belson%20riverside%20new%20jersey&st=cse.

Berger, James. *After the End: Representations of Post-Apocalypse*. Minneapolis: U of Minnesota P, 1999.

———. "There's No Backhand to This." In *Trauma at Home*. Judith Greenberg, ed. Lincoln: U of Nebraska P, 2003: 52–59.

Berlant, Lauren. *The Queen of America Goes to Washington City: Essays on Sex and Citizenship*. Durham, NC: Duke UP, 1997.

———. *Cruel Optimism*. Durham, NC: Duke UP, 2011.

Beuka, Robert. *SuburbiaNation: Reading Suburban Landscape in Recent American Fiction and Film*. New York: Palgrave Macmillan, 2004.

Beveridge, Andrew. "9/11/01-02: A Demographic Portrait of the Victims in 10048." *Gotham Gazette*. http://www.gothamgazette.com/demographics/91102.shtml.

Blakely, Edward, and Snyder, Gail. *Fortress America: Gated Communities in the United States*. Washington, DC: Brookings Institution Press, 1999.

Blythe, Will. "Men Behaving Oddly." *The New York Times Book Review* 19 July 2009: 13.

Bone, Martyn. "The Postsouthern Sense of Place in Walker Percy's *The Moviegoer* and Richard Ford's *The Sportswriter*." *Critical Survey* 12:1 (2000): 64–81.

———. "New Jersey Real Estate and the Postsouthern 'Sense of Place': Richard Ford's *Independence Day.*" *American Studies in Scandinavia* 33:2 (2001): 105–119.

"Borderline Personality Disorder." National Institute of Mental Health. http://www.nimh.nih.gov/health/topics/borderline-personality-disorder/index.shtml

Boyle, T. Coraghessan. *The Tortilla Curtain*. New York: Viking, 1995.

Boym, Svetlana. *The Future of Nostalgia*. New York: Basic Books, 2001.

Brinkley, Douglas. *The Great Deluge*. New York: William Morrow, 2006.

Brodkin, Karen. *How Jews Became White Folks—And What That Says About Race in America*. New Brunswick, NJ: Rutgers UP, 1999.

Brodsky, Robert. "Pain, Grief Still Raw 10 Years After 9/11." *Newsday* 7 September 2011. http://www.newsday.com/911-anniversary/pain-grief-still-raw-10-years-after-9-11-1.3152775.

Burns, James Macgregor, and Georgia Sorensen. *Dead Center: Clinton-Gore Leadership and the Perils of Moderation*. New York: Scribner, 1999.

Bury, Chris. "Clint Eastwood's Super Bowl Chrysler Ad Stirs Political Waters." *ABC News*. http://abcnews.go.com/blogs/business/2012/02/clint-eastwoods-chrysler-ad-stirs-political-waters.

Bush, George W. "Address to Joint Session of Congress." 20 September 2001. edition.cnn.com/2001/US/09/20/gen.bush.transcript.

Carroll, Hamilton. *Affirmative Reaction: New Formations of White Masculinity*. Durham, NC: Duke UP, 2011.

Caruth, Cathy. "Trauma and Experience: Introduction." In *Trauma: Explorations in Memory*. Cathy Caruth, ed. Baltimore: Johns Hopkins UP, 1995: 3–12.

———. *Unclaimed Experience: Trauma, Narrative, and History*. Baltimore: Johns Hopkins UP, 1996.

Caserio, Robert. "The Antisocial Thesis in Queer Theory." *PMLA* 121 (3) May 2006: 819–21.

Cave, Damien. "Experts Say 'Hero Syndrome' Not Common Among Police." *The New York Times*, August 2, 2004. http://www.nytimes.com/2004/08/02/nyregion/experts-say-hero-syndrome-not-common-among-police.html.

Cazdyn, Eric. *The Already Dead: The New Time of Politics, Culture, and Illness*. Durham, NC: Duke UP, 2012.

Chang, Yoonmee. *Writing the Ghetto: Authorship and the Asian Ethnic Enclave*. New Brunswick, NJ: Rutgers UP, 2011.

Charles, Ron. "Jonathan Franzen's New Novel, *Freedom*." *Washington Post* 25 August 2010. http://www.washingtonpost.com/wp-dyn/content/article/2010/08/24/AR2010082405326.html.

———. "Gish Jen's 'World and Town.'" *Washington Post* 10 November 2010. http://www.washingtonpost.com/wp-dyn/content/article/2010/11/09/AR2010110905603.html.

Cheever, John. *The Stories of John Cheever*. New York: Knopf, 1978.

Chen, David W., and Steven Greenhouse. "A Nation Challenged: New Jersey; As Anthrax Cases Mount, the Tranquil Rhythms of Suburban Havens Are Disrupted." *The New York Times* 1 November 2001. http://www.nytimes.com/2001/11/01/nyregion/nation-challenged-new-jersey-anthrax-cases-mount-tranquil-rhythms-suburban.html?scp=10&sq=anthrax%20princeton%20new%jersey&st=cse&pagewanted=1.

"Children of the Cul-de-sac." Roundtable Discussion with Alan Ball, Gregory Crewdson, A. M. Homes, Tamara Jenkins, Eric Mendelsohn, and David Schisgall. *The New York Times Magazine* 9 April 2000: 82–88.

Chou, Joey, and Jason Kane. "Obesity in America: By the Numbers." *PBS Newshour* 8 May 2012. http://www.pbs.org/newshour/rundown/2012/05/obesity-in-america-by-the-numbers-1.html.

Chrysler. "Imported from Detroit." 2011. Advertisement. http://www.youtube.com/watch?v=SKL254Y_jtc.

Chrysler. "It's Halftime in America." 2012. Advertisement. http://www.youtube.com/watch?v=tFAiqxm1FDA.

"Clint Eastwood Chrysler Ad I, II, II." *Saturday Night Live*, NBC, 11 February 2012.

Clover, Joshua. "Suburban Scrawl." *Village Voice* 2–8 June 1999. http://www.villagevoice.com/books/9922,clover,6162,10.html.

Cohen, Lizabeth. *A Consumers' Republic: The Politics of Mass Consumption in Postwar America*. New York: Random House, 2003.

Cohen, Samuel. *After the End of History: American Fiction in the 1990s*. Iowa City: U of Iowa P, 2009.

Cohn, D'Vera. "Census Bureau Lowers U.S. Growth Forecast, Mainly Due to Reduced Immigration and Births." *Pew Research Social & Demographic Trends* 14 December 2012. http://www.pewsocialtrends.org/2012/12/14/census-bureau-lowers-u-s-growth-forecast-mainly-due-to-reduced-immigration-and-births.

Cole, Teju. "The White Savior Industrial Complex." *The Atlantic* 21 March 2012. http://www.theatlantic.com/international/archive/2012/03/the-white-savior-industrial-complex/254843.

The Company Men. Dir. John Wells. The Weinstein Company, 2010. Film.

Connell, R. W. "Politics of Changing Men." *Australian Humanities Review*. http://www.australianhumanitiesreview.org/archive/Issue-Dec-1996/connell.html.

Cooper, Helene. "Meet the New Elite: Not Like the Old." *The New York Times* 25 July 2009. http://www.nytimes.com/2009/07/26/weekinreview/26cooper.html.

Corner, Martin. "Opening the Literal: Spirituality in Updike and Ford." In *Biblical Religion and the Novel 1700–2000*. Mark Knight and Thomas Woodman, eds and introd. Burlington, VT: Ashgate, 2006: 137–151.

Cronon, William. "The Trouble With Wilderness; or, Getting Back to the Wrong Nature." In *Uncommon Ground: Rethinking the Human Place in Nature*. William Cronon, ed. New York: Norton, 1995: 69–90.

Cumings, Bruce. *The Korean War: A History*. New York: Modern Library, 2010.

Dallek, Lance, and Len Kravitz. "The History of Fitness." http://www.ideafit.com/fitness-library/the-history-of-fitness.

Dallek, Robert. "The Medical Ordeals of JFK." *Atlantic Monthly* December 2002. http://www.theatlantic.com/magazine/archive/2002/12/the-medical-ordeals-of-jfk/305572.

———. *An Unfinished Life: John F. Kennedy, 1917–1963*. New York: Little, Brown and Company, 2003.

Darling, Janet. "Living Memorials." *House Beautiful* January 1945: 42.

Dean, Tim. "An Impossible Embrace: Queerness, Futurity, and the Death Drive." In *A Time For Humanities: Futurity and the Limits of Autonomy*. James J. Bono, Tim Dean, and Ewa Plonowska Ziarek, eds. New York: Fordham UP, 2008: 122–140.

DeLillo, Don. "In the Ruins of the Future." *Harper's Magazine* December 2001: 33–40.

———. *Falling Man*. New York: Scribner, 2007.

Di Chiro, Giovanna. "Nature as Community: The Convergence of Environment and Social Justice." In *Uncommon Ground: Rethinking the Human Place in Nature*. William Cronon, ed. New York: Norton, 1995: 298–320.

Duffy, Brian. *Morality, Identity, and Narrative in the Fiction of Richard Ford*. Amsterdam, Netherlands: Rodopi, 2008.

Edelman, Lee. *No Future: Queer Theory and the Death Drive*. Durham, NC: Duke UP, 2005.

Edgerton, Gary. "Falling Man and Mad Men." *In media res: A Media Commons Project*. 23 April 2009. http://mediacommons.futureofthebook.org/imr/2009/04/19/falling-man-and-mad-men-154.

Ellen, Ingrid Gould. *Sharing America's Neighborhoods: The Prospects for Stable Racial Integration*. Cambridge, MA: Harvard UP, 2001.

Englehardt, Tom. *The End of Victory Culture: Cold War America and the Disillusioning of a Generation* (revised, with new preface and afterword). Amherst: U of Massachusetts P, 2007.

Erian, Alicia. *Towelhead*. New York: Simon and Schuster, 2005.

Espach, Allison. *The Adults*. New York: Scribner, 2011.

Eugenides, Jeffrey. *The Virgin Suicides*. New York: Farrar, Straus and Giroux 1993.

Evans, Mei Mei. "'Nature' and Environmental Justice." In *The Environmental Justice Reader: Politics, Poetics, and Pedagogy*. Joni Adamson, Mei Mei Evans, and Rachel Stein, eds. Tucson: U of Arizona P, 2002: 181–193.

"Fact-Checking the Franzenfreude: Is the New York Times' Book Section Really a Boys' Club?" *Slate.com* 2 September 2010. http://www.slate.com/articles/double_x/doublex/2010/09/factchecking_the_franzenfreude.single.html.

"The Federal Government Takes on Physical Fitness." *The John F. Kennedy Presidential Library and Museum*. http://www.jfklibrary.org/JFK/JFK-in-History/Physical-Fitness.aspx?p=2.

Felman, Shoshana, and Dori Laub. *Testimony: Crises of Witnessing in Literature, Psychoanalysis, and History*. London: Routledge, 1991.

Ferris, Joshua. *The Unnamed*. New York: Reagan Arthur, 2010.

Fiore, Robert. Letter to the Editor. *Harper's Magazine* April 1996: 83.

Fitzpatrick, Kathleen. *The Anxiety of Obsolescence: The American Novel in the Age of Television*. Nashville: Vanderbilt UP, 2006.

Fleming, Thomas. "John F. Kennedy's PT-109 Disaster." *Military History Quarterly* 8 February 2011. http://www.historynet.com/pt-109-disaster.htm.

Folks, Jeffrey. "The Risks of Membership: Richard Ford's 'The Sportswriter.'" *Mississippi Quarterly* 52:1 (Winter 1998–1999): 73–88.

Ford, Richard. *The Sportswriter*. New York: Vintage, 1986.

———. *Independence Day*. New York: Knopf, 1995.

———. "The Worry Trap." *The New York Times* 1 November 2001: A29.

———. "A City Beyond the Reach of Empathy." *The New York Times* 4 September 2005. http://www.nytimes.com/2005/09/04/opinion/04ford.html?scp=1&sq=richard%20ford%20empathy&st=cse.

———. *The Lay of the Land*. New York: Knopf, 2006.

———. "How Does Being an American Inform What I Write?" *Writers on America*. Washington, DC: Office of International Programs, US Department of State, 2008. iipdigital.usembassy.gov/st/english/publication/2011/05/20110503155306suo.251592.html#axzz2eQQNHjAl.

———. "Nobody's Everyman." *Bookforum* April/May 2009. http://www.bookforum.com/inprint/016_01/3512.

Foser, Jamison. "Why Did Republicans Stop Acknowledging the Economic Importance of Demand?" *Political Correction.org*. http://politicalcorrection.org/print/blog/201109020008.

Frankenberg, Ruth. *White Women, Race Matters: The Social Construction of Whiteness*. London: Routledge, 1994.

Franzen, Jonathan. "Perchance to Dream: In the Age of Images, a Reason to Write Novels." *Harper's Magazine* April 1996: 35–54.

———. *The Corrections*. New York: Farrar, Straus and Giroux, 2001.

———. *How to Be Alone*. New York: Farrar, Straus and Giroux, 2002.

———. *Freedom*. New York: Farrar, Straus and Giroux, 2010.

———. "A Rooting Interest: Edith Wharton and the Problem of Sympathy." *The New Yorker* 13 February 2012: 60–65.

Freedman, Samuel. "Suburbia Outgrows Its Image in the Arts." *The New York Times* 28 February 1999. http://www.nytimes.com/1999/02/28/arts/suburbia-outgrows-its-image-in-the-arts.html?pagewanted=all&src=pm.

Friedan, Betty. *The Feminine Mystique*. 1963. New York: Laurel Books, 1983.

Fukuyama, Francis. "The End of History?" *The National Interest*, Summer 1989: 3-18.

———. *The End of History and the Last Man*. New York: Free Press, 1992.

Gans, Herbert J. *The Levittowners: Ways of Life and Politics in a New Suburban Community*. New York: Columbia UP, 1967.

Garland-Thomson, Rosemarie. *Extraordinary Bodies: Figuring Disability in American Culture and Literature*. New York: Columbia UP, 1997.

Gates, David. *Jernigan*. New York: Knopf, 1991.

———. *Preston Falls*. New York: Knopf, 1998.

Gilbert, Susan. "Private Lives and Public Issues: Anne Tyler's Prize-Winning Novels." In *The Fiction of Anne Tyler*. C. Ralph Stephens, ed. Jackson: U of Mississippi P, 1990: 136–146.

Gilman, Richard. "The Dante of Suburbia." In *The Critical Response to John Cheever*. Francis J. Bosha, ed. Westport, Greenwood Press., 1993: 175.

Giuliani, Rudy. Speech to the United Nations, 1 October 2001. http://www.americanrhetoric.com/speeches/rudygiuliani911unitednations.htm.

Goffman, Erving. *Stigma: Notes on the Management of Spoiled Identity*. New York: Prentice Hall, 1963.

Gram, Margaret Hunt. "Franzen, Fiction, and the Aggregate." Paper delivered at the MLA Annual Conference. Seattle, Washington. 7 January 2012.

Gran Torino. Dir. Clint Eastwood. Warner Bros., 2008. Film.

Gray, Richard. *After the Fall: American Literature Since 9/11*. West Sussex, UK: Wiley Blackwell, 2011.

Grossman, Lev. "Jonathan Franzen. The Wide Shot." *Time* 23 August 2010: 42–48.

Guinn, Matthew. "Into the Suburbs: Richard Ford's Sportswriter Novels and the Place of Southern Fiction." In *South to a New Place*, Suzanne W. Jones and Sharon Monteith, eds. Baton Rouge: Louisiana State UP, 2002: 196–207.

Guinness World Records. http://web.archive.org/web/20040904214302. http://www.guinnessworldrecords.com/content_pages/record.asp?recordid=54365.

Gullette, Margaret Morganroth. *Safe at Last in the Middle Years: The Invention of the Midlife Progress Novel*. Berkeley: U of California P, 1988.

Halberstam, Judith. *In a Queer Time and Place: Transgender Bodies, Subcultural Lives*. New York: NYU Press, 2005.

———. *The Queer Art of Failure*. Durham, NC: Duke UP, 2011.

Hallberg, Garth Risk. "Why Write Novels at All?" *The New York Times* 13 January 2012. http://www.nytimes.com/2012/01/15/magazine/why-write-novels-at-all.html?pagewanted=all.

Haralovich, Mary Beth. "Sitcoms and Suburbs: Positioning the 1950s Homemaker." In *Critiquing the Sitcom*, Joanne Morreale, ed. Syracuse: Syracuse UP, 2003: 69–85.

Haraway, Donna. *Simians, Cyborgs, and Women: The Reinvention of Nature*. New York: Routledge, 1991.

Harvey, David. *A Brief History of Neoliberalism*. Oxford: Oxford UP, 2005.

Hayden, Dolores. *Building Suburbia: Green Fields and Urban Growth 1820–2000*. New York: Pantheon, 2003.

Hayes, Christopher. *Twilight of the Elites: America After Meritocracy*. New York: Crown Publisher, 2012.

Heise, Ursula. *Sense of Place and Sense of Planet: The Environmental Imagination of the Global*. London: Oxford UP, 2010.

Henry, Derrick, and Janet Roberts. "Long Island Foreclosures Rise, With No End in Sight." *The New York Times* 13 May 2009. http://www.nytimes.com/2009/05/17/nyregion/long-island/17mortli.html?pagewanted=all.

Herberg, Will. *Protestant-Catholic-Jew: An Essay in American Religious Sociology*. 1955. Chicago: U of Chicago P, 1983.

Herman, Judith. *Trauma and Recovery: The Aftermath of Violence from Political Terror to Domestic Abuse*. New York: Basic Books, 1997.

Hoberek, Andrew. *The Twilight of the Middle Class: Post-World War II American Fiction and White Collar Work*. Princeton, NJ: Princeton UP, 2005.

Hobson, Fred. "The Sportswriter: Post-Faulkner, Post-Southern?" In *Perspectives on Richard Ford*. Huey Guargliardo, ed. Jackson: UP of Mississippi, 2000: 83–96.

Hodgson, Godfrey. *The Myth of American Exceptionalism*. New Haven, CT: Yale UP, 2010.

Homans, John. "Soft *Aloft*." *New York Magazine* 8 March 2004. http://nymag.com/nymetro/arts/books/reviews/n_9942.

Homes, A. M. *Music for Torching*. New York: Weisbach Morrow, 1999.

———. *May We Be Forgiven*. New York: Viking, 2012.

Howe, Irving. "This Age of Conformity." *Partisan Review* 21:1 (Winter 1954): 7–33.

———. "Realities and Fictions." *Partisan Review* 26:1 (Winter 1959): 130–31.

Hungerford, Amy. "Memorizing Memory." *Yale Journal of Criticism* 1:14 (Spring 2001): 67–92.

Hutchinson, Colin. "Jonathan Franzen and the Politics of Disengagement." *Critique: Studies in Contemporary Fiction* 50:2 (Winter 2009): 191–207.

Hutner, Gordon. *What America Read: Taste, Class, and the Novel: 1920–1960*. Chapel Hill: U North Carolina P, 2008.

It's a Wonderful Life. Dir. Frank Capra. RKO Radio Pictures, 1946. Film.

"Jack Kennedy Practices the Fitness That He Preaches." *Sports Illustrated* 26 December 1960. http://sportsillustrated.cnn.com/vault/article/magazine/MAG1134751/index.htm.

Jackson, Kenneth. *Crabgrass Frontier: The Suburbanization of the United States*. New York: Oxford UP, 1985.

Jacobson, Kristin. *Neodomestic American Fiction*. Columbus: Ohio State UP, 2010.

Jacobson, Matthew Frye. *Whiteness of a Different Color: European Immigrants and the Alchemy of Race*. Cambridge, MA: Harvard UP, 1999.

Jager, Sheila Miyoshi. "Politics of Anti-Americanism in South Korea." *Asia Times Online* 5 August 2005. http://www.atimes.com/atimes/Korea/GH05Dg03.html.

Jaggi, Maya. "Flight Checks." *The Guardian* 2 July 2004. http://www.guardian.co.uk/books/2004/jul/03/featuresreviews.guardianreview17.

Jarvis, Christina. *The Male Body at War*. Dekalb: Northern Illinois UP, 2004.

———. "'If He Comes Home Nervous': U. S. World War II Neuropsychiatric Casualties and Postwar Masculinities." *The Journal of Men's Studies* 17:2 (Spring 2009): 97–115.

Jen, Gish. *Mona in the Promised Land.* New York: Knopf, 1996.

———. *World and Town.* New York: Knopf, 2010.

Jerng, Mark C. "Nowhere in Particular: Perceiving Race, Chang-rae Lee's *Aloft*, and the Question of Asian American Literature." *MFS* 56:1 (Spring 2010): 183–204.

Johnson, Philip. "War Monuments: What Aesthetic Price Glory?" *Art News* 44 (September 1945): 9+.

Jones, Paul Christian. "A Re-Awakening: Anne Tyler's Postfeminist Edna Pontellier in *Ladder of Years.*" *Critique* 44:3 (Spring 2003): 271–283.

Junod, Tom. "The Falling Man." *Esquire* September 2003. http://www.esquire.com/features/ESQ0903-SEP_FALLINGMAN.

———. "Falling (Mad) Man." *Esquire* 30 January 2012. http://www.esquire.com/the-side/feature/falling-mad-man-6648672.

Jurca, Catherine. *White Diaspora: The Suburb and the Twentieth-Century American Novel.* Princeton, NJ: Princeton UP, 2001.

Kakutani, Michiko. "A Family Portrait as Metaphor for the 90's." *The New York Times* 4 September 2001. http://www.nytimes.com/2001/09/04/books/books-of-the-times-a-family-portrait-as-metaphor-for-the-90-s.html.

———. "The Age of Irony Isn't Over After All; Assertions of Cynicism's Demise Belie History." *The New York Times* 9 October 2001. http://www.nytimes.com/2001/10/09/arts/critic-s-notebook-age-irony-isn-t-over-after-all-assertions-cynicism-s-demise.html?ref=michikokakutani.

———. "Late Midlife Crisis, Prompted by a Violent Encounter." *The New York Times* 4 January 2010. http://www.nytimes.com/2010/01/05/books/05book.html.

Kelly, Barbara M. "The Houses of Levittown in the Context of Postwar American Culture." In *Preserving the Recent Past.* Deborah Slaton and Rebecca A. Schiffer, eds. Washington, DC: Historic Preservation Education Foundation, 1995. http://www.nps.gov/history/nr/publications/bulletins/suburbs/Kelly.pdf.

Kennedy, John F. "The New Frontier." Democratic National Convention Acceptance Speech, delivered 15 July 1960. http://www.americanrhetoric.com/speeches/jfk1960dnc.htm.

———. "The Soft American." *Sports Illustrated* 26 December 1960. http://sportsillustrated.cnn.com/vault/article/magazine/MAG1134750/index.htm.

———. "The Vigor We Need." *Sports Illustrated* 16 July 1962. http://sportsillustrated.cnn.com/vault/article/magazine/MAG1074003/2/index.htm.

Kirp, David L., John P. Dwyer, and Larry A. Rosenthal. *Our Town: Race, Housing, and the Soul of Suburbia.* New Brunswick, NJ: Rutgers UP, 1996.

Kotkin, Joel. "The Kids Will Be Alright." *Wall Street Journal* 23 January 2010. http://online.wsj.com/article/SB10001424052748704509704575018990188917592.html.

———. *The Next Hundred Million: America in 2050* (New York: Penguin, 2010).

Kneebone, Elizabeth. "The Suburbanization of American Poverty." The Brookings Institute Metropolitan Series No. 2, 19 October 2009. http://www.brookings.edu/opinions/2009/1019_poverty_kneebone.aspx.

Krist, Gary. "Burning Down the House." *The New York Times* 30 May 1999. http://www.nytimes.com/1999/05/30/books/burning-down-the-house.html?pagewanted=all&src=pm.

Krugman, Paul. "The Mensch Gap." *The New York Times* 20 February 2006: A31. http://query.nytimes.com/gst/fullpage.html?res=9504E0DC113EF933A15751C0A9609C8B63.

Larabee, Eric. "The Six Thousand Houses That Levitt Built." *Harper's* September 1948: 79–88.

Laub, Dori. "Truth and Testimony: The Process and the Struggle." In *Trauma: Explorations in Memory*. Cathy Caruth, ed. Baltimore: Johns Hopkins UP, 1995: 61–75.

———. "Not knowing is an active process of destruction. Why the testimonial procedure is of so much importance." *Trauma Research Newsletter 1*, Hamburg Institute for Social Research, July 2000. TraumaResearch.net/focus1/laub.htm.

Lazarus, David. "This Way, Consumers All. To The Cash Register." *San Francisco Chronicle* 5 November 2005. http://www.sfgate.com/business/article/This-way-consumers-all-to-the-cash-register-2593375.php.

Lee, Chang-rae. *Native Speaker*. New York: Riverhead, 1996.

———. *A Gesture Life*. New York: Riverhead, 1999.

———. *Aloft*. New York: Riverhead, 2004.

Lee, Don, "About Richard Ford: A Profile." *Ploughshares* Fall 1996. http://www.pshares.org/read/article-detail.cfm?intArticleID=4087.

Lee Rubber and Tire Company. Advertisement. *Fortune* 30 (August 1944).

Leonhardt, David. "Income Inequality." *The New York Times* 21 August 2009. http://topics.nytimes.com/top/reference/timestopics/subjects/i/income/income_inequality/index.html?scp=9&sq=leonhardt&st=cse.

Lewis, Sinclair. *Babbitt*. 1922. New York: Penguin, 1996.

Lipsitz, George. *The Possessive Investment in Whiteness: How White People Profit From Identity Politics*. Philadelphia: Temple UP, 1998.

Luhby, Tami. "Poverty Pervades the Suburbs." *CNN Money* 23 September 2011. http://money.cnn.com/2011/09/23/news/economy/poverty_suburbs/index.htm.

Majeski, Sophie. "Richard Ford: The Salon Interview." 1996. http://www.salon.com/1996/07/07/interview_18.

"Making Hillary Clinton an Issue." *Nightline*. Jackie Judd, correspondent. Ted Koppel, anchor. 26 March 1992. Transcript. http://www.pbs.org/wgbh/pages/frontline/shows/clinton/etc/03261992.html.

Marshall, John. "Chang-rae Lee: Nice Guy Triumphant." *The Seattle Post Intelligencer*. 17 March 2004. http://www.seattlepi.com/ae/books/article/Chang-rae-Lee-Nice-guy-triumphant-1139801.php

Massey, Douglas S., and Nancy A. Denton. *American Apartheid: Segregation and the Making of the Underclass*. Cambridge, MA: Harvard UP, 1993.

Mather, Mark. "Fact Sheet: The Decline in U.S. Fertility." *World Population Data Sheet 2012*. Population Reference Bureau. http://www.prb.org/Publications/Datasheets/2012/world-population-data-sheet/fact-sheet-us-population.aspx.

McCarthy, Cormac. *The Road*. New York: Knopf, 2006.

McGirr, Lisa. "The New Suburban Poverty." *The New York Times* 19 March 2012. http://campaignstops.blogs.nytimes.com/2012/03/19/the-new-suburban-poverty.

McGrath, Charles. "Heading Home to Adultery and Angst." *The New York Times* 1 April 2004: E1+.

McGurl, Mark. "Philip Roth's Modest Phase." Paper delivered at the MLA Annual Conference. Seattle, WA. Saturday, 7 January 2012.

McKenzie, Evan. *Privatopia: Homeowner Associations and the Rise of Residential Private Government*. New Haven, CT: Yale UP, 1996.

Meyer, Stephen Grant. *As Long As They Don't Move Next Door: Segregation and Racial Conflict in American Neighborhoods*. New York: Rowman and Littlefield, 2000.

Michaels, Marguerite. "Anne Tyler: Writer 8:05 to 3:30." In *Critical Essays on Anne Tyler*. Anne Petry, ed. New York: G. K. Hall & Co., 1992: 40–44.

Moody, Rick. *The Ice Storm*. New York: Little Brown and Company, 1994.

Mordock, Deroy. "Giuliani's Finest Hour." *National Review* 14 September 2001. http://www.nationalreview.com/articles/205017/giulianis-finest-hour/deroy-murdock.

Morrison, Toni. *Playing in the Dark: Whiteness and the Literary Imagination*. Cambridge, MA: Harvard UP, 1992.

Mumford, Lewis. "Monuments and Memorials." *Good Housekeeping* January 1945: 17+.

Murphy, Bernice M. *The Suburban Gothic in American Popular Culture*. New York: Palgrave Macmillan, 2009.

Murphy, Robert. *The Body Silent*. New York: Henry Holt and Company, 1987.

Nelson, Dana. *National Manhood: Capitalist Citizenship and the Imagined Fraternity of White Men*. Durham, NC: Duke UP, 1998.

Nystrom, Derek. "Haut-Bourgeois Precarity in Boston: The Company Men." *Post45* 24 January 2013. http://post45.research.yale.edu/2013/01/haut-bourgeois-precarity-in-boston-the-company-men.

Ohmann, Richard. "The Shaping of a Canon: U.S. Fiction, 1960–1975." *Critical Inquiry* 10:1 (September 1983): 199–223.

"Oprah's Book Club Announcement: *Freedom* by Franzen." 17 September 2010. http://www.oprah.com/oprahshow/Oprahs-Book-Club-Announcement-Video.

Perrotta, Tom. *Little Children*. New York: St. Martin's, 2004.

Petry, Alice Hall. *Understanding Anne Tyler*. Columbia: U of South Carolina P, 1990.

———. "Tyler and Feminism." In *Anne Tyler as Novelist*. Dale Salwak, ed. Iowa City: U of Iowa P, 1994: 33–42.

Peyser, Mark. "Worst Predictions #6: Graydon Carter Proclaims the End of Irony." *Newsweek* 2010. http://2010.newsweek.com/top-10/worst-predictions/graydon-carter.html.

Picoult, Jodi. "NYT raved about Franzen's new book. Is anyone shocked? Would love to see the NYT rave about authors who aren't white male literary darlings." 16 August 2010, 5:26 a.m. Tweet.

Pinter, Jason. "Jodi Picoult and Jennifer Weiner Speak Out on Franzen Feud: Huff-Post Exclusive." *HuffPost Books*. 26 August 2010. http://www.huffingtonpost.com/jason-pinter/jodi-picoult-jennifer-weiner-franzen_b_693143.html.

Posnock, Ross. "All's Well That Ends." *Raritan: A Quarterly Review* 1 June 2006: 51–63.

Pozorski, Aimee. *Roth and Trauma: The Problem of History in the Later Works (1995–2010)*. London: Continuum, 2011.

Prashad, Vijay. *The Karma of Brown Folk*. Minneapolis: U of Minnesota P, 2000.

Prysner, Michael. "Iraq Veteran: Racism and U. S. War." From the Michael Moore Website. 26 December 2009. http://www.bibliotecapleyades.net/sociopolitica/sociopol_waronterror29.htm

"Public Attitudes Toward the War in Iraq, 2003-2008." *Pew Research Center* 19 March 2008. http://www.pewresearch.org/2008/03/19/public-attitudes-toward-the-war-in-iraq-20032008/

Puchner, Eric. *Model Home*. New York: Scribner, 2010.

Putnam, Robert. *Bowling Alone: The Collapse and Revival of American Community*. New York: Simon and Schuster, 2000.

Randall, Eric. "'The Death of Irony' and its Many Reincarnations." *The Atlantic Wire* 9 September 2011. http://www.theatlanticwire.com/national/2011/09/death-irony-and-its-many-reincarnations/42298.

Reich, Robert. "Secession of the Successful." *The New York Times Magazine* 20 January 1991: 42+.

Rich, Frank. "The Way We Live Now: 9–30–01: Close Reading: Elements of War; The Father Figure." *The New York Times* 30 September 2001. http://www.nytimes.com/2001/09/30/magazine/the-way-we-live-now-9-30-01-close-reading-elements-of-war-the-father-figure.html.

Riesman, David. *The Lonely Crowd*. New Haven, CT: Yale UP, 1950.

Roberts, Sam. "White Flight Has Reversed, Census Finds." *The New York Times* 22 September 2008. http://www.nytimes.com/2008/09/23/nyregion/23census.html.

Robbins, Bruce. "The Worlding of the American Novel." In *The Cambridge History of the American Novel*. Leonard Cassuto, ed. New York and Cambridge: Cambridge UP, 2011: 1096-106.

Robinson, Sally. *Marked Men: White Masculinity in Crisis*. New York: Columbia UP, 2001.

Roediger, David. *Working Toward Whiteness: How America's Immigrants Became White. The Strange Journey from Ellis Island to the Suburbs*. New York: Basic Books, 2005.

Rome, Adam. *The Bulldozer in the Countryside: Suburban Sprawl and the Rise of American Environmentalism*. Cambridge: Cambridge UP, 2001.

Rosenblatt, Roger. "The Age of Irony Comes to an End." *Time* 24 September 2001. http://www.time.com/time/magazine/article/0,9171,1000893,00.html.

Ross, Andrew. "The Great White Dude." In *Constructing Masculinity*. Maurice Berger, Brian Wallace, and Simon Watson, eds. New York: Routledge, 1995: 167–175.

Roth, Philip. *Portnoy's Complaint*. New York: Random House, 1969.

———. *The Breast*. New York: Holt, Rinehart and Winston, 1972.

———. *The Anatomy Lesson*. New York: Farrar, Straus and Giroux, 1983.

———. *American Pastoral*. New York: Houghton Mifflin, 1997.

———. *Everyman*. New York: Houghton Mifflin Harcourt, 2006.

Rothberg, Michael. "'There Is No Poetry In This': Writing, Trauma, and Home." In *Trauma at Home*. Judith Greenberg, ed. Lincoln: U of Nebraska P, 2003: 147–157.

———. "Decolonizing Trauma Studies: A Response." *Studies in the Novel* 40:1/2 (Spring/Summer 2008): 224–234.

———. "A Failure of the Imagination: Diagnosing the Post-9/11 Novel: A Response to Richard Gray." *American Literary History* 21:1 (Spring 2009): 152–158.

Rothman, Hal. *The Greening of a Nation*. New York: Norton, 1991.

Sawyers, June. " 'Everyman' Bascombe Returns." SFGate.com. 5 November 2006. http://www.sfgate.com/books/article/Everyman-Bascombe-returns-2485514.php.

Schivelbusch, Wolfgang. *The Culture of Defeat: On National Trauma, Mourning, and Recovery*. Jefferson Chase, trans. New York: Picador, 2004.

Schryer, Stephen. *Fantasies of the New Class: Ideologies of Professionalism in Post-World War II Literature*. New York: Columbia UP, 2010.

Schuessler, Jennifer. "In Book Circles, A Taming of the Feud." *The New York Times* 4 June 2011. http://www.nytimes.com/2011/06/05/weekinreview/05feuds.html.

Schwarz, Benjamin. "Mad About *Mad Men*." *The Atlantic* November 2009. http://www.theatlantic.com/magazine/archive/2009/11/mad-about-mad-men/307709.

Scott, A. O. "Still Wild About Harry." *The New York Times* 19 November 2000. http://www.nytimes.com/books/00/11/19/reviews/001119.19smcgt.html.

Shanken, Andrew. "Planning Memory: Living Memorials in the United States During World War II." *Art Bulletin* 84:1 (March 2002): 130–147.

Sheehy, Gail. *Middletown, America: One Town's Passage from Trauma to Hope*. New York: Random House, 2003.

Showalter, Elaine. "The Female Frontier." *The Guardian* 9 May 2009. http://www.guardian.co.uk/books/2009/may/09/femail-novelists-usa/print.

———. *Jury of Her Peers: American Women Writers from Anne Bradstreet to Annie Proulx*. New York: Knopf, 2009.

Silverman, Kaja. *Male Subjectivity at the Margins*. New York: Routledge, 1992.

Sittenfield, Curtis. "*Freedom* by Jonathan Franzen." *The Observer* 18 September 2010. http://www.theguardian.com/books/2010/sep/19/freedom-jonathan-franzen-review.

Sklenicka, Carol. *Raymond Carver: A Writer's Life*. New York: Scribner, 2009.

Smiley, Jane. "Say It Ain't So, Huck: Second Thoughts on Mark Twain's 'Masterpiece.'" *Harper's Magazine* January 1996: 61–67.

———. "Feminism Meets the Free Market." In *The Mommy Wars: Stay-at-Home and Career Moms Face Off on Their Choices, Their Lives, Their Families*. Leslie Morgan Steiner, ed. New York: Random House, 2006: 201–212.

Song, Min Hyoung. *Strange Future: Pessimism and the 1992 Los Angeles Riots*. Durham, NC: Duke UP, 2005.

———. "The Children of 1965: Allegory, Postmodernism, and Jhumpa Lahiri's *The Namesake*." *Twentieth Century Literature*, 53:3 (Fall 2007): 345–370.

Spigel, Lynn. *Welcome to the Dreamhouse: Popular Media and Postwar Suburbs*. Durham, NC: Duke UP, 2001.

Stamelman, Richard. "September 11: Between Memory and History." In *Trauma at Home*. Judith Greenberg, ed. Lincoln: U of Nebraska P, 2003.

Stevens, Wallace. *The Necessary Angel: Essays on Reality and the Imagination*. 1951. New York: Vintage, 1965.

Thatcher, Margaret. "Aids, education, and the year 2000!" Doug Keay, interviewer. *Women's Own* 31 October 1987: 8–10. http://www.margaretthatcher.org/speeches/displaydocument.asp?docid=106689.

Tocqueville, Alexis de. *Democracy in America*, vol. 2. 1840. New York: Vintage Classics, 1990.

Tongson, Karen. *Relocations: Queer Suburban Imaginaries*. New York: NYU P, 2011.

Tyler, Anne. *The Accidental Tourist*. 1985. New York: Ballantine, 2002.

———. *Digging to America*. New York: Knopf, 2006.

———. *The Beginner's Goodbye*. New York: Knopf, 2012.

Updike, John. *Rabbit, Run*. 1960. New York: Ballantine Books, 1996.

———. *Rabbit Redux*. 1971. New York: Ballantine Books, 1996.

———. *Rabbit at Rest*. New York: Knopf, 1990.

———. "Rabbit Remembered." In *Licks of Love*. New York: Knopf, 1990.

———. "Loosened Roots." In *Anne Tyler as Novelist*. Dale Salwak, ed. Iowa City: U of Iowa P, 1994: 120–124.

———. *Rabbit Angstrom: A Tetralogy*. New York: Everyman's Library, 1995.

Varon, Jeremy. "History Gets in Your Eyes: *Mad Men*, Misrecognition, and the Masculine Mystique." In *Mad Men, Mad World: Sex, Politics, Style, and the 1960s*. Lauren M. E. Goodlad, Lilya Kaganovsky, and Robert A. Rushing, eds. Durham, NC: Duke UP, 2013: 257–278.

Walsh, Bryan. "Recycling the Suburbs." *Time* 12 March 2009. http://content.time.com/time/specials/packages/article/0,28804,1884779_1884782_1884756,00.html.

Walker, Karen Thompson. *The Age of Miracles*. New York: Random House, 2012.

Waller, Willard. *Veteran Comes Back*. New York: Dryden Press, 1944.

Warren, David and Robert Puentes. "One Fifth of America: A Comprehensive Guide to America's First Suburbs Data Report." Washington, DC: The Brookings Institution Metropolitan Policy Program, February 2006. http://www.brookings.edu/reports/2006/~/media/Files/rc/reports/2006/02metropolitanpolicy_puentes/20060215_firstsuburbsdata.pdf.

Weiner, Jennifer. Call for non-Franzen novels about love, identity, families, The Way We Live Now. I pick Anne Tyler's DIGGING TO AMERICA. 23 August 2010, 10:34 a.m. Tweet.

Weinger, Mackenzie. "Phil Gingrey: Affordable Care Act is 'Un-American.'" *Politico* 29 June 2012. http://www.politico.com/news/stories/0612/78022.html.

Whitehead, Colson. "The End of the Affair." *The New York Times* 3 March 2002. http://www.nytimes.com/2002/03/03/books/the-end-of-the-affair.html?pagewanted=all&src=pm.

Whyte, William. *The Essential William Whyte*. Albert Lafarge, ed. New York: Fordham UP, 2000.

Wiegman, Robyn. *American Anatomies: Theorizing Race and Gender*. Durham, NC: Duke UP, 1995.

Wilhite, Keith. "Contested Terrain: The Suburb as Region." *American Literature* 84:3 (September 2012): 617–644.

Williams, Jeffrey J. "The Rise of the Academic Novel." *American Literary History* 24:3 (Fall 2012): 561–589.

Wolfe, Alan. *One Nation, After All: What Middle-Class Americans Really Think About God, Country, Family, Racism, Welfare, Immigration, Homosexuality, Work, the Right, the Left, and Each Other*. New York: Viking, 1998.

Wood, James. "Keeping It Real." *The New Yorker* 15 March 2010: 71. http://www.newyorker.com/arts/critics/atlarge/2010/03/15/100315crat_atlarge_wood.

Yates, Richard. *Revolutionary Road*. 1961. New York: Vintage, 2000.

Yen, Hope. "White Flight? Suburbs Lose Young Whites to Cities." AP 9 May 2010. http://www.huffingtonpost.com/2010/05/09/suburbs-losing-young-whit_n_569226.html.

Yudice, George. "What's a Straight White Man to Do?" In *Constructing Masculinity*. Maurice Berger, Brian Wallace, and Simon Watson, eds. New York: Routledge, 1995: 267–283.

Žižek, Slavoj. *Welcome to the Desert of the Real: Five Essays of September 11 and Related Dates*. London: Verso, 2002.

INDEX

THE NEW AMERICAN CANON

Violet America: Regional Cosmopolitanism in U.S. Fiction since the Great Depression
by Jason Arthur

The Legacy of David Foster Wallace
edited by Samuel Cohen and Lee Konstantinou

American Unexceptionalism: The Everyman and the Suburban Novel after 9/11
Kathy Knapp

Reading Capitalist Realism
edited by Alison Shonkwiler and Leigh Claire La Berge